COLLECTANEA CLIFFORDIANA.

First published in 1817 by Arthur Clifford, Esq.
and printed by M.Nouzou, 9, Rue de Cléry, Paris.

© 1980 published by Skipton Castle Limited,
Skipton-in-Craven, North Yorkshire.

ISBN 0 9506975 0 8

PUBLISHER'S NOTE

The reappearance of this scarce book at a fraction of the current cost of an original copy will, we hope, make the work available to a much wider audience.

———

At the head of the pages some numbers are duplicated because this volume contains several books or sections.

For readers of this Reprint edition, to make quick reference back to any point of interest, quite separate numbering has been added to the fore-edge foot of each page. These numbers are continuous from the beginning to the end of the book.

Printed in Great Britain by F.H. Brown Limited
Litho Division, Burnley, Lancashire.

COLLECTANEA CLIFFORDIANA,

IN THREE PARTS:

~~~~~

CONTAINING

I. ANECDOTES of Illustrious Personages of the name of CLIFFORD.

II. HISTORICAL and GENEALOGICAL NOTICES respecting the Origin and Antiquity of the CLIFFORD FAMILY.

III. CLIFFORD, a TRAGEDY.

Tu facito, mox quum matura adoleverit ætas,
Sis memor, et te animo repetentem exempla tuorum,
Et pater Æneas, et avunculus excitet Hector.
VIRGIL, Æn. B. xii.

~~~~~~~~~~~

BY ARTHUR CLIFFORD, ESQ.

PARIS:

PRINTED BY M. NOUZOU, 9, RUE DE CLÉRY.

1817.

5

COLLECTÁNEA CLIFFORDIANA.

PART THE FIRST:

CONTAINING

ANECDOTES OF ILLUSTRIOUS PERSONAGES

OF THE

NAME OF CLIFFORD.

CONTENTS.

	PAGE.
Dedication	i

PART THE FIRST—Anecdotes of illustrious Personages of the name of Clifford.

I. Anecdotes of George Clifford, Lord Clifford of Westmorland, third Earl of Cumberland . 7

His education, and naval expeditions

One of the founders of the East India Company 8

The favourite champion of Queen Elizabeth

Assisted at the trial and death of Mary Queen of Scots 9

Sonnet by Spenser

Extract from Lloyd's "Worthies" . . 10

His character from the "Heroologia" . . 11

His Portrait in "Purchas's Pilgrims" . . 12

Description of his last voyage to the West Indies from Camden's "Life of Queen Elizabeth'

His character from a manuscript at Appleby-castle 13

His death and monument . . . 14

Genealogy of the Cliffords of Ugbrook, and of Tixall 15

II. Anecdotes of Lady Anne Clifford . . 16

Lines from the "Pleasures of Memory" . . 18

Her death and monument

List of authors who have mentioned her . . 19

PAGE.

III. Henry, Lord Clifford of Westmorland, first Earl of Cumberland, cousin and cotemporary to King Henry VIII.   .   .   .   20

Created Earl of Cumberland

Letter to Pope Clement VII.

Made a knight of the Garter   .   .   .   21

Warden of the marches of Scotland, and Lord President of Wales

His son's marriage with King Henry's niece   . .   22

The succession to the throne of England settled on their issue   23

His death and marriages

Countess of Cumberland   24

IV. Henry, Lord Clifford of Westmorland, second Earl of Cumberland   .   .   .   25

His marriages and issue   . . .   26

Dissipation and learned retirement   . .   27

Remarkable anecdote   . . .   28

Entail of his estates on Clifford of Ugbrook   . .   26

The prospect which his family had of succeeding to the crown of England   . . .   30

V. Henry, Lord Clifford, of Westmorland, surnamed the Shepherd   . . .   32

The "Nut-brown Maid"   . . .   35

Battle of Flodden-field

His first wife   36

His death   . . .   37

VI. Anecdotes of the *ancestors* of Lord Clifford the Shepherd   . .   38

Lord Clifford's speech to Henry VI. from Shakspeare   . . .   39

Thomas Lord Clifford, ancestor of the Cliffords of Ugbrook, and Tixall   . .   41

A favourite of King Richard II.

(iii)

	PAGE.
Famous for tilting and turnaments . .	42
Killed in Lithuania . . .	43
Summons to parliament—Marriage and issue	
John, Lord Clifford of Westmorland . .	44
Feats of chivalry	
Battle of Agincourt . . '.	45
Much esteemed by King Henry V. . .	46
Built the Gatehouse of Appleby-castle	
His marriage with the daughter of Hotspur	
Singular covenant of Lady Clifford, his widow .	47
Her misfortunes	49
Thomas, Lord Clifford of Westmorland . .	50
Wars with Scotland and France—Curious stratagem	51
York and Lancaster . . .	52
Repaired Appleby-castle . . .	53
Sir Robert Clifford and Perkin Warbeck . .	54
John, Lord Clifford of Westmorland . .	55
Battle of Wakefield—His character vindicated .	56
Hero of the Tragedy of Clifford . .	57
Battle of Towton—Lord Clifford's death . .	59
His marriage—Father of Lord Clifford the Shepherd	61
VII. Anecdotes of the *descendants* of Lord Clifford the Shepherd . . .	62
Petition of Lady Anne Clifford, Countess of Dorset	63
Francis Clifford, fourth Earl of Cumberland .	65
Henry Clifford, fifth and last Earl of Cumberland .	67
Civil war between Charles I. and the parliament	
His death—Monument of his children . .	68
His poetical character . . .	69
Extinction of the male line of the Cliffords, Earls of Cumberland	
VIII. Anecdotes of the Cliffords of Ugbrook, in the county of Devon . . .	70
Preservation of the name of Clifford, and of the male line, in a younger branch of the family .	81

(iv)

PAGE·

Their descent from the Cliffords, Lords of Westmorland 73
Sir Lewis Clifford, knight of the Garter
Friend of John of Gaunt, and a chief of the Wickliffites 74
His descendants, seated at Borscomb, in the county of Wilts 77
Thomas Clifford, Esq. of Ugbrook . . 78
Sir Thomas Clifford, Knt. first Lord Clifford of Chudleigh 81
His naval exploits . . . 82
History of the ministry called the Cabal . . 84
Created a baron, and appointed lord high treasurer 88
Speech of Lord Shaftesbury . . 89
Death—Grants from King Charles II.—Marriage and issue 90
Hugh, second Lord Clifford of Chudleigh
Dryden's dedication of his translation of Virgil's Pastorals 91
His marriage, and children . . . 93
Alliance of his family with that of Constable, Viscount Dunbar 94
Epitaph on the Hon. Amy Constable
Hugh, third Lord Clifford of Chudleigh . . 96
His marriage and issue
Cliffords of Tixall, in the county of Stafford . 97
Hon. Thos. Clifford—His marriage
Some account of the ancient and noble family of Aston 98
Families of Constable, Viscount Dunbar, and Tunstall of Wycliff
Surviving sons of the Hon. Thomas Clifford of Tixall 99
PART THE SECOND—Origines et Antiquitates Cliffordienses

12

PAGE.

I. Of the origin of the name of Clifford . . 103

Clifford-castle, in the county of Hereford . . 104

Ralph de Toeny—Walter Fitz-Ponts . . 105

Different possessors of Clifford-castle . . 106

Its ruins, and description from Domesday-book . 107

Other places called Clifford, in Domesday-book . 108

II. Of the origin and antiquity of the Clifford family 111

Supplement to Collins's Peerage

Mistakes of Collins corrected . . 113

Count of Eu, in Normandy

Ponts, son of the Count of Eu—Origin of his name 114

A descendant of Rollo

Rollo, first Duke of Normandy—His history . 115

William I. second Duke of Normandy . . 123

Richard I. third Duke of Normandy . . . 124

Roman du Rhou, by Robert Wace . . 125

William, Count of Eu . . . 126

His adventures, and marriage . . 128

Ponts—His children—Progenitor of the Clifford family 129

Richard Fitz-Ponts, his son . . 131

Walter Fitz-Ponts, surnamed " De Clifford," of
    Clifford-castle 132

Margaret de Toeni, his wife.—Their issue . 134

Their daughter, called " Fair Rosamund" . . 135

A discourse about Fair Rosamund, by Hearne . 137

Her children by King Henry II. . . 158

Cliffords of Frampton, in the County of Gloucester 160

Walter de Clifford, second Lord Clifford of Clifford-
    . castle 162

Agnes, his wife—Her benefactions to the church . 163

Walter, third and last Lord Clifford of Clifford-cast-
    castle 165

Tomb of his wife, in Aconbury church . . 168

PAGE.

Roger de Clifford, his brother . . . 169

Letter concerning them from King Henry III. to 170
the Pope

Sir Roger de Clifford, Knt. fourth Lord Clifford . 172

The barons' wars—Battle of Evesham . . 174

Crusade to the Holy Land—Countess of Lorraine 176

Justiciary of all Wales—Death, and that of his son 177

Estates in Ireland 178

II. Of the origin and antiquity of the Clifford family
in the county of Westmorland . . 179

Recapitulation

The Lord of Vipont

Grants to him from King John . . . 180

Robert de Vipont's two daughters . . 181

Roger de Clifford, the younger, of Brougham-castle in Westmorland . . . 184

Isabella de Vipont, his wife—Sheriffess of Westmorland

Robert, fifth Lord Clifford of his name, and first
Lord Clifford of Westmorland

Expeditions into Scotland . . . 185

Grants and honours from king Edward I. . 187

Summons to parliament . . . 188

Death of Edward I.—His injunctions to Lord Clifford 189

Appointed Earl Marshal of England, by king Edward II.

Captain-General, and Governor of all Scotland

Skipton-castle, and Fee . . . 190

Piers Gaveston put to death by Lord Clifford and
others 192

Treaty of peace between Lord Clifford and king
Edward II. 193

Battle of Bannockburn . . . 195

Character of Lord Clifford . . 196

14

PAGE.

Of the descendants of Robert, first Lord Clifford of
    Westmorland   .   .   . 197

His eldest son Roger, beheaded at York   . . 198

Succeeded by Robert his brother

Hunting visit from the king of Scotland . . 199

Captain-General in the North

Isabel de Berkeley his wife   .   .   . 200

Robert, Lord Clifford, his son and successor

Fought at Crecy and Poitiers

Succeeded by his brother Roger, fifth Lord Clif-
    ford of Westmorland   .   . . 201

Expeditions into Gascony and Ireland • . 202

A knight banneret, and admiral   .   . 203

His arms, and those of his wife, on Brougham-castle

His death, and character

Sir Thomas de Clifford, his brother   .   . 204

Richard de Clifford, bishop of London

Made a cardinal, and nominated for the papacy . 205

Conclusion

IV. Of the armorial bearings of Clifford . . 206

V. The genealogy of the Clifford family deduced
    from Rollo, first duke of Normandy, with expla-
    natory notes   212

PART THE THIRD.

Clifford, an Historical Tragedy, in five acts

APPENDIX.

I. History of the Clifford family, from Dugdale's
    " Baronage of England,"

II. Passages relating to the Clifford family, from
    Collins's Peerage

III. Descriptions of places that belonged to them,
    from Camden's " Britannia"

IV. Scenes from Shakspeare's tragedy of king Henry
    the Sixth

V. Extract from the " Biographie Universelle"

TO THE

Right Honourable Charles, Lord Clifford,

Baron Clifford, of Chudleigh, in the County

of Devon:

AND

To Sir Thomas Clifford, Baronet, of Tixall,

in the County of Stafford:

Who are the Descendants by the Male Line

O F

Walter De Clifford,

. O F

CLIFFORD-CASTLE,

IN THE

COUNTY OF HEREFORD,

The first who assumed the Name of

DE CLIFFORD,

About the middle of the Twelfth Century :

TO

His Grace, William, Duke of Devonshire,
who is the Representative of the last Male
Line of the Cliffords, Earls of Cumberland :

TO THE

Right Honourable John, Earl of Thanet,
hereditary High Sheriff of Westmorland,
by descent from the Cliffords, Lords of
Westmorland; and Proprietor of the Castles of Appleby, and Skipton, the Ancient
Mansions of the Elder Branch of the

CLIFFORD FAMILY·

TO THE

Right Honourable Edward Southwell, Lord
De Clifford, who enjoys the Ancient Title
and Barony of De Clifford, first conferred
on Robert de Clifford, of Westmorland,
by Summons to Parliament, from King
Edward I.

AND

To all the other Honourable Descendants
and Connexions of the Ancient and Noble
Family of Clifford,

THIS WORK

Is most respectfully dedicated

By

THE AUTHOR.

COLLECTANEA CLIFFORDIANA.

I.

ANECDOTES

O F

GEORGE CLIFFORD,

LORD CLIFFORD OF WESTMORELAND, AND THIRD EARL OF
CUMBERLAND, KNIGHT OF THE GARTER.

GEORGE CLIFFORD, third Earl of Cumberland,
who flourished in the reign of Queen Elizabeth,
was one of the most remarkable and illustrious personages of his time ; and was particularly celebrated for his naval exploits and adventures.   He
was educated at the University of Cambridge,
where he had Dr. John Whitgift, afterwards Archbishop of Canterbury, for his tutor; and his chief
delight being in the study of mathematics, he
thence acquired a decided taste for navigation.
He made nine voyages by sea, *all at his own expence*, chiefly to attack the Spanish settlements in
America; and is said to have built the largest
ship that had till that time been seen in England.
His first voyage was in 1587, to the relief of
Sluys, in Flanders, then besieged by the Duke of
Parma; and in the following year, the Spanish ar-
mada threatening an invasion of England, he fitted

out several ships at his own charge; with which having joined the grand fleet, under the command of
Lord Thomas Howard, Lord Admiral, he greatly
distinguished himself on that memorable occasion,
and contributed very much to the capture and
destruction of the Spanish vessels. It would appear, that to his adventurous spirit, the English
nation is partly indebted for the first establishment of the East India Company: for it is recorded, that on the 5oth of December, in the year
1600, Queen Elizabeth granted the first charter
of the " English East India Company, to George
Earl of Cumberland, and 215 knights, aldermen,
and merchants: incorporating them into one
body politic and corporate, by the name of ' The
Governor and Company of Merchants trading to
the East Indies." '(a)

The Earl of Cumberland was not only a skilful
navigator, an intrepid commander, and a disin-
terested patriot, but moreover an accomplished
courtier. On his return from one of his naval expeditions, he obtained an audience of Queen Elizabeth, during which her Majesty dropped one
of her gloves. The Earl having picked it up, and
presented it to her, she ordered him to keep it as
a mark of her regard. He had it set with diamonds,
and used to wear it in his hat on all public occasions. Queen Elizabeth also appointed him her
champion in all public tilts and tournaments; and
the massy, ponderous, and richly ornamented ar-

(a) Mortimer's " Elements of Commerce," p. 23.

mour which he wore at these entertainments, is still preserved and shewn at Appleby Castle, in Westmoreland, one of his principal seats. These tilts, and tournaments, in which the Earl of Cumberland exhibited, as the champion of Queen Elizabeth, were the last public entertainments of the kind in England. The age of chivalry died with Elizabeth.

The Earl of Cumberland was one of the Lords who sat on the trial of Mary Queen of Scots, and one of the four Earls who were appointed to seè the sentence carried into execution. A few years after which he was made a knight of the garter. (*b*)

Among the sonnets prefixed by Spencer to his Fairy Queen, and which are all addressed to some of the greatest personages then in England, is the following to George Clifford, Earl of Cumberland:

To the Right Honourable the Earl of Cumberland.

Redoubted lord! in whose corageous mind,
The flower of chivalry now blooming fair
Doth promise fruit worthy the noble kind,
Which of their praises have left you the heir :
To you this humble present I prepare,
For love of virtue, and of martial praise :
To which though nobly you inclined are,
As goodly well you showed in late essays ;
Yet brave examples of long-passed days,
In which true honour you may fashioned see,
To like desire of honour may you raise,
And fill your mind with magnanimity.
Receive it, therefore, Lord, as it was meant,
For honour of your name, and high descent.

(*b*) See Biogr. Brit. and the Gen. Biogr. Dict. Art. Clifford.

Extract from Lloyd's " Worthies."

" When King James came first out of Scotland
to York, the Earl of Cumberland attended him
with such an equipage of followers for number
and habit, that he seemed rather a king than Earl
of Cumberland. Here happened a contest between the Earl and the Lord President of the
North, about carrying the sword before the king in
York; which office, upon due search and enquiry,
was adjudged to the Earl as belonging to him:
And whilst Clifford's Tower is standing in York,
that family will never be therein forgotten." *(c)*

It may here be observed, that the Cliffords,
Lords of Westmoreland, and Earls of Cumberland, were for many centuries in the north-west
of England, what the Percies, Earls of Northumberland were, and still are in the north-east;
but the vast possessions of the Clifford family, in
the north of England, have gone by females into
other families.

In the " Heroologia," a scarce and curious
work, with valuable engravings by the celebrated
Pass, there is a striking portrait of George Clifford, third Earl of Cumberland. He has a bold
and warlike countenance, and appears to be dressed
in the robes and insignia of the order of the gar-

(c) Lloyd's Worthies, vol. ii. p. 9.

ter. Ronnd the portrait are the words : "Georgius Clifford, Cumbriæ Comes." Above, is an earl's coronet, and below, the word *Desormais*, the ancient motto of the elder branch of the Clifford family. On the opposite page is the following sketch or character of this illustrious nobleman :

Fortis eques bello, dux imperterritus hosti,
Mors nisi Victoris sisteret atra gradum.

GEORGIUS CLIFFORD.

Georgius Clifford, Cambriæ, sive Cumbriæ Comes, Baro Clifford, Bromflete, et Vescy ; Dominus de Skipton, et Turris Bardenæ in Provinciâ Eboracensi ; Westmorlandiæ snmmus Vicecomes hereditarius : quibus in honoribus suo patri successit. Multis expeditionibus, in re navali imprimis, feliciter confectis, Regina Elizabetha, beatæ memoriæ, equitibus cum Georgianis, sive " Aureæ Periscelidis" annum eravit.

Quique, si jam in vivis esset, in secundum militari laude excellentium ordinem ascribi se vix aut ne vix quidem sustineret : illud semper Homericum in animo habens.

Ανεν αρισ Ίευειν και υπειροχον εμμεναι αλλων
Μηδε γενος παΊερων αισχυνεμεν.

Et ne ejus laudes imminuamus, si terrestrem navalemque militiam consideres, unus erat è summis Regni heroibus, et in plerisque molitionibus suis felicissimus. *Ex ungue Leonem,* ut dicitur, et martiam ex facie prolem facilè agnosceres.

In morbum prolapsus est, supremamque obit diem Londini, anno Domini 1605, tertioque regni serenissimi Domini nostri Regis Jacobi.

Est commune mori, nulli mors parcit honori.
           Nihilominus
                 Vivit post funera virtus.

25

In the first edition of " Purchas's Pilgrims," (one of the earliest collections of voyages and travels in the English language) there is an engraved title page, on which is a great number of very small portraits of the most illustrious navigators and travellers. Among them is that of George Clifford, Earl of Cumberland. He is placed between Mandeville and Christopher Columbus ; and this small portrait very much resembles the larger one above-mentioned in the " Heroologia."

In the same collection are also to be found many details respecting the various expeditions, and naval adventures of the Earl of Cumberland. But the following account of his last voyage to the West Indies, is extracted from Camden's " Life of Queen Elizabeth."

" He furnished out a fleet of eleven ships *at his own proper expence*, in order to intercept the Portugual carracks, as they sailed from the river Tagus to the East Indies ; but they hearing thereof, staid so long in the river, under the protection of Fort St. Julian, that they lost their voyage for that season. Whereupon the earl sailed away, first for the Canaries, where he took and plundered the isle and town of Lancerota ; from whence he steered for Boriquen; and landing his men made an attack upon Portorico, taking the town and forts, with the loss of not above thirty men, though there were in the town above 400 soldiers, besides inhabitants. This place, being for the advantage of its situation, accounted by the Spaniards the key of America, he resolved to make it the seat of the war, and removed all the inhabitants out of it, though they offered a great ransom for their houses. But shortly after, the English were so wretchedly handled by the bloody flux, and the griping of the guts, that in their forty days stay there, seven hundred men were swept away by those distempers, which forced him to return home with more honour than booty, though he carried from thence above sixty pieces of brass cannon. However, he did considerable damage to the Spaniards in hindering their carracks from making their voyage to the Indies that year, and by preventing the return of the Plata fleet from America."

In a history of the Clifford Family, drawn up under the directions of Lady Anne Clifford, only daughter of George, Earl of Cumberland, and which is still preserved in manuscript, at Appleby-castle, the following character is given of him : " This noble Earl was endowed with many perfections; he had an active and strong body, with a quicknes of wit, and apprehension, and an affable disposition and behaviour, which made him generally beloved through the whole kingdom; so that when he went to sea, he was accompanied by several persons of great quality, and many of the gentry, who voluntarily tendered their service to him."

On the acccession of James I., the Earl of Cum-

berland was sworn of the privy council, but being
exhausted with fatigue and disease, chiefly brought
on by his numerous and laborious expeditions to
such distant countries, and bad climates, he
was seized soon after with a lingering illness
which put a period to his life at the age of forty-
seven. He died at the Savoy, in London, in
the year 1605, and was buried in the family-vault
of the Cliffords, in the church of Skipton, in Craven; where a stately monument of black marble
was erected to his memory by his daughter the
Countess of Dorset. On the top of this monument, is a long inscription, in which it is said
that he was the seventeenth of his blood, that was
lord and hereditary high-sheriff of Westmoreland,
and thirteenth lord of the honour of Skipton.
Round the sides of the tomb are the following
shields, or coats of arms, showing the marriages
of many generations of the Clifford family for
more than three centuries: .

1. Clifford and Russel, within the garter, an
earl's coronet above.—2. Clifford between Brandon and Dacre.—3. Clifford and Percy within the
garter; a coronet above.—4. Vipont and Buly.—
5. Vipont and Ferrers.—6. Vipont and Fitz-
John.—7. Clifford and Vipont.—8. Clifford and
Clare.—9. Quarterly, Clifford and Vipont.—10.
Clifford and Beauchamp.—11. Clifford and Roos.
—12. Clifford and Percy within the garter.—
13. Clifford and Dacre.—14. Clifford and Brom-
flet (de Vesci).—15. Clifford and St. John of Bletsho.—16. Clifford and Berkeley.—17. Clifford and
Nevill.

" I much doubt," says Dr. Whitaker, " whether such an assemblage of noble bearings can be found on the tomb of any other Englisman." (*d*)

The eleventh shield on this monument of George Clifford, Earl of Cumberland, (Clifford and Roos) shows the marriage of Thomas, Lord Clifford, of Westmoreland, with Elizabeth, daughter of William, Lord Roos, of Hamlake, who was one of the competitors for the crown of Scotland : being great-grandson of Robert, Lord Roos, and his wife Isabel, daughter of William, king of Scotland.   By her Lord Clifford had three sons, John his heir, William, and Lewis.

From Sir Lewis Clifford, the third son, who was a knight of the garter, are descended the Cliffords of Ugbrook, in Devonshire, and of Tixall, in Staffordshire. They are the only descendants by the *male line*, of " Walter de Clifford," of Clifford-castle, in Herefordshire, the father of " Fair Rosamund," and the first who assumed the name of Clifford, about the middle of the 12th century.

Sir Lewis Clifford, knight of the garter, died in the year 1404

(*d*) History of Craven, p. 317.

II.

ANECDOTES

OF

LADY ANNE CLIFFORD,

COUNTESS OF DORSET, PEMBROKE AND MONTGOEMRY.

George Clifford, third Earl of Cumberland, married Lady Margaret Russel, daughter of Francis Russel, second Earl of Bedford; by whom he had two sons who died in their infancy, and one daughter, the celebrated Lady Anne Clifford; who was first married to the Earl of Dorset, and secondly, to the Earl of Pembroke and Montgomery.

The limits which I have prescribed to myself in this little work, will not allow me to indulge as I could wish, on the history of this high-born, high-spirited, and venerable lady. I must therefore content myself with selecting two anecdotes concerning her, which show at once the greatness of her spirit, and the tenderness of her heart: two qualities which are rarely found united to such an exalted degree in the same individual.

Lady Anne Clifford had experienced great injustice from a decision of King James I., respecting her right of succession to some estates of her father, which were thereby transferred to her un-

cle, Francis, fourth Earl of Cumberland. During
the usurpation of Cromwell, she had also received some threatening messages from him, respecting her castles in the north of England, which
she had fortified for King Charles I. After the restoration, a corrupt minister of Charles II. attempted
to force her to return a ministerial member for
one of her boroughs, contrary to her own sentiments. On this occasion, she returned the following laconic answer, which breathes all the spirit
of a Spartan heroine :

"I have been dictated to by a king, I have been
bullied by a usurper, but I will not submit to a
subject. Your man shall not stand,

"ANNE,

"Dorset, Pembroke, and Montgomery."

The other anecdote which I have to relate of
Lady Anne Clifford, is not less creditable to her
sensibility and piety. On the road side, between
Penrith, and Appleby, near Brougham Castle,
which was a part of her property, stands a small
pillar with this inscription :

"This pillar was erected in the year 1656, by
Anne, Countess Dowager of Pembroke, for a memorial of her last parting in this place, with her
good and pious mother, Margaret, Countess Dowager of Cumberland, on the 2d of April 1616:
in memory whereof, she hath left an annuity of 4l.
to be distributed to the poor of the parish of

B

Brougham, every second day of April, for ever, upon a stone-table placed hard by. Laus Deo."

This simple but affecting incident has afforded a pleasing illustration to the author of that elegant poem, " The Pleasures of Memory," in the following lines :

> Hast thou through Eden's wild wood vales pursued
> Each mountain scene magnificently rude,
> To note the sweet simplicity of life,
> Far from the din of Folly's idle strife;
> Nor, with Attention's lifted eye, revered
> That modest stone which pious Pembroke reared?
> Which still records beyond the pencil's power
> The silent sorrows of a parting hour;
> Still to the musing pilgrim points the place
> Her sainted spirit most delights to trace.

Lady Anne Clifford was first married to Richard Sackville, Earl of Dorset, by whom she had two daughters ; and 2diy, to Philip Herbert, Earl of Pembroke and Montgomery, by whom she had no issue. She lived to the age of eighty-five, and died in the year 1675, in her castle at Appleby. She was buried in the church of that town, near her mother, in a vault which she caused to be made during her lifetime, and over which she erected a stately monument of black and white marble. Lady Anne Clifford was a woman of admirable judgment, and extremely charitable and hospitable. She was a great benefactress to the town of Appleby, and to many churches, schools, and hospitals in the counties of Cumberland and Westmoreland, where her memory is still revered.

The curious reader will find some interesting memorials concerning Lady Anne Clifford, together with various portraits of her in the following works :

Pennant's " Tour to Scotland ;" vol. 3. p. 355 : Gilpin's " Tour to the Lakes of Cumberland ;" vol. 2. p. 151 : Whitaker's " History of Craven ;" p. 277. See also Walpole's " Catalogue of Royal and Noble Authors ;" and " The Biographia Britannica." Art. Clifford.

III.

HENRY,

LORD CLIFFORD, OF WESTMORELAND,

FIRST EARL OF CUMBERLAND.

Henry, Lord Clifford, afterwards Earl of Cumberland, was descended from a long line of noble and illustrious ancestors, and was born in the year 1493. His mother was the Lady Anne St. John, only daughter to Sir John, St. John of Bletsho ; and by the half-blood cousin-german to King Henry VII. her father being half-brother to that king's mother, Margaret, Countess of Richmond and Derby. Lord Clifford was cotemporary with king Henry VIII., for he was born about two years after that prince, and died about four years before him. In his childhood, and youth,

B 2

he was for the most part bred up with Henry VIII.
then Duke of York; who conceived an affection
for him which continued to the end of his life;
and which was further increased by their rela-
tionship, Henry the Seventh being cousin-german
to Lord Clifford's mother.

In the year 1525, 17 Hen. VIII. Lord Clifford
was created Earl of Cumberland, in the king's
palace at London, called Bridewell.

Down to this period it appears, that Lord Clifford lived with great magnificence and profusion in
the court of Henry VIII., who was a great lover
of pomp and shew, and certainly possessed a real
taste for regal splendour; but when the title of
Earl was conferred upon him, he quitted his habits of prodigality, and lived with proper economy
during the remainder of his life.

In the twenty-second year of Henry the Eighth's
reign, the Earl of Cumberland was one of the peers
who in parliament subscribed that letter to Pope
Clement the Seventh, in which they represented,
" That having for a long time expected his answer concerning the king's divorce from Catherine
his queen, they therefore were obliged to repeat
their request; although the justice of the cause,
and the approbation of the learned of most of the
universities of England, France, and Italy, as well
as of other learned men, were sufficient, without

any intreaty, to prevail on his Holiness to confirm
the sentence. But that on his refusal, they should
be obliged to attain this end by other means."

What those means were is sufficiently known
to every reader. About two years after, he was
elected one of the kinghts companions of the most
noble order of the garter, and was installed at
Windsor, the 17th May, 1537, as appears by his
plate there in St. George's chapel. Ashmole, in
his " History of the Garter," relates it as a remarkable precedent, that the Earl of Cumberland
being absent when elected, his investiture with
the garter, and his installation were dispatched at
the same time.

In the year 1539, he was appointed Warden of
the west of Scotland, also governor of the town
and castle of Carlisle, and president of the king's
council in the north. During the time he held
these high offices, the Yorkshire men having made
an insurrection, which they called the " Pilgri-
mage of Grace," they called on the Earl of Cumberland, who was then in his castle at Skipton,
to join with them, which he resolutely refused ;
and immediately wrote to the king, that though
the 500 gentlemen, *whom he retained at his own
cost*, had forsaken him, he would still continue his
majesty's true subject, and would defend his castle,
in which he had great ordnance, against them all.

As Warden of the West Marches, on the borders of Cumberland, he continually had a com-

mand in all expeditions sent out of England into
Scotland ; in which he was always distinguished
for his military skill and valour, and discharged the
trust reposed in him with great honour. He was
also frequently appointed Lord President of Wales,
a dignity which his ancestors had often borne before him.

But the greatest proof of affection which
Henry VIII. shewed for the Earl of Cumberland,
was in the inclination which that king expressed for
the marriage of his niece, the Lady Eleanor Brandon, with Henry, Lord Clifford, the earl's eldest
son. The Princess Mary, second daughter of
Henry VII. had married Lewis XII. King of
France, and on his decease, had taken for her
second husband, Charles Brandon, Duke of Suffolk. The Lady Eleanor was their youngest
daughter, and her marriage with Henry Lord
Clifford, was celebrated in the house of her father,
the Duke of Suffolk, near St. Mary Overy's, in
Southwark, the king himself being present, in the
year 1537. In order to entertain this Lady Eleanor
with greater magnificence, when she arrived at
Skipton, in Craven, her father-in-law, the Earl of
Cumberland, caused the great gallery at Skipton,
and the tower at the east-end of it, to be built from
the ground in the space of three months, together
with a passage from the great castle to the gallery.
Here she was entertained for four or five months,
by the Earl of Cumberland, and the Countess his
wife, with all imaginable affection, respect, and

grandeur. They both lived to see this young lady
have children, though all her issue male died in
their infancy, and none lived to the age of maturity, except Lady Margaret Clifford, who was
married to Henry, Earl of Derby.

———

Henry VIII. carried his regard for the Earl of
Cumberland and his family still farther, for having procured an act of parliament, by which he
was empowered to settle the succession to the
throne of England, according to his own will
and pleasure, he accordingly, by his last will and
testament, settled the succession on his son Edward, and on his two daughters, Mary and Elizabeth ; and in case of failure of issue from them, on
the issue of Henry Lord Clifford, by his niece the
Lady Eleanor. But she dying without male issue,
on the death of Queen Elizabeth, James VI. of
Scotland, who was descended from Henry the
Eighth's eldest sister, ascended the throne of England.

———

The Earl of Cumberland died in his castle of
Skipton, in Craven, in the year 1542, being
about 50 years of age, and was buried in the family vault of the Cliffords, in Skipton church.
By his last will he directed that 24*l.* should be distributed to the poor at his funeral, but that not
above 300 marks should be expended on it; and
he also ordered an Obit to be observed yearly in
the church of Skipton, and a dirge and mass to be

there sung for his own soul, for his wife, his children, his ancestors, and for all Christian souls: which shows, that he had not entirely adopted the new doctrines of the Reformation.

———

Henry Clifford, first Earl of Cumberland, was twice married—first, to Lady Margaret Talbot, eldest daughter of George, fourth Earl of Shrewsbury; who died young, without children, not long after her marriage, and was buried at Skipton.

His second wife was Lady Margaret Percy, sole daughter of Henry, fifth Earl of Northumberland, and sister to Henry, the sixth earl, called the Unthrifty Earl. She had given her by her father in dower, and afterwards confirmed by her brother, all those lands in Craven, called "The Percy Fee;" by which name they are mentioned in Domesday-Book, and are now the property of the Duke of Devonshire.

This Lady Margaret Percy's mother was Catherine, daughter and co-heiress of Sir Robert Spencer, Knight, by Eleanor, his wife, daughter and co-heiress of Edmund Beaufort, Duke of Somerset; so that she was lineally descended from John of Gaunt, Duke of Lancaster, and consequently from King Edward the Third.

But, besides her great birth, this Countess of Cumberland was a lady of singular piety, virtue, and goodness, living for the most part a retired life in the north of England, though her husband chose to live at court. She had only five children who lived to the age of manhood, and had the happiness to see her eldest son Lord Clifford, form so great an alliance by his marriage with the Lady Eleanor, daughter of the Duke of Suffolk, by the Princess Mary, Queen Dowager of Louis XII. King of France, and sister to Henry VIII. The Countess of Cumberland died about two years after her husband, and was buried by his side, in the fam ly vault at Skipton, in Craven.

IV.

HENRY,

LORD CLIFFORD, OF WESTMORELAND,

SECOND EARL OF CUMBERLAND.

Henry, Lord Clifford, second Earl of Cumberland, was born in the year 1517. At the age of sixteen, he was made a knight of the bath, by King Henry VIII. on the coronation of Queen Anne Boleyn; and when he was twenty years old, he was married to the Lady Eleanor, King Henry's niece. With this lady he lived about ten years, for she died at Brougham-castle, in Westmoreland, in the year 1547, and was buried in the family vault of the Cliffords, in the church of Skipton, at Craven. She left only one child at her death, the Lady Margaret Clifford, afterwards Countess of Derby, from whom the Stanleys, Earls of Derby, are descended, and some other great English families.

This Earl of Cumberland married to his second wife, Anne, daughter of William, Lord Dacre, of Gillesland; by whom he had issue George Clifford, third Earl of Cumberland, Francis, the fourth Earl, and Lady Frances Clifford, who married Philip, Lord Wharton. From them descended the celebrated Duke of Wharton, the friend of Addison and Young, and whose character is so ably delineated in one of the satires of Pope.

——————————

It is recorded of the second Earl of Cumberland, that in his youth he lived like his father at the court of Henry VIII. with great magnificence; and so much involved his property, that he was obliged to sell a part of the family estates, and in particular the great manor of Tenbury, situated, part in Worcestershire, and part in Herefordshire; which in the time of Henry II. was the property of Walter de Clifford, first Lord Clifford, of Clifford-castle, the father of "Fair Rosamund:" and consequently, was one of the most ancient possessions in the Clifford family.

But soon after the death of Henry VIII. he left the court, and took to a country life, when living with proper economy, he retrieved his affairs, and grew so rich that he made many purchases of great value.

During his retirement in the country, he addicted himself very much to the study of chemistry or alchymy, as it was then called, and was a great encourager of all learned pursuits. He collected an excellent library for that period, both of manuscripts and printed books ; and appears to have been so delighted with his literary and philosophical studies, that after the death of his first wife, the Lady Eleanor, he only went to London three times, and on the following occasions :

First, at the beginning of Queen Mary's reign, in order to assist at her coronation :

Secondly, on the marriage of his only daughter, by the Lady Eleanor, Lady Margaret Clifford, who was married in the year 1555, to Lord Stanley, afterwards Earl of Derby ;

The third and last time that he went up to London, was to see Queen Elizabeth, and to present his duty to her on her accession to the throne.

In the twelfth year of the reign of Queen Elizabeth, happened the famous insurrection of the Earls of Northumberland and Westmoreland, on which occasion the Earl of Cumberland fortified Carlisle, and raised a body of men to oppose them. This was the last public service which he performed, for he departed this life soon after, in the year 1569, at Brougham-castle, in Westmoreland, being only fifty-three years of age. He was buried in the family vault of Skipton church, by the side of his first wife, the Lady Eleanor.

A remarkable anecdote is related of this second
Earl of Cumberland, respecting a violent illness
with which he was attacked soon after the death of
his first wife. He fell into a languishing state,
and was reduced to such an extreme degree of weakness, that his physicians thought he was dead. His
body was already stripped, laid out upon a table,
and covered with a hersecloth of black velvet; when
some of his attendants, by whom he was greatly
beloved, perceived symptoms of returning life.
He was once more put to bed, and by the help of
warm cloths without, and cordials within, gra-
dually recovered. But for a month or more, his
only sustenance was milk which he sucked from a
woman's breast; and for three or four months
after that, he lived upon asses' milk. This regi-
men completely restored him to health before the
end of the year; he became a strong man, and
continued without any other indisposition till the
last illness which put a period to his life.

In the first year of the reign of Philip and Mary,
the Earl of Cumberland executed a special deed of
entail, by which in default of issue from George,
his son and heir, afterwards third Earl of Cumberland, he settled the greatest part of his estates on
his two brothers; and in default of issue from them,
on Henry Clifford, Esq. of Borscomb, in Wiltshire, eldest son of Anthony Clifford, Esq. of Borscomb, in Wiltshire, and of Ugbrook, near Chud-

leigh, in the county of Devon. This Anthony
Clifford, Esq. was great-grandson of Sir Lewis
Clifford, knight of the garter, who, as I have men-
tioned above, was the youngest son of Thomas
Lord Clifford, of Westmoreland, ancestor of the
Earl of Cumberland.

This deed of entail he confirmed by his last will
and testament, which extended it to Francis Clifford,
his youngest son, who was afterwards fourth Earl
of Cumberland. He bequeathed to the Lady Frances Clifford, his daughter, if she married an earl,
or an earl's son and heir, his lands not entailed, and
two thousand pounds, equivalent to ten or twelve
thousand at the present day; if she married a
baron, 2,000 marks ; and 800 only if she married
a knight. He further bequeathed two hundred
pounds for mending the highways in Craven, and
in the county of Westmoreland.

His executors were his brother-in-law, the Viscount Montagu, Sir Edward Saunders, Knt. lord
chief baron of the exchequer, Wm. Tancred, Esq.
one of the queen's majesty's council in the north
parts, Wm. Farrand, *groom of his chamber*, and
Laurence Preston, his *auditor*.

I cannot take leave of Henry, Lord Clifford, the
second Earl of Cumberland, without observing
that his family had a very near chance of being
seated on the throne of England. There is not
perhaps in all history, a similar instance of a private family which in a regular and constitutional

way, had so fair a prospect of inheriting the crown
of their native land. For, in the first place, the
succession to the crown was settled upon them, by
the will of Henry VIII. authorised by act of parliament, in case of failure of issue from his three
children Edward, Mary, and Elizabeth, and they
all did die without issue.

In the second place, Mary, Queen of Scots,
grand-daughter of Henry the Eighth's eldest sister,
was the only other pretender to the crown of England, from which she was excluded by Henry the
Eighth's will, which gave the preference to the
issue of his second sister, the Queen Dowager of
France, by the Duke of Brandon. Moreover,
Mary, Queen of Scots, married first, Francis II.
King of France, who died very young without
issue. But, had she had a son by him, that son
would have been King of France; and it is not to be
believed, that the English nation would have suffered themselves to fall under the dominion of a
King of France, or have allowed the British isles to
have formed one monarchy with that kingdom.
In this case, the children of Lord Clifford and
the Lady Eleanor, would then have been the only
legitimate heirs to the crown of England, either by
blood, or settlement.

In the third place, though James VI. son of
Mary, Queen of Scots, by Lord Darnley, succeeded to the throne of England, on the death
of Queen Elizabeth; yet, if the Earl of Cumberland's son, by Lady Eleanor, had grown up
to manhood, and been brought up in the court

of Queen Elizabeth, (like his son George, third Earl of Cumberland, by his second wife) if we consider the jealousy which Queen Elizabeth always bore to the Queen of Scots, with the aversion which the English naturally had to a foreign sovereign, having been so long governed by their native princes, it is very probable, I say, that Queen Elizabeth, desirous also to maintain her father's will, by which she held her own right to the crown, would have considered the Earl of Cumberland's son, by the Lady Eleanor, as her rightful heir, and have had him declared such by parliament. And in fact, she could hardly have done otherwise. For, Mary, Queen of Scots, and her issue, being formally excluded from the succession, by the will of Henry VIII., the only legitimate heirs to the throne that could be found, were the children of Lord Clifford, second Earl of Cumberland, and the Lady Eleanor, King Henry the Eighth's niece. However, Providence decreed it otherwise, the sons of Lady Eleanor died in their infancy, and instead of the Clifford family, the unfortunate race of the Stuarts, and the house of Brunswick, their descendants, by the female line, were destined to rule over the English nation.

V.

HENRY,

LORD CLIFFORD, OF WESTMORELAND,

SURNAMED THE SHEPHERD.

The life of Henry, Lord Clifford, surnamed the
Shepherd, father of the first Earl of Cumberland,
exhibited a memorable example of the awful vicissitudes of human grandeur. He is known in history by the name of Lord Clifford, the Shepherd,
an appellation which he obtained from the following circumstance. His father, John Lord Clifford,
being killed in the fatal battle of Towtn, in the
year 1460, fighting for Henry VI. and the house of
Lancaster; and Edward Duke of York, obtaining the crown, the young Lord Clifford, who
was then only seven years old, was exposed to such
imminent peril from the victorious party, that his
mother Lady Clifford found it necessary to conceal
him at a farm-house, in the dress of a shepherd's
boy. The memory of his father, and grand-fa-
ther, who was also killed in battle, was so hateful
to the house of York, that all their property was
confiscated, and their titles attainted; and had
young Henry been discovered, he would most probably have been put to death. He was first com-

mitted to the care of a shepherd's wife, who lived at Lonsborough, in Yorkshire, the seat of Lady Clifford, his mother, who was a great heiress, and Baroness Vescy in her own right. This woman was particularly chosen for the purpose, as she had formerly been nursery-maid at Skipton-castle; and therefore the young lord being well acquainted with her, and very fond of her, he the more readily submitted to his hard condition, and to be seperated from his disconsolate mother. And she being examined about her children, replied, that she had given positive directions to have them transported beyond the seas, into the Low Countries, there to be educated, and she knew nothing further about them. This answer was the more readily believed, as she had taken the precaution, immediately on her husband's death, to send both her children to the sea-side, and the youngest was actually sent into the Low Coutries, there to be educated, where he soon after died.

In this manner, therefore, young Henry lived in complete disguise, near his mother at Lonsborough, till he was fourteen years of age; when his grandfather, Lord Vescy, dying, a fresh rumour prevailed in the court of Edward IV. that the young Lord Clifford was alive; and strict enquiry being made after him, his mother, with the help of Sir Launcelot Threlkeld, her second husband, had him removed, together with the same shepherd and his wife, into Cumberland, where a farm was taken for him on the borders of Scotland. Here

C

he lived as a shepherd for about 91 years; but his good father-in-law often came on purpose to see him, and he was sometimes visited very privately by his affectionate mother. Is it possible to fancy a more romantic and more interesting situation?

The greatest inconvenience which resulted to Lord Clifford from this mode of life was, that his education was entirely neglected; as his mother was afraid even to have him taught to read or write for fear of discovery; and it was not till he had been restored to his lands and honours that he learnt even to write his own name. But notwithstanding the total neglect of his education, he always appeared to be a very intelligent man, and was an excellent economist in the management of his estate, and fortune. He also became a great builder, and thoroughly repaired all his castles in the north of England, and in other parts; which having been in the hands of strangers for five and twenty years had fallen greatly into decay. Skipton-castle, and the lands about it had been given by King Edward the Fourth, to Sir Wm. Stanley; and the county of Westmoreland to Richard Duke of Gloucester, afterwards King of England, by the name of Richard III. In this distressful situation, therefore, he lived as a shepherd till he was thirty-two years of age; when Henry VII. of the house of Lancaster, obtaining the crown, Lord Clifford was restored in blood and honours, and to all his baronies, lands, and castles, by an act of parliament in the first of King Henry's reign, by which his attainder was reversed, and his property restored.

Dr. Whitaker, in his valuable history of Craven, has conjectured with great appearance of probability, that the romantic adventures of Lord Clifford, the shephered, gave rise to the beautiful old ballad of the " Nutbrown Maid," modernised by Prior, in his poem of " Henry and Emma."

Lord Clifford having passed his youth in this lowly condition among the mountains, appears to have acquired a decided taste for rural retirement; for he passed the remainder of his life at a romantic spot called Barden Tower, in Craven, where he addicted himself with great assiduity and delight, to the studies of astronomy and chemistry, in which he was assisted by the monks of the neighbouring priory of Bolton. However, he was drawn out of his retreat in the year 1513, when near sixty years old, and was one of the principal commanders in the great victory obtained over the Scotch, at Flodden-field, when he shewed that the military genius of the family had neither been chilled in him by age, nor damped by the strange misfortunes of his youth, nor extinguished by long habits of peace.

In the old metrical history of Flodden-field, the following description is given of the followers of Lord Clifford the Shepherd:

> From Penigent to Pendle Hill,
> From Linton to Long Addingham,
> And all that Craven cotes did till
> They with the lusty Clifford came.

C 2

All Staincliff hundred went with him
With striplings strong from Wharledale,
And all that Hanton hills did climb
With Longstroth eke, and Litton Dale ;
Whose milk-fed fellows fleshy bred,
Well browned with sounding bows upbent,
All such as Horton fells had fed
On Clifford's banner did attend.

Lord Clifford, the Shepherd, received a summons to the first parliament held in the reign of Henry VII., and to all the succeeding parliaments of that reign, 'as well as those of Henry VIII. until his death. But in the twenty-first year of the reign of Henry VII. he fell under the displeasure of that avaricious and umbrageous monarch, for having taken part with the commons against the tax-gatherers ; so that the king ordered him to produce all his evidences, in order to show by what right he held his lands in Westmoreland, as well as the office of hereditary high sheriff of that county, which he performed to the complete satisfaction of the king and his council.

This Lord Clifford, of Westmoreland, was twice married. His first wife was Anne, only daughter of Sir John St. John, of Bletsho, and cousin-german to King Henry VII. She was a lady of singular virtue, goodness, and piety ; and so great a housewife, that she was one of the first who caused those tapestry hangings to be made, which are so often mentioned by Shakespeare, and other early writers, by the name of *Arras;* but which in this Lady Clifford's time, were a great rarity in England. Some of these hangings, with her arms and those of Lord Clifford. wrought upon them, were remaining at Skipton-castle, in the time of Charles I., but they appear to have been destroyed during the civil war between the king and the parliament. By this lady, Lord Clifford had three sons, and four daughters. His eldest son and heir, who was afterwards Earl of Cumberland, was born in the year 1493.

Lord Clifford's second wife was Florence, or Florentia, daughter of —— Pudsey, Esq. of an ancient family in Craven. By her he had two or three sons who died young, and one daughter named Dorothy, who was married to Sir Hugh Lowther, of Lowther, in Westmoreland, from whom the present Earl of Lonsdale is descended.

Lord Clifford's widow survived him many years, and took to her second husband, Richard, Lord Gray, a younger son of Thomas, first Marquis of Dorset.

By his last will and testament, Lord Clifford appointed that his body should be interred by that of his grandfather, Henry Bromflete, Lord Vescy, in the monastery of the White Friars, within the suburbs of London, provided he died in that city or neighbourhood. But in case he died in the north of England, he ordered his body to be buried in the abbey of Shapp, in Westmoreland, or in Bolton-abbey, in Craven, to both of which he was a great benefactor. He died in one of his castles in the north of England, and ended his memorable life on the 23d of April, in the year 1523.

VI.

ANECDOTES

OF THE

ANCESTORS OF LORD CLIFFORD,

THE SHEPHERD.

The father, grandfather, and great-grandfather of Lord Clifford, the Shepherd, were all killed in battle, as several of their ancestors were before them. There never was a more martial family than that of the Cliffords. In the Tragedy, which forms the third part of this work, and in which the father of Lord Clifford, the Shepherd, is the principal personage, one of the speakers in the dialogue is made to say with great truth—

> In an old book of genealogies,
> I've read that scarcely any of the Cliffords
> Died in their beds at home, but mostly fell
> Fighting like heroes in the tented field.

The father and grandfather of Lord Clifford, the

Shepherd, make a distinguished figure in Shakespeare's play of Henry VI. part the second, act
the fifth, and part the third, act second and third.

The following speech, which Shakspeare puts
into the mouth of Lord Clifford, has always been
justly admired as a specimen of persuasive oratory
and as a forcible appeal to the king, both as a sovereign and a man.

Lord Clifford's Speech to Henry VI.

My gracious liege, this too much lenity,
And harmful pity must be laid aside.
To whom do lions cast their gentle looks?
Not to the beasts that would usurp their den.
Whose hand is that the forest-bear doth lick?
Not his that spoils her young before her face.
Who 'scapes the lurking serpent's mortal sting?
Not he that sets his foot upon her back.
The smallest worm will turn being trodden on,
And doves will peck in safeguard to their brood.
Ambitious York did level at thy crown;
Thou smiling, while he knit his angry brows.
He, but a duke, would have his son a king,
And raise his issue like a loving sire:
Thou, being a king, blest with a goodly son,
Didst yield consent to disinherit him;
Which argued thee a most unloving father.
Unreasonable creatures feed their young;
And though man's face be fearful to their eyes,
Yet, in protection of their tender ones,
Who hath not seen them, (even with those wings
Which sometimes they have used in fearful flight)
Make war with them that climbed unto their nest,
Offering their own lives in their young's defence?
For shame, my liege, make them your precedent.
Were it not pity that this goodly boy
Should lose his birthright by his father's fault?

And long hereafter say unto his child—
What my great-grandfather, and grandsire got,
My careless father fondly gave a way !
Ah ! what a shame were this ! Look on the boy—
And let his manly face, which promiseth
Successful fortune, steel thy melting heart,
To hold thy own, and leave thy own to him.

I have mentioned above, that the father, the grandfather, and the great-grandfather of Henry, Lord Clifford, the Shepherd, were all slain in battle. They are called by the genealogists the tenth, eleventh, and twelfth Lord Clifford, of Westmoreland.

I now propose to relate some anecdotes of each of them, but shall first premise some account of Thomas, the ninth Lord Clifford, of Westmoreland, from whom are descended the Cliffords of Ugbrook, in Devonshire, and of Tixall, in Staffordshire.

VII.

THOMAS,

NINTH LORD CLIFFORD,

OF WESTMORELAND.

======

Thomas, Lord Clifford, was the only son and heir of Robert, Lord Clifford, and Isabel de Berkeley, only daughter to Maurice, Lord Berkeley, of Berkeley-castle. He was born in the year 1365, the 39th of the reign of King Edward III. In his youth, he was much at court, and being a favourite of that unfortunate prince King Richard II. he is said to have indulged too much in the dissipation and extravagance for which the court at that time was so remarkable. Yet he was always a gallant man, and continually exercised himself in military affairs.

In the 8th year of the reign of King Richard II. being a knight of the king's chamber, he was appointed governor of Carlisle-castle for life, and the year following was joined with Lord Nevill in the custody of that castle and city.

But not finding sufficient occupation for his military spirit, at Carlisle, Lord Clifford obtained a general leave from King Richard II. to exercise himself in all deeds of arms, as well on foot, as on horseback, in any place within the marches of Scotland, between the 28th of January, and the

Easter following. In consequence of this permission he entered Scotland, and having shown off his prowess, for some months, among the chivalrous knights of that country, he next determined to try those of France ; and accordingly, sent a cartel to a famous French knight, called " Le Sire de Burjisande," in which he invited him to try his skill in the exercise of arms ; and added a letter under his own seal, in which he specified the exercises he proposed to perform. This invitation being accepted by the French knight, Lord Clifford prevailed on the king to send Northampton herald, into France, in order that the ceremony might be arranged according to the laws of chivalry, and with suitable pomp and splendour. These arrangements being made, Lord Clifford went over to Calais, and thence to the place appointed for the tournament, where he met the Sire de Burjisande, and manifested his skill in jousting and tilting, to the great honour of English knighthood.

Having thus made himself conspicuous for his courage and gallantry in feats of arms, Lord Clifford received frequent challenges, from French and Scottish knights, to meet them at feats and tournaents, which they gave in his honour, in the district between Boulogne and Calais, and in the Marches of Scotland. Lord Clifford, who was Warden of the East and West Marches, an office at that time, of great consequence, trust, and honour, always attended these entertainments with a pompous retinue of knights and squires, and with all the parade of chivalry. But not being satisfied merely with the show of war and battle, he accompanied Thomas, of Woodstock, Duke of Gloucester, King Richard the Second's uncle, on an expedition into Prussia, against the infidels of Lithuania, where he was unfortunately slain in the flower of his age, being only thirty years old, in the year 1395.

This gallant man had summons to all the parliaments in the reign of King Richard, and was concerned in all the truces and treaties which were made during his time with Scotland.

Thomas, Lord Clifford, married Elizabeth, daughter of Thomas, Lord Roos, of Hamlake, as I have mentioned above, by whom he had three sons, John, his heir, William, and Lewis; and a daughter called Matilda, married to Richard, Duke of Cambridge, afterwards Duke of York, who disputed the throne of England with Henry VI. of the house of Lancaster.

JOHN,

TENTH LORD CLIFFORD,

OF WESTMORELAND.

John, Lord Clifford, was, like his father, a favourite of King Richard II. who gave him a confirmation of the grants of the town of Appleby, and Brough, in Westmoreland, to hold to him and his heirs, which had originally been given by King John, to Robert de Vipont, Lord Clifford's ancestor.

On the accession of King Henry the Fifth, Lord Clifford received an invitation to assist at the coronation, and had an order of council, as was customary in those times, for six ells of fine scarlet cloth for his robes on that occasion.

In the second year of the reign of Henry V. he was of the expedition that was made into France ; but returning to England the same year, he obtained from the king " letters of safe-conduct," for Sir Wm. Douglas, of Drumlanrig, in Scotland, in order that he might come to the town of Berwick, to perform feats of arms, with the Lord Clifford, and six other Englishmen. But instead of going to Berwick, they met at Carlisle, where Lord Clifford and six other Englishmen, encountered as many Scotch; namely, Lord Clifford, with Sir Wm. Douglas, Sir William Harrington, with Sir David Mynges, Sir Ralph Greystock, with Wm. Edmundson, Esq. Sir Christopher Curwen, with David Halyburton, Esq. whom he hurt in the neck ; and Sir John Lancaster, with Sir John St. Leger. In this chivalrous exercise, Lord Clifford was greatly distinguished for his strength and prowess, and the English bore away the prize.

A few years afterwards, he again attended King Henry the Fifth into France ; was with him at the battle of Agincourt, and at the siege of Harfleur, and Cherbourg ; which latter place, together with the castle, was surrendered to him by the governor.

Lord Clifford was summoned to all the parliaments which were held in the reigns of Henry IV. and V. : and in the year 1421, was elected one of the knights companions of the most noble order of the garter. But the year following he was unfortunately slain at the siege of Meaux, in France, being only 33 years old.

The expedition of Lord Clifford to France, and his untimely death, are thus described in the Tragedy, which forms a part of this volume.

> Fired with the heat of youth, and love of arms,
> And placing in his eye the wide-spread fame,
> And exploits of his great progenitors,
> With our late sovereign he embarked for France;
> Conducting to his aid a chosen band
> Of hardy mountaineers, the flower and pride
> Of Westmoreland, and Craven's rough domains.
> There by his side, in many a toilsome march,
> And furious skirmish, did they win their way
> Resistless, till on Agincourt's proud plain,
> They rode triumphant o'er their crest-fallen foes
> And trampled in the dust the power of France.
>
> Oft have I heard, that in that glorious fight,
> With his own hand the gallant Clifford slew

Twelve of their bravest captains—but alas!
Not all his valour could secure his life
Againstthe fated accidents of time.
For, while his beauteous lady here at home,
Expected his return, with joyful smiles
To greet her lord, and hail him conqueror—
He, at the siege of some strong citadel,
Was, by the sudden bursting of a gun,
Deprived of life! O fatal, dreadful stroke!

"Through the whole course of his life," says Collins, "he was truly great, and justly favoured and esteemed by his sovereign for his magnanimity, and his experience in martial affairs: He was one of the first that attended King Henry the Fifth into France; and that king, at the coronation of his consort, Queen Catherine, daughter to Charles VI. King of France, honoured him with the office of butler, at that solemnity."

He built the strong and beautiful arched gate-house, at Appleby-castle, in Westmoreland, whereon were carved in stone, the arms of Vipont, and Clifford, and those of Percy, which were the arms of his wife. This stately building was standing in the reign of Charles I., but was defaced and taken down during the civil war, in the year 1648.

This John, Lord Clifford, married Elizabeth, daughter of Lord Henry Percy, eldest son of the Earl of Northumberland, and who is so renowned in English history, and in one of Shakespeare's plays, by the name of Hotspur. Hotspur's wife, the mother of Lady Clifford, was the eldest daughter of Edmund Mortimer, third Earl of March, by his wife Philippa Plantagenet, only daughter and heir to Lionel, Duke of Clarence, second son of King Edward III.

Lord Clifford had by his wife Lady Elizabeth Percy, Thomas, his son and heir; Henry, who died without issue, and Mary, married to Sir Philip Wentworth, Knt. ancestor of the Lords Wentworth, and the Earls of Strafford, of that name.

———————

A few years after Lord Clifford's death, his widow, Lady Clifford, entered into an arrangement, which would appear very extraordinary in these times, with Thomas, Lord Dacre, of Gillesland, for the marriage of her eldest son, Lord Clifford, who was then only about ten years of age. By a regular indenture, dated 2 Hen. VI. between herself and Lord Dacre, she covenanted, that Thomas, son and heir of John, Lord Clifford, should marry Joan, daughter of the said Lord Dacre: And if that daughter should die before marriage, then he should espouse Margaret, another daughter of the said Lord Dacre: And in case the said Thomas, Lord Clifford, should die before marriage, then Henry, his brother, should be obliged to marry in the same manner. For this marriage, Lord Dacre agreed to pay to the Dowager Lady Clifford, the sum of 1,100 marks sterling; and Lady Clifford, on her part, was to deliver up her son to the custody of Lord Dacre, to be educated by him. It was also agreed, that after the marriage was celebrated, the young married couple should be kept and entertained acccording to their degree and estate, at the expence of the Lord Dacre, till Lord Clifford was of age; Lord Dacre receiving the allowance which was granted by the king to Lady Clifford, for the maintenance of her eldest son. But if the said Thomas, Lord Clifford, or Henry, his brother, should not agree to the marriage, at the age of fourteen, and a divorce should ensue, then the Dowager Lady Clifford was to pay to Lord Dacre, the sum of 200 marks, within a year after the divorce : And if either Joan or Margaret, his lordship's daughters, should die before marriage, then the Lord Dacre agreed to deliver at Skipton, in Craven, within a year after, the said Thomas, Lord Clifford, or Henry, his brother, whichsoever should be in his custody ; and upon such delivery, the Dowager Lady Clifford was to repay to the Lord Dacre, the sum of 700 marks sterling.

This covenant, which would appear very singular in our days, arose out of the military tenures and institutions of the feudal system, with which the whole business of life was complicated in those ages, and which were only repealed in the reign of Charles II.

In the fourth year of the reign of Henry VI. Lady Clifford married a second time, and took to her husband Ralph, Lord Nevill, the second

Earl of Westmoreland ; by whom she had issue an only son, the Lord Nevill, who was slain with his nephew John, Lord Clifford, at the fatal battle of Towton, in the year 1460.

This Lady Clifford, from the lustre of her birth and marriages, being nobly descended, and as nobly matched, had a fair prospect of being one of the greatest and happiest ladies of her time ; but happening to live in the melancholy period of the civil wars between the houses of Lancaster and York, she lost her children, and all her nearest relatives in the field of battle. Like a second Niobe, she might almost have exclaimed—

> An insulated monument of woe,
> Of all my house I am the sole survivor!

Her grandfather, Henry, Earl of Northumberland, being taken prisoner at Bramham-Moor, with the Lord Bardolf, in the year 1408, in a rebellion against Henry IV. was beheaded on the spot ; his son, her father, who was called Hotspur, was killed at the battle of Shrewsbury ; her husband fell at the siege of Meaux, in France ; and her son Thomas, Lord Clifford, with John, Lord Nevill, her son by her second husband, as also her grandson John, Lord Clifford, all perished in the civil war !

Lady Clifford died in the fifteenth year of the reign of Henry VI., and was buried in the church of Stanthrop, in the bishopric of Durham, where are interred several of the Neviles, Earls of Westmoreland, and their wives.

D

THOMAS,

ELEVENTH LORD CLIFFORD,

OF WESTMORELAND.

Thomas, Lord Clifford, eldest son of John, Lord Clifford, and the Lady Elizabeth Percy, was only seven years old at the time of his father's death. Like his ancestors, he was frequently employed against the Scotch, who were very troublesome neighbours in the north of England; and in the 13th year of the reign of Henry VI., there being a great apprehension that the Scotch would lay siege to Berwick, and to other strong holds in the Marches, Lord Clifford was commissioned to arm and array all knights, esquires, and yeomen, in the counties of York, Nottingham, Derby, Northumberland, Cumberland, and Westmoreland; and also to march with them for the safeguard of those parts.

These warlike prepartions were afterwards terminated by a truce for three years, from 1451 to 1454, between the two kingdoms; on which occasion Lord Clifford was joined in the commission with the Bishop of Durham, and the Earl of Salisbury, to treat with the ambassadors of James I. King of Scotland. He was also appointed one of the conservators of the truce, with power to inspect and examine, if other conservators should

by themselves, or their deputies, neglect the trust
reposed in them.

This Lord Clifford greatly distinguished himself
in the war in France, and did signal service to the
English cause, particularly at the siege of the strong
town of Pontoise, near Paris, where he employed
a stratagem, which might be added to those collected by Polyœnus, and would probably have
been much admired among the Greeks and Romans. The English had lain for some time before the town, without much hopes of success,
when a heavy fall of snow coming on in the night-
time, Lord Clifford dressed his men in white, and
made them advance close to the ditches and ram-
parts of the town, which they did without being
discovered. At day-break he ordered them to scale
the walls, and make a sudden attack on one of the
gates, in which they were completely successful,
and in this manner surprised the town. This event
happened in the year 1438.

Two years afterwards, Lord Clifford was again at
Pontoise, when it was attacked by the French King
Charles VII. in person ; but he valiantly defended
it against all the forces which the French could
bring forward.

———————————

Lord Clifford not only signalized his valour,
and military skill, in the wars of France, but
also in the unhappy civil war which broke out in
his time in England, between the houses of York
and Lancaster. He embraced the cause of the

D 2

house of Lancaster, with great zeal and alacrity, and though nearly allied to Richard, Duke of York, yet with that steady and active loyalty for which his ancestors had always been distinguished, he took part with Henry VI. and maintained his cause to the last with the greatest courage and perseverance. He gained the first victory on the king's side, but was unfortunately slain in the battle of St. Albans, in the year 1454, with his uncle the Earl of Northumberland, and many other noblemen. They were all buried in the chapel of our Lady, in the conventual church of that ancient city. Lord Clifford was only forty years of age at the time of his death.

Notwithstanding he was so much engaged in military affairs, Lord Clifford found time to attend to his estates in the north of England, and in particular to the repair of his castles in those parts, which had often suffered during the wars between England and Scotland. One of his principal castles was that of Appleby, in Westmoreland, which is beautifully situated on a high cliff, at the foot of which runs the river Eden. Some part of this castle is very ancient, for the great tower, called Cæsar's Tower, was undoubtedly built by the Romans, when they were masters of Britain ; and the principal apartment in it was built long before the time of this Lord Clifford, as it was called the Knight's Chamber, or the Baron's Chamber, in the reign of Henry III. and Edward I. However, Lord Clifford repaired Appleby-castle, and built the best part of it to the east, as the hall and chapel show ; in the windows of which are to be seen the arms of Vipont, and Clifford, and also those of Dacre, impuling those of Clifford. In the hall window are the arms of Lord Clifford's father and mother impaled, and also his own and those of his wife, and the single coat of Vipont. In the windows of the chapel are the arms of Clifford, quartering those of Bromflete, and at the bottom of the principal window is this inscription :

" This chapel was built by Thomas Lord Clifford, Anno Domini One Thousand fower Hundred fifty fower."

Thomas, Lord Clifford, married Joan, or Joanna, daughter of the Lord Dacre, of Gillesland, according to the covenant above-mentioned, made by his mother in his childhood. When this marriage was made, Lord Clifford could not be above ten years old, and was not more than nineteen, when his eldest son was born. His wife's mother was Philippa, daughter of Ralph Nevill, the first Earl of Westmoreland, by Lady Margaret, his wife, daughter of Hugh, Earl of Stafford. By this lady, Lord Clifford had four sons and five daughters, of whom, Robert, the third son is remarkable in the history of England, for the part which he took in the famous imposture of Perkin Warbeck, in the reign of King Henry VII. He was so deeply engaged in this affair, that, as Lord Bacon relates in his History of Henry VII., " His majesty thought it his interest to assail, sap, and work into the constancy of Sir Robert Clifford, and to win him, if they could ; he being the man that knew most of their secrets, and who being won away, would most appal and discourage the rest, and in a manner break the knot. Being won to be assured to the king, he therefore divulged and spread abroad the imposture and juggling of Perkin Warbeck's person and travels, with the circumstances thereof, throughout the realm. Being beyond the seas, he was sent for over by the king, to whose presence being admitted at a select council, he fell down at his feet, and in all humble manner begged the king's pardon, which the king then granted, though he were indeed assured of his life before. Then being commanded to tell his knowledge, he did, amongst others, appeach Sir William Stanley, the lord chamberlain of the king's household. The king seemed to be much amazed at the naming of this lord, as if he heard the news of some strange and wonderful prodigy. To hear a man that had done him service of so high a nature, as to save his life, and set the crown upon his head; a man that enjoyed by his favour and advancement so great a fortune, both in honour and riches : no ways disgraced, no ways discontent, no ways put in fear, should be false unto him! Clifford was required to say over, again and again, the particulars of his accusation; being warned, that in a matter so unlikely, and that concerned so great a servant of the king's, he should not in any wise go too far. But the king finding that he did sadly and constantly, without hesita-

tion, or varying, and with those civil protesta-
tions that were fit, stand to that he had said, offering to justify it upon his soul and life, he caused
him to be removed, and Sir Wm. Stanley being
convicted, suffered death."

JOHN,

TWELFTH LORD CLIFFORD,

OF WESTMORELAND.

John, Lord Clifford, father of Henry, Lord Clifford, surnamed the Shepherd, was twenty years
old at the death of his father, who as I have mentioned above, was slain in the first battle of St.
Albans, in the year 1454. In the 38th year of his
reign, Henry VI. appointed him commissary-
general of the Marches towards Scotland, and one
of the conservators of the truce with that kingdom,
which was made for five years.

Lord Clifford entered warmly into the interest
of the house of Lancaster, and greatly contributed
by his enthusiastic valour and courage to the support
of Henry VI. In the battle of Wakefield, where
Richard, Duke of York was slain, Lord Clifford
was very instrumental in obtaining the victory, and
was said by his enemies of the house of York, to
have made so great a slaughter, that he was thence-

forth called "Black Clifford" and the butcher. A stain has also been thrown upon his character, by the writers of that party, who accuse him of having stabbed the young Edmund Plantagenet, Earl of Rutland, third son of Richard, Duke of York. But in the manuscript history of the Clifford family above-mentioned, it is observed, that the Earl of Rutland was at least 16 or 17 years of age ; that he might be considered as one of the officers or leaders in his father's army ; that he was engaged in the action sword in hand against Henry the Sixth, his lawful sovereign, and that he was slain by Lord Clifford, not in cold blood, but in the heat and passion of a defeat and pursuit, exasperated by all the vindictive circumstances of a civil war. The cotemporary historians of this dreadful contest, were all attached to the house of York, and wrote under the reign of Edward IV. It is no wonder therefore, that the character of Lord Clifford has descended to posterity with this unmerited imputation ; and some pretext indeed was wanted for the cruelties which were exercised upon his family. Though Lord Clifford was slain in battle, fighting under the banners of his lawful sovereign, Henry VI., who had succeeded his father and grandfather on the throne of England, and had reigned himself nearly forty years, yet on Edward IV. obtaining the crown, Lord Clifford was attainted, all his property was confiscated, and his eldest son, the representative of such a long and noble line of illustrious ancestors, was condemned

to live above thirty years in the condition of a pea-
sant.

In the second battle of St. Albans, in which the
Lancastrians were victorious, Henry VI. who had
been taken prisoner by the Yorkists was set free,
and again restored to his queen and family. They
met in Lord Clifford's tent after the battle, and
the scene was very affecting; but it was observed
that wherever the king was, the enterprises were
unfortunate.

This Lord Clifford is the hero, or principal character, in the tragedy of " Clifford ;" or " The
Battle of Towton," now first printed in this volume, and his services to King Henry VI. and the
house of Lancaster, are enumerated in the following speech, which is put into the mouth of the
king :

> Clifford, it is from me that thanks are due.
> In my unhappy cause, alas ! your father,
> And other much-lamented kinsmen fell.
> Who on my side first gained a victory ?
> Who, with his heaven-directed falchion slew
> Richard of York, that overbearing chief,
> And father of this hydra-headed race ?
> Who, in the battle at St. Albans town,
> A second time dispersed my enemies,
> Released me from my hard captivity,
> And gave me back once more, with joy and triumph,
> To the embraces of my wife and child ?
> Who still supports my rights, and in the north,
> Preserves the people loyal to their king ?
> To you, my lord, and to your friends, through you,
> I am indebted for these countless services.

After the victory of St. Albans, the Lancastrians found it necessary to retreat into the north to recruit their forces, where Lord Clifford's interest was so strong, and his friends so daring and vigilant, that Queen Margaret was soon enabled to form an army of 60,000 men. The command of the whole army was given to Lord Clifford, the Duke of Somerset, and the Earl of Northumberland. In the mean time, King Edward IV. having assembled another powerful army, left London, and advanced by easy journeys to Pomfret, where he rested, and appointed the Lord Fitzwalter to keep the pass of Ferry-bridge. Lord Clifford, who was eager to revenge the death of his father, and friends, was well prepared to receive his enemies ; and it being determined that King Henry, with his qneen and son, should for their better safety be left in the city of York, it was then resolved that the pass of Ferry-bridge should be recovered at all hazard. This daring enterprise was committed to Lord Clifford, who departing from the main army with a competent number of light horsemen, very early in the morning, on the Saturday before Palm Sunday, made such expedition, that he gained the bridge, and slew the guard. The Lord Fitzwalter, hearing the noise, rose out of his bed, as did the bastard of Salisbury, brother to the Earl of Warwick, who suspected it was a mutiny among the soldiers ; but they were immediately attacked by the Lancastrians and slain. Upon this, King Edward encouraging his men, and thinking loss of time might endanger the rest of his forces, resolved to bring his fortune immediately to the trial of a battle. Finding it impossible to force the passage of Ferry‐bridge, he ordered his vanguard to pass the river three miles above it, at Castleford. Lord Clifford observing this movement, was retiring on the main army of the Lancastrians, when he was suddenly encompassed by the enemy; and perceiving no hope of escape, he encouraged his men to sell their lives as dearly as possible. He defended himself with his small force for a considerable time, with the greatest bravery, to the astonishment and even envy of his enemies ; but feeling himself overcome with heat and fatigue, he had unloosed his gorget, when he was shot through the throat with an arrow, and instantly fell dead on the field.

Next day, being Palm Sunday, both armies were in sight of each other, between Saxton and Towton, King Henry's forces being computed at 60,000 men, and those of King Edward at near 50,000. Our historians have given a particular account of this dreadful battle, which lasted three days ; and in which were slain on both sides, 36,776 persons, all Englishmen. The Earl of Northumberland, led the advanced guard, and perceiving that the snow which fell in the faces of his men prevented them from discerniug how they shot, he led his forces on to the charge sword in hand, when a bloody conflict. continued for ten hours, with doubtful success. But the Lancastrians, dispirited by the death of Lord Clifford, and their other chiefs, were completely defeated. The battle

of Towton was the Pharsalia of England, and it is
on the preceding historical facts, that the tragedy
of Clifford, in this volume, is founded.

Lord Clifford was only twenty-six years old
when he was killed, and had not enjoyed his lands
and honours more than five years after the death of
his father. His body was buried presently after
his death, together with that of his cousin the Earl
of Northumberland, and many other lords, knights,
and gentlemen, near the river Ayre, not far from
Ferry-bridge, where a little chapel was afterwards
erected, but which is long since decayed and gone
to ruin.

The fourth act of the tragedy of Clifford, con-
cludes with the following lamentation of the Earl
of Northumberland over the dead body of Lord
Clifford :

> Bright flower of chivalry ! Brave son of war !
> Most valiant leader, anchor of our hopes !
> The rock and tower of our loyal cause !
> The shield and bulwark of our Henry's throne !
> Fallen ! ah ! fallen ! fallen in his prime,
> A bloody victim to remorseless fate !
> O woe of woes! O grief above all grief !
> O Clifford ! Clifford ! flow, flow on my tears,
> Never, ah ! never was a loss like this !
> Why did I live to see this fatal day ?
> Here point your weapons, York, and Warwick, here
> With joy would I receive the stroke of death.
> O Skipton-castle ! dreadful, killing thought !
> A tender husband, father, brother—oh !
> My friend in arms, my loved companion slain !
> Sad sight of horror ! dismal, woeful sight !
> Pale, cold, and breathless, dead ! mere senseless clay !

A bleeding corpse! ah! who shall shield thee now!
Who shall protect thy honoured, loved remains!
Alas! alas! was ever loss like this!
Where shall I turn me now? ho, help there, ho.
Now could I gladly here upon this heath
Pierced through with deadly wounds resign my breath.
Our cause is hopeless, all is ruined, gone,
Proud York triumphant, Lancaster undone!

John, Lord Clifford, married the Lady Margaret
Bromflett, only daughter and heir of Henry Bromflett, Lord Vescy. She was Baroness Vescy, in
her own right, and brought that title into the Clifford family, together with Lonsborough House,
in Yorkshire, and other valuable estates which are
now the property of the Duke of Devonshire.

Her eldest son, was Lord Clifford, the Shepherd, whose memorable history I have already
related. She had the happiness to live to see him
restored to his lands and honours, and died in her
own house at Lonsborough, in the year 1493. Her
body was interred in the church of Lonsborough
before the high altar, as appears by the following inscription engraved on her tomb:

Orate pro animâ MARGARETÆ DOMINÆ de CLIF-
FORD et VESCY et WESTMORLAND filiæ et hœredis
HENRICI BROMFLETE quondam Domini VESCY ac
etiam Matris HENRICI Domini de CLIFFORD, WEST-
MORELAND, et VESCY Quæ obiit xv die Mensis
Aprilis Anno Domini Mcccc Nonagesimo tertio
Cujus Corpus sub hoc marmore est humatum.

VIII.

ANECDOTES

OF THE

DESCENDANTS OF LORD CLIFFORD,

THE SHEPHERD.

The descendants of Lord Clifford, the Shepherd, were the three first Earls of Cumberland, above-mentioned, Francis the fourth earl, and Henry, the fifth and last Earl of Cumberland. Of the two last, I shall now proceed to give some account, but must first inform the reader, that on the death of George Clifford, third Earl of Cumberland, without male issue, in the year 1605, the titles of Clifford, Westmoreland, and Vescy, descended to his only daughter Lady Anne Clifford, being dignities, which took their first rise by summons of her ancestors to parliament; and were moreover vested in her by virtue of the entail of the lands and castles belonging to those titles, of which she was the true and lineal heir. However it appears that her uncle Francis, who had succeeded his brother George, in the title of Earl of Cumberland, laid claim also to the title of Lord Clifford; to prevent which, Lady Anne Clifford, who was then Countess of Dorset, presented the following petition to the House of Peers, which is thus recorded on the Journals :

Die Veneris, viz. decimo sexto die Maii, 1628.

The petition of Countess Dowager of Dorsett, was read *in hœc verba*.

To the King's most excellent Majesty.

The humble petition of Anne, Countess Dowager of Dorsett, late wife of Richard Earle of Dorsett, deceased, and daughter and sole heire of George Earle of Cumberland, Lord Clifford, Westmerland, and Vescy.

Sheweth,

That Henry Lord Clifford, Westmerland, and Vescy, was right heire of *Robert de Clifford*, summoned to Parliament by that Name in the eight and twentieth yeere of Edward the First, as a Baron ; which Henry had also, and enjoyed the Names, Stiles, and Dignities, of Lord Westmerland and Vescy ; all which he had in Fee Simple descended from his Ancestors. The same Henry was by the late King Henry the Eight created Earl of Cumberland ; to have to him and the Heires Males of his body issuing. After the death of the said Henry, and of Henry his Son and Heire, and of George his Sonne and Heire, Father of the Peticioner, without Heire Male issuing of his Bodie, the said Earledome descended to Francis Earl of Cumberland, Brother of the said George : And the Name, Stiles, and Dignities, as well of Clifford, as of Westmerland, and Vescy, are descended to the Peticioner, and she of right ought to enjoy those names, Stiles, and Dignities, and by them bee called.

Yet so it is, (may it please your most excellent Majesty) that the said Francis Earl of Cumberland hath published, that the name of Lord Clifford, and also (as the Peticioner is enformed) the name of Lord Vescy, and Westmerland, doe perteine unto h'm. And that Henry Clifford, his sonne and Heire Apparent, by the name of Henry Clifford, Chivalier, was summoned to the present parliament; and calleth, and styleth himselfe by the name of Lord Clifford, and claimeth and useth the place of the title of Lord Clifford, belonging as aforesaid to the Peticioner, to her great wronge and disherison.

She therefore prayeth, that your Majestie will admitt of her clayme of the said styles, Dignities, and Places of Clifford, Westmerland, and Vescy; that shee and her Heires may have and beare these Stiles and Dignities, and use the place belonging to them; and to give Order and Direccion, that the said now Earle of Cumberland, and the said Henry his sonne and Heire, may from henceforth forbeare to style themselves by any of those names, and shee shall dayly pray, etc."

" Charles R.

It is our pleasure, that the Lords Spiritual and Temporal assembled in Parliament, calling both the Peticioner, and the within named Henry, eldest Sonne of the Earl of Cumberland, and also the said Earle, should examine the Contents of this Peticion, and certefie us, what they thinke in Justice doth perteine. And thereupon full justice shall be done to these parties."

On the 26th May, 1628, the hearing of her petition was appointed in the beginning of the next session ; but I do not find that there were any further proceedings.

FRANCIS CLIFFORD,

FOURTH EARL OF CUMBERLAND.

Francis Clifford, fourth Earl of Cumberland, was the second son of Henry, Lord Clifford, of Westmoreland, second Earl of Cumberland, by his second wife, Anne, daughter of William, Lord Dacre, of Gillesland. He was born in Skipton-castle, in Craven, in the year 1559, and was forty-six years of age, when he succeeded his brother George, third Earl of Cumberland, the celebrated naval adventurer in the reign of Queen Elizabeth.

In the fifteenth year of the reign of King James I. Francis, Earl of Cumberland, was joined with Lord Sheffield, the Lord President of the North, in two commissions for suppressing all murders, felonies, robberies, riots, etc. on the borders between England and Scotland ; and three years afterwards he was appointed to another commission with Toby, Archbishop of York, to correct and amend all

E

errors, heresies, schisms, contempts, etc. which
by any spiritual or ecclesiastial power might law-
fully be reformed or redressed.

This Earl of Cumberland, unlike the generality
of his ancestors, led a quiet, regular, and tranquil life; and as he was the last but one of his
noble and illustrious race, so he was the longest-
lived of them all. He reached the advanced age
of eighty-two, and died in Skipton-castle, where
he was born, in the year 1641, just before the
breaking out of the civil war between Charles I.
and the Parliament. He was buried among his ancestors in the vault of the chancel of Skipton-
church, where a monument was erected to his
memory.

Francis, fourth Earl of Cumberland, married
in the year 1589, the widow of Edward Nevill,
Lord Bergavenny; by whom he had issue Henry,
his son and heir, and two daughters, Lady Margaret Clifford, married to Sir Thomas Wentworth,
afterwards the famous Earl of Stafford, who was
beheaded· in the reign of Charles I., and Lady
Frances Clifford, who was the second wife of Sir
Gervase Clifton, knight and baronet.

HENRY CLIFFORD,

EARL OF CUMBERLAND.

Henry Clifford, fifth Earl of Cumberland, was born in Lonsborough House, in Yorkshire, in the year 1592. On the breaking out of the civil war between Charles I. and the Parliament, he continued steadfast in his loyalty to the king; and retiring with his majesty to York, was one of the peers who signed those public declarations of their principles which were issued from that city. He likewise raised forces to assist the king: and Whitlock writes, that the king's party grew strong under the Earl of Cumberland, who forced Hotham to retreat to Hull. The same author informs us, that when the Earl of Essex took the command of the parliamentary forces, his instructions from the parliament were, " To declare pardon to those who should withdraw from the king, except the Duke of Richmond, the Earl of Cumberland, and seven others specially named."

The Earl of Cumberland being thus actively employed in the service of the king, was unfortunately seized with a violent fever in one of the prebend's houses, in the city of York, where he resided, and where he departed this life, on the 11th of Decem-

E 2

ber, 1643; being just fifty-one years, ten months,
and ten days old at his death; and had enjoyed the
title of Earl of Cumberland, only two years, ten
months, and twenty-one days. He was buried in
the family-vault of the Cliffords, in the church of
Skipton; and his lady dying on the 14th of February following, in the same house at York, was
buried in the cathedral of that city. Henry, last
Earl of Cumberland, married in the year 1610,
the Lady Frances Cecil, only daughter to Robert
Cecil, Earl of Salisbury, and lord high-treasurer
of England. By her he had three sons, who all
died in their infancy, and to whom he erected a
monument in Skipton-church, with the following
inscription, " which," says Dr. Whitaker, " has a
beautiful simplicity and pathos :"

Immensi doloris monumentum angustum!

Henricus pater deflet

Franciscum

Carolum

Henricum

A.D. M. DC. XXXXI.

Echard, in his History of England, mentions the
death of the Earl of Cumberland, in the following
terms :

" 1643. Died Henry Clifford, Earl of Cumberland, a loyal gentleman, who being of a peaceable
and affable disposition, had few enemies; and
was distinguished by the various copies of verses

he wrote, which obtained him the character of the best poet among the nobility."

It is to be presumed that none of these verses of the Earl of Cumberland were ever published, since they have escaped the researches of all the collectors of the poetry of that period; nor is his name mentioned by Walpole, in his " Catalogue of Royal and Noble Authors," though there is an article in that work on Lady Anne Clifford, who was first cousin to the Earl of Cumberland, and survived him many years. It is to be regretted that the poetical productions of a nobleman, who had " the character of the best poet among the nobility," should have been allowed to remain in manuscript, or perhaps perish altogether; and the more so, as the poetry of that memorable period of our history has always been much esteemed, and is highly extolled by Ellis, in his " Specimens of early English Poetry."

Besides his three sons who died in their infancy, the Earl of Cumberland had by his wife Lady Frances Cecil, an only daughter Lady Elizabeth Clifford, who was born in Skipton-castle, in the year 1613, and was married in the year 1635, to Richard Boyle, Lord Viscount Dungarvan, son and heir to Richard, Earl of Cork : and from them is descended the Duke of Devonshire.

Thus ended the male line of this noble and illustrious race; which had flourished in England, under the name of Clifford, in a regular succession from father to son, with the highest lustre and renown, for the space of five hundred years; from the middle of the twelfth century, when the name was first assumed by Walter de Clifford, of Clifford-castle, in the county of Hereford, to the middle of the seventeenth century, when the name and line became extinct, in the elder branch of the family, by the death of Henry, Lord Clifford, fifth and last Earl of Cumberland, without male issue.

IX.

ANECDOTES

OF THE

CLIFFORDS OF UGBROOK,

IN THE COUNTY OF DEVON.

I have mentioned above, that the Duke of Devonshire, and Lord de Clifford, of King's-Weston, in the county of Gloucester, are descended by the female line from the Cliffords, lords of Westmoreland, and earls of Cumberland. I now proceed to lay before the reader some account of the families of Clifford of Ugbrook, in the county of Devon, and of Tixall, in the county of Stafford, who are the only descendants in England, by the male line, of Walter de Clifford, of Clifford-castle, in the county of Hereford, who first assumed the name of Clifford, and was the great progenitor of all the families who have borne that name.

Dr. Whitaker, in his excellent "History of the Deanery and Antiquities of Craven," having noticed the untimely death of the three infant sons of Henry, Lord Clifford, the last Earl of Cumberland, makes the following observation on that melancholy event :—" By cutting off five heirs male in the compass of three generations, Providence seems to have decreed the extinction of the name of Clifford." This observation may be allowed to be perfectly just, if it be confined to the elder branch of the Clifford family, of whom alone Dr. Whitaker treats, and to the extinction of their name in the north of England, where they had flourished with great glory for so many centuries. But, on the other hand, might we not assert, with equal submission to the inscrutable decrees of Divine Providence, that, when it had decreed the extinction of the elder branch of the Clifford family, which had now run its full career of honour and renown, it reserved a compensation for their loss, by raising up, at the time time, an illustrious individual of another branch of the same family, who, by the splendour of his abilities, and his eminent services to his king and country, was destined to shed a new lustre on the name of Clifford, and to transmit it with new titles, and new honour, to the latest posterity? This distinguished personage was Sir Thomas Clifford, of Ugbrook, in the county of Devon, who, a few years after the death of the last Earl of Cumberland, and during the lifetime of Lady Anne Clifford, Countess of Dorset, was appointed by King Charles II. lord high-trea-

surer of England, and was raised to the dignity of
a peer of the realm, by the title of Lord Clifford,
Baron Clifford of Chudleigh, in the county of
Devon.

—— Uno avulso non deficit alter
Aureus, et simili frondescit virga metallo:

Though from the tree one branch be torn away,
Another flourishes without delay ;
The new sprung shoots with equal lustre shine,
And shed fresh glories on the golden line.

I now proceed, therefore, to lay before the reader
some passages of the history of Sir Thomas Clifford, of Ugbrook, first Lord Clifford, of Chudleigh, in the county of Devon ; but shall first
shew how he was lineally descended by the male
line, from the same original stock as his illustrious
relations of the name of Clifford, in the north of
England ; and shall then relate some anecdotes of
is immediate ancestors.

SIR LEWIS CLIFFORD,

KNIGHT OF THE GARTER.

In a preceding part of this work, I have shown that Thomas, ninth Lord Clifford, of Westmoreland, married Elizabeth, daughter of Thomas, Lord Roos, of Hamlake, by whom he had issue three sons : John, tenth Lord Clifford, of Westmoreland, (ancestor of the Earls of Cumberland,) William, his second son, and Lewis, ancestor of the Cliffords of Ugbrook, in the county of Devon.

Sir Lewis Clifford, who flourished in the brightest age of chivalry, was made a knight by that illustrious monarch, King Edward the Third, and was much employed by that sovereign, as well as by his grandson and successor King Richard II. in all their military expeditions. Froissart relates, that Sir Lewis Clifford was a constant companion of John of Gaunt, Duke of Lancaster, and attended that prince in the expedition which he made into France, towards the end of Edward the Third's reign.

In consideration of his high descent, and distinguished services, Sir Lewis Clifford was chosen one of the knights companions of the most noble order of the Garter, which had then been lately instituted by King Edward III. A grand festival of this noble order been kept by King Richard II. in the

seventh year of his reign, on the feast of St. George,
the patron of England; on this occasion, Sir Lewis
Clifford, and the other knights of the garter, had
surtouts given them by the king of *violet in grain;*
which was the custom of those times.

In the ninth year of the reign of King Richard II.
Sir Lewis Clifford was commander in chief of the
city of Carlisle, when it was attacked by a large
army of the Scotch and French; but he valiantly
defended it, and forced them to retire. His brother Sir William Clifford was at the same time
governor of Berwick, which, together with Carlisle, were at that period, the two most important fortresses in the kingdom. Their being
commanded at the same time, by these two brothers, shows how great was the consequence of
the Clifford family in the state, at that early period
of our history, and evinces at the same time the military spirit by which they were animated.

In the year 1390, Sir Lewis Clifford, who constantly took an active part in all state affairs,
signed, together with the king, the peers, and
other great men of the realm, a letter of remon-
strance to the pope, in which they strongly com-
plained of the exorbitances and encroachments of
the apostolic see. This was the age of Wickliff,
and the Lollards, whose doctrines were espoused
and protected by John of Gaunt; and Sir Lewis Clifford, appears to have been one of their chiefs. In the
last year of the reign of Edward III. some of the
Wickliffites, and followers of John of Gaunt, having affronted the Bishop of London, a tumult en-

sued, and a riotous mob beset the Duke of Lancaster's palace, called the Savoy, which was also at that time the residence of the Princess of Wales, widow of the Black Prince, and mother of King Richard II. The princess perceiving the fury of the mob, sent three of her knights, of whom Sir Lewis Clifford was one, to entreat them to be reconciled to the Duke. Sir Lewis Clifford having expostulated for some time with their leaders, they returned an answer, " That for the honour of the princess they would obey, and with all reverence be ready to do whatever she should please to require."

In the fifteenth year of King Richard II. Sir Lewis Clifford was sent ambassador with Lord Percy to the King of France, to declare to him the sincere desire of the king, his master, for a peace between the two kingdoms, and also to request the French king to appoint a place to treat of the preliminaries, which was accordingly fixed at Amiens. A few years after the conclusion of the peace, Sir Lewis Clifford was sent again on an embassy into France, in order to treat of a marriage between the Princess Isabella, daughter of the French king, and the King of England, on which occasion he appeared at the French court with great magnificence. But soon after his return to England, he witnessed the downfall of that unfortunate King Richard II. whose fatal end he did not long survive; for he died in the year 1404, the fourth year of King Henry the Fourth.

Sir Lewis Clifford is much taken notice of by the

English historians, for the decided part which he took with the zealots or reformers of that period, who were called Lollards. He appears to have been one of their principal leaders, but in his latter days, it is said, he became sensible of the dangerous tenets he had espoused, and confessed his error with cordial repentance to the Archbishop of Canterbury. However that may be, his last will and testament, which is still preserved in the prerogative court of the archbishopric of Canterbury, shows that he died with great sentiments of Christian humiliation. Of this curious will, the reader will find a transcript in the Appendix.

DESCENDANTS OF

SIR LEWIS CLIFFORD,

KNIGHT OF THE GARTER.

By his wife Eleanor, Sir Lewis Clifford had a daughter, who was married to Sir Philip La Vache, and a son, William Clifford, Esq. who married Elizabeth, daughter and coheir of Sir Arnold Savage, and widow of Sir Reginald Cobham.

William Clifford, Esq. son and heir of Sir Lewis, had issue by his wife two sons, Lewis and John. From Lewis the eldest, descended the Cliffords of Holm, in the county of Kent, now extinct.

John, the second son of William Clifford, Esq. son and heir of Sir Lewis, was the ancestor of the Cliffords of Ugbrook, in the county of Devon. He married Florentia, daughter of John St. Leger, Esq. and died in the 16th year of the reign of King Henry the Sixth.

Thomas Clifford, Esq. his son and heir, great grandson of Sir Lewis, was seated at Borscomb, in the county of Wilts ; which continued for a long period to be the residence of this branch of the Clifford family. Being descended, from a younger son of a younger brother, their patrimony could not be very considerable, and they appear to have lived for several generations in the rank of esquires, or private country gentlemen.

Henry Clifford, of Borscomb, Esq. grandson of Thomas, last-mentioned, was the person on whom Henry, Lord Clifford, of Westmoreland, second Earl of Cumberland, entailed his lands and estates, in default of issue from his own brothers, as I have related in another place. This deed of entail was executed in the reign of Philip and Mary, about the year 1555.

Henry Clifford, of Borscombe, Esq. was succeeded by his son and heir Anthony Clifford, Esq. who died in the reign of Queen Elizabeth, in the year 1580, and was buried in the cathedral at Exeter.

By his wife, daughter of Sir Peter Courtney, of Ugbrook, in the Parish of Chudleigh, in Devonshire, he had issue three sons, Henry, William, and Thomas.

From Henry, the eldest son, descended the Cliffords of Ugbrook, and King's-Teignton, the last of which name there, James Clifford, Esq. left issue an only daughter and heir, Mary Clifford, who married Colonel Bampfield, only son of Sir Coplestone Bampfield, Bart. of Poltimore, in the county of Devon.

Thomas Clifford, Esq. the third son of Anthony, had the seat of Ugbrook, in Devonshire ; and was the first of his family that was seated in that beautiful spot. He was a man of a very vigorous mind, and great activity of body ; and his life was remarkable from the variety of his pursuits, and the different situations in which he was engaged. In his youth he served in the Netherlands, during the contest which the United Provinces maintained against Philip II. in defence of their independence, and in which they were so vigorously assisted by Queen Elizabeth. At the conclusion of this war, finding no further employment for his military talents, Clifford of Ugbrook engaged with the same earnestness in literary pursuits. He became a scholar in the university of Oxford, but was drawn from his studious retirement by Queen Elizabeth, who sent him twice as envoy extraordinary, to some of the German and Italian princes. In the latter part of Queen Elizabeth's reign, he again took up arms in order to attend the Earl of Essex in his naval expedition to Cadiz, but on his return to England, he resumed .his literary labours, and gave up his time once more to learning and science. When he was past fifty years of age, he turned his mind to the study of divinity; and became so great a proficient in theological science, that, after having performed all the accustomed exercises, he took the degree of doctor of divinity in the university of Oxford. On this occasion he preached a Latin sermon, which was greatly admired, and continued his ecclesiastical functions, but without any preferment in the church. Though he would accept of no living or preferment, yet he preached frequently, with a view, as he often said, to show others the way of avoiding those rocks whereon he himself had in his youth sometimes run. He died in the year 1634, having married Amy, daughter and heir of Hugh Staplehill, Esq. of Bremble, in the county of Wilts, by whom he left two sons, Hugh and Thomas, and four daughters.

This family of Staplehill, of which Thomas Clifford, Esq. of Ugbrook, married the heiress, was of great antiquity in the county of Devon; and I have met with the following remarkable anecdote respecting the armorial bearings of the family.

In the reign of Edward the First, Staplehill and Prideaux, being two English commanders at the battle of Houlkirk, where 20,000 Scotch were slain, and perceiving by their standards that each bore the same coat, they resolved to try by single combat to whom the arms belonged. But the king being unwilling to hazard the loss of such valiant soldiers, commanded them to cast lots who should bear the addition of *three labels in chief gules;* and the lot fell to Prideaux.

The arms which Staplehill bore were quarterly; 1st and 4th argent, a chevron sable · 2d and 3d gules, three fishes naiant, argent.

Hugh, eldest son of Thomas Clifford, Esq. of Ugbrook, succeeded his father. With that active loyalty for which all the branches of this noble family have been ever distinguished, on the rebellion of the Scotch in the year 1639, he immediately took up arms for King Charles I. and was appointed colonel of a regiment of foot. But falling sick, during the march of the army in the north of England, he returned home and died the same year.

Hugh Clifford, Esq. of Ugbrook, married Mary, daughter of Sir George Chudleigh, Bart. of Ashton, in the county of Devon; by whom he had two sons, Thomas, who was created Lord Clifford; and George, who married Elizabeth, daughter of George Price, Esq. of Esher, in Surrey.

SIR THOMAS CLIFFORD, KNIGHT,

FIRST LORD CLIFFORD

OF CHUDLEIGH.

Thomas, first Lord Clifford of Chudleigh, was born at Ugbrook, in Devonshire, the seat of his father, in the year 1630. He was endowed with great natural parts, and having received an excellent education, he became a very diligent student of the law in the Middle Temple, in London ; and soon obtained so great a reputation for his legal knowledge, and for his general acquaintance with state affairs, that the borough of Totness, in Devonshire, elected him their member in the memorable parliament which restored King Charles II. In the house of commons his eloquence was greatly admired ; and in the thirteenth year of the reign of Charles II. he was again returned to parliament, when he received the honour of knighthood.

Sir Thomas Clifford, like his grandfather abovementioned, had no less ardour for military exploits, than for the pursuits of science, or political administration. On the breaking out of the war with Holland, he attended the Duke of York, afterwards James II. in the great sea-fight with the Dutch, which happened on the 3d of June, in the year 1665, when the English were victorious, and Sir Thomas Clifford was highly

F

distinguished for his ardour and courage. After the action, he continued with the fleet, which was then commanded by the Earl of Sandwich, as vice-admiral, and was on board the squadron which was sent out in the month of August following, to attack the Dutch in the port of Bergen, in Norway. Sir Thomas Clifford was sent privately into the town, in order to treat with the Danish government on the subject; but the impetuosity of the English sailors, who refused to wait till the governor of Bergen received instructions from his court, entirely ruined the business. When the instructions arrived, the governor sent once more to desire Sir Thomas Clifford to come on shore, which he did; but notwithstanding the ability with which he managed the negociation, it fell to nothing. Soon after, however, he was sent as envoy and minister plenipotentiary to the courts, both of Sweden and Denmark, with full powers to treat, and to make new alliances with them.

In the year 1666, the English had another action with the Dutch, which continued the four first days of June, to the great honour of the English navy, whose memorable heroism on that occasion was celebrated by Dryden, in some beautiful stanzas of a poem, entitled " Annus Mirabilis." The fleet was commanded by Prince Rupert, and the Earl of Albemarle. Sir Thomas Clifford was present in the action, and likewise in another on the 25th of July following, in both of which he was always foremost in every service of danger.

On his return from these remarkable and adven-

turous enterprises, Sir Thomas Clifford was appointed comptroller of his majesty's household ;
and on the 5th of December following, was sworn
a member of the privy council, according to the
expressions in the Gazette, " for his singular zeal,
wherein he had, on all occasions, merited in his
majesty's service, and more eminently in the honourable dangers in the then late war against the
Dutch and French, where he had been all along
a constant actor, and as it was observed, had made
it his choice to take his share in the warmest part of
those services." And, in fact, to see a country gentleman of family and fortune, who had morever
closely addicted himself to the study of the law, engage in the sea-service, and display all at once the
bravery and skill of a naval officer, with the abilities
of a statesman and negociator, was a phenomenon
which could not but strike the eyes of all who beheld
it. The eulogium passed by Pope on the great Duke
of Argyle, might, with equal propriety, be applied
to Sir Thomas Clifford :

Argyle, the state's whole thunder born to wield,
And shake alike the senate and the field.

New honours and dignities now flowed on Sir
Thomas Clifford. On the death of the Earl of Southampton, lord treasurer of England, he was appointed one of the lords commissioners for execut-
ing that high and honourable office ; and in the
year 1668, the king bestowed upon him the place
of treasurer of the household.

I now come to a period in the life of Sir Tho-

F 2

mas Clifford, in which his name was intimately connected with a very remarkable era in English history ; but which unfortunately has been so much disfigured by party-prejudice, that it is now almost impossible to discover the truth. Macpherson, in his " History of England, from the Restoration to the Accession of the House of Hanover," declares, that the spirit of party was so violent and excessive during that period, that " history was more the engine of faction than the vehicle of truth :" And Echard, after having given the character of Sir Thomas Clifford, from a French work, " The History of the Revolutions of England" by Père d'Orléans, adds, " The French Jesuits' short account of the cabal seems more material than most of the English pamphlets and secret histories that have been wrote on that occasion." For these reasons therefore, after having given the character of Sir Thomas Clifford, from Macpherson, I shall add the account of the ministry called the Cabal, by the Père d'Orléans.

Every one who has read the history of Charles the Second, knows, that in a few years after his restoration, that king appointed a ministry, consisting of five distinguished English noblemen, who were called the Cabal. These five noblemen were Clifford, Arlington, Buckingham, Ashley, and Lauderdale. The following character of Sir Thomas Clifford, is from Macpherson.

" Clifford, whom his name was placed at the

head of the cabal, deserved that pre-eminence from another cause. To a boldness, which shrunk from no political danger, he added an openness which approached to honesty. He was a violent enemy, yet a sincere friend ; and though his prejudices led him into errors, yet he atoned for them in some measure, by avowing his conduct to the world. His eloquence in the house of commons first brought him into notice ; his intimacy with Arlington first raised him into office. Ardent and impetuous in his councils, he deserved to be trusted from his spirit. His perseverance in any plan acquired him a firmness in all. The only symptom of weakness which he exhibited, was his avowed adherence to a system of faith which the laws of his country did not recognise. But, few men had then arrived at a degree of philosophy sufficient to remove religion from the channel of their temporary concerns."

The following account of the ministry called the cabal, is from the " History of the Revolutions of England," by Père d'Orléans.

" It was in the year 1670, that the court of England, perceiving that the republican spirit was again insinuating itself into the parliament, undertook to remedy this evil, which presaged many others. The authors of this enterprise were five lords, who were called the cabal, from the union which appeared among them, and because the initial letters of their names formed the word cabal. One of them was the king's favourite, and the four others his ministers ; and all the four were employed in the first offices of the state, and had great weight in the council. These five men, considered each in particular, were not without their faults ; but taken altogether, they formed a body which wanted but few of those things on which the success of great designs depends. The Duke of Buckingham, the king's favourite, was very fit for a minister, if his application had corresponded with his talents; if his understanding, which was excellent, had not been distracted by his libertinism which was extreme, and by a love of pleasure, which rendered frivolous a man who had the best natural parts for sober business. The Duke of Lauderdale, a Scotchman, and secretary of state for the affairs of Scotland, was a man of great versatility of genius, and a profound politician. Lord Clifford, the lord high treasurer, only wanted a theatre on which reason and virtue were more practised than they were in his country during his age, in order to render him superior to the others. The Earl of Arlington, secretary of state for England, had the least talents of the five; but this was compensated by his experience, and above all by his knowledge of foreign affairs. Anthony Ashley Cooper, Earl of Shaftsbury, and Lord Chancellor, was the fittest of them all to conduct a great enterprise; and in fact, he was the soul of this. He was endowed with a comprehensive, and enlightened mind, bold and intriguing, and equally firm in prosperous or adverse circumstances, as long as those to whom he was attached, gave him no reason to change his opinions. A constant friend, but an implacable enemy, he was the more dangerous, as being perfectly unconcerned about religion or conscience, he was the less embarrassed in his choice of the means of doing mischief; for he was neither alarmed by the enormity nor the multitude of any crimes which he thought necessary either for his own preservation, or for the ruin of those who had incurred his hatred.

These lords, attached to their sovereign by their places, and by his benefits, could not behold without indignation, the rapid strides which the republican spirit had been making in parliament, for some years past, against the royal authority.— Among other things, the triple alliance, which the republican party had forced the king to make against his will, appeared to them an audacious enterprise against royalty, of which it was absolutely necessary to prevent the consequences. Full of these *just sentiments*, they persuaded the king to be master in his own kingdom, *as far as the prerogatives of the crown, and the laws of the country gave him a right;* to confine parliament within the limits prescribed by established customs ; and to prevent that outrageous combination of republicanism and monarchy, and that usurpation of the subject on the sovereign, the infallible result of which would be a monstrous anarchy, that would expose England a second time, to fall into that dreadful chaos from which it was hardly emerged."

From this account of the objects and views of the ministry called the cabal, it seems fair to conclude, that like Cicero, during the convul-

sions of the Roman republic in his time, and like
all the wise and honest statesmen of every nation,
in which the popular party has had a share in the
government, Sir Thomas Clifford, and his associates, endeavoured to throw the ascendancy of
state affairs into the hands of the executive power,
*as far as was consistent with the laws of the coun-
try, and the liberties of the people.* And indeed
the experience of all history, with the examples of
our own days, sufficiently prove, that a contrary
mode of administration in a government, will in-
fallibly be followed by anarchy, bloodshed, and
desolation.

But whatever judgment may be formed of the views
or conduct of Sir T. Clifford, at this period, there
can be but one opinion respecting his claims to the
honours and rewards, which were so justly bestowed upon him by his sovereign. In the year
1672, he was appointed principal secretary of state,
and about the same time was advanced to the dignity of a baron of the realm, by the title of Lord
Clifford, of Chudleigh. In the month of Novem-
ber following his majesty made him lord high treasurer of England, by the delivery of the white
staff, and by constituting him at the same time by
letters patent, treasurer of the exchequer.

This important office of lord high treasurer of
England, had been held several years in commission, but Lord Clifford having received the white
staff from the king's own hands, he went with
mighty solemnity, and a pompous attendance, to
be sworn at Westminster-hall, where he was re-

ceived by the Earl of Shaftsbury, one of his col-
leagues in the ministry, who had lately been appointed lord chancellor. After having made some
observations on the nature of his high office of lord
treasurer, the chancellor addressed Lord Clifford
as follows: " I may justly say, you are in a place
of the very first rank as to dignity, power, trust,
and influence of affairs ; a place that requires such
a man as our great master's wisdom has found for
it: from whose natural temper we may expect
courage, quickness, and resolution; and from
whose extraction, (that noble and illustrious house
of the Cliffords) an heroic mind, a large soul, and
an unshaken fidelity to the crown."

The foregoing pages of this little volume sufficiently show, that either with respect to Lord
Clifford, or the family from which he descended,
there was no exaggeration in the flattering eulogium
thus pronounced upon them by the lord chancellor.

Lord Clifford continued in the place of lord high
treasurer till the month of June 1673, when he determined to relinquish entirely all public affairs,
and pass the remainder of his life in rural retirement. He accordingly resigned his staff into the
hands of the king, together with all his other employments, and retired to his seat at Ugbrook, in
the county of Devon.

In consideration of his faithful services, his majesty King Charles II. granted him a lease of Creslow
Pastures, near Aylesbury, in Buckinghamshire ;
and gave to him and his heirs the manors of Can-
nington and Rodway, in the county of Somerset.

But Lord Clifford did not long enjoy the honours and favours of his sovereign, for being seized with a mortal illness soon after his retreat into the country, he died in the month of September 1673. He was buried in the chapel at Ugbrook, a handsome building which he himself had erected, and which had been consecrated by the Bishop of Exeter.

Lord Clifford married Elizabeth, daughter and coheir of William Martin, Esq. of Lindridge, in the county of Devon, by whom he had issue seven sons and eight daughters. He was succeeded in his title, and estates, by Hugh, his fifth son, the others having died before him.

HUGH,
SECOND LORD CLIFFORD,
OF CHUDLEIGH.

Lord Clifford, the treasurer, amidst the varied employments of his active and laborious life, was not forgetful of the interests of literature. He was the decided patron of Dryden, whom he invited to his seat at Ugbrook ; and there that illustrious poet afterwards completed his translation of Virgil's Pastorals, which he dedicated to Hugh, second Lord Clifford, son and heir of the treasurer. This dedication of Dryden is so flattering to Lord Clifford and his family, that I shall here transcribe some passages from it :

My Lord,

I have found it not more difficult to translate Virgil, than to find such patrons as I desire for my translation. For though England is not wanting in a learned nobility, yet such are my unhappy circumstances, that they have confined me to a narow choice. Yet I have no reason to compla:n of fortune, since in the midst of that abundance I could not possibly have chosen better, than the worthy son of so illustrious a father. He was the patron of my manhood, when I flourished in the opinion of the world, though with small advantage to my fortune, till he awakened the remembrance of my royal master. He was that Pollio, or that Varus, who introduced me to Augustus : and though he soon dismissed himself from state affairs, yet in the

short time of his administration he shone so power-
fully upon me, that, like the heat of a Russian summer, he ripened the fruits of poetry in a cold cli-
mate ; and gave me wherewithal to subsist at least,
in the long winter which succeeded.

My Lord, I know to whom I dedicate, and could
not have been induced by any motive to put this
part of Virgil or any other into unlearned hands.
You have added to your natural endowments,
which, without flattery, are eminent, the super-
structures of study, and the knowledge of good
authors. Courage, probity, and humanity, are
inherent in you. These virtues have ever been ha-
bitual to the ancient house of Cumberland, from
which you are descended ; and of which our chro-
nicles make so honourable mention, in the long wars
betwixt the rival families of York and Lancaster.
Your forefathers have asserted the party they chose
till death, and died for its defence in the fields of
battle. You have besides the fresh remembrance
of your noble father, from whom you never can
degenerate.

—— *Nec imbellem feroces*
Progenerant aquilæ columbam.

May you ever continue your esteem for Virgil ;
and not lessen it for the faults of his translator ;
who is, with all manner of respect and sense of
gratitude,

My Lord,
Your Lordship's most humble, and
Most obedient Servant,
JOHN DRYDEN.

It is certain that Dryden in his latter days was frequently at Ugbrook, and a spot is shown in the Park, one of the most beautiful in England, which is dignified by the name of Dryden's Seat.

Hugh, second Lord Clifford, of Chudleigh, married Anne, one of the daughters and coheiresses of Sir Thomas Preston, Bart. of Furness, in the county of Lancaster, by whom he had issue nine sons, and six daughters.

Francis, the eldest son, born in the year 1686, died an infant.

Thomas, the second son, married Charlotte, Countess of Newburgh, in her own right, by whom he had only two daughters, one of whom died unmarried. The other, Lady Anne Clifford, married Count O'Mahony, of the kingdom of Naples, and had an only daughter, who married Prince Justiniani of Rome, from whom the present Prince of that name is descended.

Hugh, the seventh son, born in the year 1708, succeeded his father in his title and estates, and was the third Lord Clifford, of Chudleigh.

Of the *daughters* of Hugh, second Lord Clifford, Elizabeth, the eldest, was married to William Constable, Lord Viscount Dunbar, who died without issue in the year 1718.

Catherine and Mary, were nuns at Ghent, in Flanders.

Anne, the fourth daughter, married George Carey, Esq. of Torr-abbey, in the county of Devon.

Amy, the fifth daughter, married Cuthbert Constable, Esq. of Burton-Constable, near Hull, in Yorkshire, and of Wycliffe, in the same county.

Cuthbert Constable, Esq. was the son of Francis Tunstall, Esq. of Wycliff, by Cecily, daughter of John, Lord Viscount Dunbar; and assumed the name of Constable, by the will of his maternal uncle, William, Lord Viscount Dunbar, above-mentioned, who left him his great estates at Burton-Constable, in the county of Holderness, in the East Riding of Yorkshire.

His wife, the Honourable Amy Clifford, fifth daughter of Hugh, second Lord Clifford, died at the age of 26, and was buried in the church-yard of Pancras, near London, which is the general place of interment for all the Roman Catholics who die in the metropolis. A handsome marble monument was erected to her memory by her afflicted husband on the spot where she was interred, with the following epitaph:

Here lieth all that was mortal of
The Honourable Amey Constable,
The worthy daughter of Hugh Lord Clifford of
Chudleigh, and the much lamented wife of
Cuthbert Constable, Esq.
Of Burton-Constable, in Holdernesse:
A Lady
who, in the flower of her youth, employed her whole time and thoughts in the care of her soul, the Christian education of her children,

and an engaging behaviour to her husband and friends.

She was agreeable without art,
Cheerful without levity,
Grave without affectation,
Witty without censoriousness;
Obliging to all, without flattery,
Patient and courageous, without ostentation.

An enemy to nothing but what was vicious or base,
A friend only to Virtue and Truth.

She finished her course on the 25th of July, A. D. 1731, and the 26th year of her age.

Her disconsolate husband erected this monument of her uncommon merit, and his irreparable loss.

HUGH,

THIRD LORD CLIFFORD,

OF CHUDLEIGH.

Hugh, third Lord Clifford, was born at Ugbrook, in the year 1700. He married Elizabeth, daughter and coheiress of Edward Blount, Esq. of Blagdon, in the county of Devon, and sister to the Duchess of Norfolk. By her, he had issue four sons: Hugh, father of the present Lord Clifford, Edward, who died unmarried, Henry, who died an infant, and Thomas, born after his decease. Also two daughters, Elizabeth, who died an infant, and Mary, married to Sir Edward Smythe, Bart. of Acton-Burnell, in the county of Salop.

CLIFFORDS OF TIXALL,

IN THE

COUNTY OF STAFFORD.

The Honourable Thomas Clifford, youngest son of Hugh, third Lord Clifford, of Chudleigh, was born after the death of his father, in the year 1732. In his youth he was for some years in the French service, during the reign of Lewis XV., and was an officer in one of the regiments of the king's household, called " Les Mousquetaires," into which only persons of noble birth were admitted. On the breaking out of a war between France and England, about the middle of the last century, he returned to England; and soon after married the Honourable Barbara Aston, youngest daughter and coheir of James, fifth Lord Aston, Baron of Forfar, in Scotland. This lady was of very high and noble descent, for her mother was the Lady Barbara Talbot, daughter of George, fourteenth Earl of Shrewsbury, and her grandmother the Lady Mary Howard, sister to Thomas and Edward, both Dukes of Norfolk. The ancestors of her father, Lord Aston, who were allied to some of the first families in the realm, had flourished at Tixall, in the county of Stafford, and at Haywood, in the immediate neighbourhood of it, for

G

many centuries. They were constantly returned as knights of the shire to parliament, from the reign of Henry III., when the house of commons was first established, down to the reign of Charles I.; when Sir Walter Aston, of Tixall, who had been twice ambassador in Spain, in very critical times, was, for his eminent services, and in consideration of his noble and illustrious lineage, advanced to the peerage, by the title of Lord Aston, Baron of Forfar, in the kingdom of Scotland. His descendant, James, fifth Lord Aston, had issue by his wife, the Lady Barbara Talbot, only two daughters and coheiresses : Mary, who married Sir Walter Blount, Bart. of Sodington, and Mawley, in the county of Worcester ; and Barbara, the wife of the Hon. Thomas Clifford.

The estate of Tixall became the property of the youngest daughter the Hon. Mrs. Clifford; and the old family mansion of the Astons, being in a very ruinous state, her husband, the Hon. Thomas Clifford, erected a new and elegant modern house, near the scite of the old ruins, in one of the most beautiful situations in the county of Stafford.

The Hon. Thomas Clifford died in the year 1787, having lost his wife the year before. By her he had issue eight sons and five daughters, of whom the eldest, Sir Thomas Clifford, Bart. is the present possessor of the estate of Tixall, in the county of Stafford.

———————————

The marriage of two daughters of Hugh, second Lord Clifford, of Chudleigh, with the family of Constable, above-mentioned, was not only a very honourable and noble alliance, but proved eventually of great consequence to the Clifford family. William, last Viscount Dunbar, who married the eldest daughter of Lord Clifford, died without issue in the year 1718, leaving his estates in Holderness, in the county of York, to his nephew, Cuthbert Tunstall, Esq. of Wycliffe, who had married another daughter of Lord Clifford, and who in consequence assumed the name of Constable. Cuthbert Constable, Esq. had issue by his wife, the Hon. Amy Clifford, only one son, the late William Constable, Esq. of Burton-Constable, and of Wycliffe in the county of York; who having no issue settled all his estates on his two nephews, the late Edward Sheldon, Esq. who asssumed the name of Constable, and the present Francis Constable, Esq.: And in default of male issue from them, on the seven surviving sons of the Honourable Thomas Clifford, and the Honourable Barbara Aston, of whom four are now living; namely,

Sir Thomas Clifford, of Tixall, Bart.

James Clifford, Esq. of the Navy Pay-Office, Plymouth.

Arthur Clifford, Esq. Author of this Work; and

George Clifford, Esq. of Foxearth, in the county of Stafford.

Thus was established a new branch of the Clifford family, the descendants of which, together

G 2

with the Cliffords of Ugbrook, in the county of Devon, are, as I have stated above, the only representatives and descendants by the male line, of Walter de Clifford, of Clifford-castle, in the county of Hereford, the first who assumed the name of Clifford, about the middle of the twelfth century.

END OF THE FIRST PART.

COLLECTANEA CLIFFORDIANA,

PART THE SECOND:

CONTAINING

Historical and Genealogical Notices respecting the
Origin and Antiquity

OF THE

NAME AND FAMILY

OF

C L I F F O R D.

When we read of a family so ancient, that it has no beginning, so worthy that it ought to have no end, we sympathise in its various fortunes ; nor can we blame the generous enthusiasm, or even the harmless vanity of those who are allied to the honour of its name.   GIBBON.

ORIGINES

ET

ANTIQUITATES CLIFFORDIENSES.

I.

OF THE ORIGIN OF THE
NAME OF CLIFFORD.

It is generally allowed by all our antiquaries, and genealogists, that surnames or family names, were not common, nor well established in England, till the reign of Henry III. nearly two centuries after the Conquest. One of the earliest and most ancient of these surnames is that of Clifford, which was already celebrated in England, in the reign of King Henry II. before the middle of the 12ᵀᴴ century, and which belongs to a noble and illustrious family, of the longest continuance of almost any in the kingdom.

The name of Clifford, which is of Anglo-Saxon origin, was derived from Clifford-castle, in the county of Hereford, a fortress erected on a cliff, or steep rock, overhanging the river Wye, at the foot of which is a ford. This was probably called the Cliff-Ford, and gave its name to the adjacent village of Clifford, which appears to have existed before the Conquest. Clifford-castle was erected soon after that memorable event, by William Fitz-Osbern, a Normanbaron of great distinction, and nearly allied to the Conqueror. He commanded the advanced guard of the Norman army at the famous battle of Hastings, and greatly contributed to the victory which decided the fate of England, and placed William the Conqueror on the throne of that kingdom. Fitz-Osbern was rewarded for his services by a grant of the earldom of Hereford, and numerous manors. But he did not long enjoy these great possessions and honours; for being sent by King William on an expedition into Flanders, he was there slain in the year 1070.

The origin of Clifford-castle is celebrated in the following stanzas of a poem, composed in imitation of the old English ballad:

> In Herefordshire there lies a spot,
> To travellers often shown;
> Where once a lordly mansion stood,
> Though now by time o'erthrown.

> High on a cliff, hard by a ford,
> This warlike structure frowned;
> And hence 'twas Clifford-castle called
> By all the country round.

> With turrets, battlements, and towers,
> It proudly shone afar;
> And fenced with moat and drawbridge, seemed
> Completely armed for war.

After the death of Earl Fitz-Osbern, Roger de Bretteville, his third son, inherited the earldom of Hereford, and all his father's lands in England, with the lordship of Clifford among the the rest. This is evident from a deed in Dugdale's Monasticon, in which Roger de Bretteville grants to the church of Blessed Mary, in Clifford, and to the monks thereunto belonging, free licence to buy or sell, without toll or other restraint, in all his tenements within Wye. But in the year 1078, this Roger de Bretteville being detected in a conspiracy against King William, was sentenced to lose all his possessions, and to be imprisoned for life.

It appears from the celebrated survey of England, called Domesday-book, which was completed in the year 1086, that the castle of Clifford, and the castellany, or lordship belonging to it, was at that time, in the possession of Ralph de Toeny, another noble Norman, whose sister Adelisa, Earl Fitz-Osbern had married. Clifford-castle was probably bestowed on Ralph de Toeni by William the Conqueror, on the forfeiture of Roger de Bretteville, in the year 1078.

We now come to a third noble Norman, Walter Fitz-Ponts, who married Margaret, granddaughter of Ralph de Toeni. By this marriage, Walter Fitz-Ponts obtained possession of Clifford-castle, and assumed the name of De Clifford, which he transmitted to his posterity. In what year this marriage took place does not appear ; but, in Powell's History of Wales, Fitz-Ponts is recorded to have been governor of Llandovery-castle, in that country, in the year 1157, by the appellation of Walter de Clifford; and before that period, the name of Clifford, as a surname, or family-name, is no where to be found.

Clifford-castle, which thus gave its name to one of the most illustrious families in England, continued to be the residence of the descendants of Walter de Clifford, for some generations; but in the reign of Edward I. it devolved to Matilda, only daughter and heiress of Walter de Clifford, his grandson. Matilda de Clifford married her cousin William Longsword, Earl of Salisbury, who was grandson of King Henry II. by the celebrated Rosamund Clifford, commonly called Fair Rosamund. By him, Matilda had an only daughter called Margaret, who inherited Clifford-castle, and was married to Henry de Lacy, Earl of Lincoln. But he dying without issue, in the year 1312, Clifford-castle, according to the custom of those feudal times, then fell to the crown; and was given by King Edward II. to his celebrated favourite, Hugh le Despenser, and after his attainder, to Mortimer, Earl of March. Clifford-castle appears to have remaned in the illustrious family of Mortimer, for many generations; for it is enumerated by Dugdale, among the vast possessions which devolved to Richard, Duke of York, father of King Edward IV., upon the death of Edmund Mortimer, last Earl of March, in the year 1425. Of the possessors of Clifford-castle from this period, I can give no information. Like other remarkable edifices, which have been ennobled and illustrated by the heroes who erected

them, or the noble families who have inhabited
them, Clifford-castle has been subjected to that mu-
tability and vicissitude, which sooner or later, is
the certain lot of all the monuments of human
grandeur.

> Shades that to Bacon could retreat afford,
> Become the portion of some booby lord ;
> And Hemsley, once proud Buckingham's delight,
> Slides to a scrivener, or a city knight.

One ruined tower is now nearly all that remains
of the ancient magnificence of Clifford-castle, and
of this a view may be seen in Britton's work, entitled
" The Beauties of England and Wales."

Instead of dwelling on the ruins of Clifford-castle, I shall now lay before the reader the description of it in its primitive state, from Domesday-
book :

Herefscire—Terra Radulfi de Toeni.

Radulfus de Toeni tenet castellum de Cliford.
Willielmus comes fecit illud in wastâ terrâ, quam
tenebat Bruning tempore Regis Edwardi. Ibi
habet Radulfus terram ad tres carucatas, sed non
est nisi una caruca. Istud castellum est de regno
Angliæ, non subjacet alicui hundret, neque in
consuetudine.

Gislebertus vice-comes tenet illud ad firmam,
et burgum, et carucam. De toto reddit sexaginta
solidos.

In castellaniâ de Clifford tenet Rogerius (de Lacy)
quatuor carucatas terræ. Pater ejus tenuit. Wastæ
fuerunt et sunt.

Herefordshire—The land of Ralf de Toeni.

" Ralf de Toeni holds Clifford-castle. Earl William built it on waste land, which Bruning held in the time of King Edward : Ralf holds there three plough-lands, but there is only plough. This castle is of the kingdom of England, is not subject to any hundred, or any customary service.

Gilbert, the viscount, keeps it, together with the farm and the borough, and the plough-land. For the whole he pays sixty shillings.

In the lordship of Clifford, Roger (de Lacy) holds four plough-lands. His father held them. They were and are waste."

It may be observed, that the reason why Clifford lordship lay nearly all waste, was that it was border-land, and was therefore constantly exposed to the inroads of the Welsh.

———

Four other places bearing the name of Clifford, occur in Domesday-book :

1. Clifford, in Yorkshire, a township in the parish of Bramham, three miles from Tadcaster, and 192 from London. It still bears the name, and contains at this day, 107 houses, and 660 inhabitants.

2. Clifford, in Warwickshire, which consists of two members; the larger part called Clifford Cham-

bers, is situated in Gloucestershire, on the borders of Warwickshire, two miles from Stratford-upon-Avon, and ninety-four from London.

The other part was known in the reign of Henry I. by the name of Clifford Minor, but is called by Dugdale, in his "History of Warwickshire," Ruin Clifford. This is a place of great antiquity, as appears from the following passage in Dugdale's history above-mentioned : " In the year 988, Oswald, Bishop of Worcester, and Archbishop of York, gave to his servant Ethelward, three manses here at Clifford, with the meadows, pastures, and waters, thereto belonging. In the Conqueror's time, Robert de Statford, or Stafford, possessed one hide, and a virgate of land here, then held of him by one Hugh, whose posterity residing there, assumed hence the surname of Clifford : the last male branch of which family was John de Clifford, who (temp. Hen. 3.) passed away all his lands here to Ralph le Poer, son of Margery his sister, which makes me conclude he had no children of his own."

From this passage of Dugdale, and from what I have said above respecting Clifford-castle, in Herefordshire, it is clear, that the name of Clifford was known in England, as the name of a place, before the Norman conquest, and for many centuries most probably, before it became the surname of an individual or family.

3. and 4. Two places in Devonshire, are cited in Domesday-book, bearing the name of Clifford, and are now called East and West Clifford, in Wonford Hundred. West Clifford is a hamlet in the

'parish of Drews-Teignton. It is evident, that these four places had no connexion with the Cliffords of Clifford-castle, who, as I have shewn above, did not assume the name of Clifford, till many years after the survey called Domesday-book was com-.pleted.

Four miles and a half from the town of Northampton, is a spot called Clifford-hill, of which I find the following account in Brydges's History of Northamptonshire :—" In the parish of Houghton, on the bank of the river Nyne, stands Clifford-hill. That there was formerly a ford below the hill, in that part of the river where it is divided into two streams, is supported by general tradition. There is also a hill now named the Cliff, not far from Brayfield, from whence we may suppose it to have taken the name of Clifford."

II.

OF THE ORIGIN AND ANTIQUITY

OF THE

CLIFFORD FAMILY.

In the " Supplement" to Collins's Peerage, published at London, in the year 1750, there is an article entitled " Clifford, Baroness Clifford," which
extends through seventy pages of close small print,
and appears to have been composed with great care
and attention, from ancient records, authentic manuscripts, the principal English historians, and
other approved authorities, which are abundantly
and faithfully quoted by Collins, in almost every
page. This ample and circumstantial account of
the Clifford Family, seems to have been inserted
by Collins in the Supplement to his Peerage, in
consequence of the barony of Clifford having been
granted by King George II. in the year 1734, to
the Lady Margaret Tufton, wife of Thomas Coke,
Esq. of Holkham, in the county of Norfolk, who
was afterwards created Lord Lovel, Viscount
Coke, and Earl of Leicester. His wife, the Countess of Leicester, was daughter of the Earl of Thanet, and great grand-daughter of Lady Anne Clifford, Countess of Dorset, Pembroke, and Montgomery, whose right to the barony of Clifford has

been shown in the First Part of this Work. The titel having fallen in abeyance between the five daughters of the Earl of Thanet, his majesty King George II. was pleased to confirm it to the third daughter, the Countess of Leicester, above-mentioned. This noble lady, who had a just and exalted opinion of her high and illustrious descent, appears to have communicated to Collins all the documents in her possession, respecting the Clifford family ; and, in particular, a manuscript history of the family, in three volumes folio, which, as I have mentioned already, was drawn up with the greatest care, by the orders, and under the inspection of the celebrated Lady Anne Clifford, and is still preserved at Appleby-castle, in Westmoreland, the seat of Lord Thanet.

This article concerning the Clifford family, in the Supplement to Collins's Peerage, begins in the following manner :

Clifford, Baroness Clifford.

"Clifford-castle, in Herefordshire, built by William Fitz-Osborn, Earl of Hereford, in William the Conqueror's reign, gave surname to this great and noble family. Walter, son of Richard Fitz-Pons, having acquired it by marriage with Margaret, daughter and heir of Ralph de Toeny, a descendant from the said William Fitz-Osborn.

In the Conqueror's Survey, Walter and Drugo, and Richard, are called sons of Pons, who was son of William, Earl of Angus, in Normandy, second son to Richard, Duke of Normandy ; and was surnamed Pons, of an island called Ponor."

In this passage of Collins, there are two mistakes in the orthography of the names " Angus" and " Ponor." Pons, more properly Ponts, who is mentioned in the Conqueror's Survey, was the son of William, Earl of " Eu," in Normandy ; and " Eu" in Latin, (the language of the old Norman Historians) is called " Auga" or " Augum," which would easily be corrupted into " Angus," which has more of an English sound, and is a name both of places and families well known in Scotland.

The earldom or county of Eu, in Normandy, has always had two dependencies, called Tréport, and Pons, which are known by the same names at this day. Pons is a poor straggling village, situated on the banks of the little river Brêsle, which separates Normandy from Picardy ; and at this spot, divides into two branches, forming an island, which is connected with the banks on each side by *two bridges*, over which is the road of communication with Picardy. This circumstance of the *two bridges*, *les deux ponts*, in French, or *pontes* in Latin, was probably the origin of the name of the village, and also of the island which Collins erroneously calls *Ponor*. This mistake, as well as that of *Angus*, instead of *Eu*, has been copied into other peerages and other genealogies of the Clifford family. The ancient castle of the counts of Eu, a venerable ivy-mantled ruin, is still to be seen at that place, but the island of " Pons," in the river Brêsle, is now occupied by a great cotton-manufactory.

When William the Conqueror invaded England, Robert the second Count of Eu, attended him on

H

that expedition, and got possession of several extensive estates in the county of Sussex, which are enumerated under his name in Domesday-book. As the sons of his younger brother, called " Pons," are also mentioned in that survey, it is probable that their father, the youngest son of William, first Count of Eu, also attended the Conqueror, to whom he was nearly allied. Surnames, or family names, were at this time unknown both in England and Normandy, but in the latter country it was usual for the barons or great men to add to their christian names the name of some place or estate which belonged to them or their family. In this manner the youngest son of William, Count of Eu, assumed the name of Ponts, or Pontes; and that he derived it from the *two bridges* above-mentioned, is still further confirmed by a charter preserved in Dugdale's " Monasticon," in which two sons of Ponts, Richard, and Osbern, who were benefactors to the priory at Malvern, in Worcestershire, are called, Ricardus *Pontium*, and Osbernus *Pontium ;* or as we should say now, Richard and Osberne Bridges.

Ponts, therefore, whose sons are mentioned in Domesday-book, was the son of William, first Count of Eu, in Normandy. William, Count of Eu, was son of Richard, third Duke of Normandy, who was grandson of the famous Rollo ; a Danish or Norwegian chieftain, who conquered the country called Normandy, from Charles the Simple, King of France, and became sovereign of it under the title of duke.

Ponts, the descendant of Rollo, was grandfather of Walter Fitz-Ponts, of Clifford-castle, in the county of Hereford, above-mentioned, the first who assumed the name of Clifford, about the year 1150, and the great progenitor of all the families in England of the name of Clifford. It therefore seems proper to deduce the genealogical history of the Clifford family, from Rollo, the first Duke of Normandy, who was the ancestor of William the Conqueror, and of his royal descendants the kings of England.

ROLLO,

FIRST DUKE OF NORMANDY.

Suetonius relates in his life of Julius Cæsar, that that great man, though born and bred a republican, entertained a lofty idea of the dignity and consequence of high and noble descent; for at the funeral of his aunt Julia, he pronounced an oration, according to custom in the *Forum*, before the people, in which he used the following expressions concerning her descent, and the origin of his family :—" Amitæ meæ Juliæ maternum genus ab regibus ortum, paternum cum Diis immortalibus conjunctum est. Nam ab Anco Marcio sunt Marcii reges quo nomine fuit mater : a Venere Julii, cujus gentis familia est nostra. Est ergo in genere et sanctitas regum, qui plurimum inter homines

H 2

pollent, et ceremonia Deorum, quorum ipsi in potestate sunt reges."

" The maternal line of my aunt Julia was sprung from kings, but by her paternal descent, she was connected with the immortal gods. For the Marcian kings, of whose race was her mother, were descended from Ancus Marcius; and the Julii, which is my family, sprung from Venus. There is therefore in our line, the sacred dignity of kings, who possess great influence over mankind, and the religious veneration of the gods, in whose power are kings themselves."

It would perhaps not be more difficult to show, that Rollo the Norwegian, was descended from Thor and Friga, the Jupiter and Venus of the Scandinavians, than that Julius Cæsar was descended from the Jupiter and Venus of the Greeks; but leaving aside these celestial genealogies, I shall here relate what appears most probable respecting the history and family of this illustrious adventurer, whose descendants flourished for a considerable length of time, with great renown, for their wisdom and valour, as dukes of Normandy, and whose posterity by the female line, is still seated on the throne of Great Britain.

It would be no very difficult task to prove, that none of the historians, who have written on the early history and first conquests of the Normans, were rightly informed on the subject which they undertook to treat; nor had they in their possession the necessary documents, for establishing the truth of the facts which they relate. The first Norman chroniclers, or annalists, were all monks, and ignorance or prejudice had corrupted the sources of their information.

A considerable number of incursions made by the men of the North, had preceded that of Rollo, whom the monkish chroniclers represent in the first instance as a ruffian, because he destroyed the monasteries, but whom they afterwards extol, when he caused them to be re-built after his conversion, and became their benefactor. This illustrious chieftain had nothing of the barbarian but his name ; and it is to be regretted that so much diversity, uncertainty, and confusion prevail among the writers who have treated of his native country, of his family, and character. As nothing satisfactory can be found in the Norman historians, on the motives or circumstances of the eternal farewell which Rollo was induced to take of his native land, it seems more proper to have recourse to the Icelandish and Norwegian histories, called " Sagas,' which are likely to contain the only certain documents respecting those remote ages, since some of their writers were cotemporary with Rollo himself.

Rollo, according to the " Sagas," called in the language of his country, " Gongu Hrolff," was the sixth son of Rognwald, Jarl, or Governor of Sundmoër, in Norway, and of Hilda, daughter of Hrolf-nefjo. He was born in the year 843, during the reign of Harald Harfager ; and served in the army, at an early age, under the command of his father. He soon took to the profession of a pirate, which in those days, and in his country, as in ancient Greece, was not dishonourable, and was the only one suited to his restless, enterprising, and warlike disposition. According to the " Harald's Saga," he was tall and well made, and unequalled in strength. His first piratical expeditions were in the Baltic ; and one day, having made a descent on a part of the country which now belongs to Sweden, he seized several head of cattle, and distributed them among his followers, who began to be in want of provisions. King Harald had forbid piracy in his own states, and was therefore very indignant when he was informed that Rollo had transgressed his prohibitions. He ordered him to be summoned before the public assembly of the nation, by whom he was sentenced to be banished from Norway. Hilda, the mother of Rollo, used all her efforts to pacify the king, but in vain ; he remained inflexible, and Rollo having lost all hope of pardon, determined to leave his country for ever. Having assembled his adventurous followers, he began by pirating in the north-western seas, towards the Shetland and Orkney Isles ; after which he made a descent upon France, and conquered the province which has since borne the name of Normandy.

Rollo was a Norwegian by birth, but the hardy adventurers, who accompanied him on his perilous and memorable expeditions, were probably an assemblage of persons from the different northern nations, who were called Normans, because they came from the North Seas. Thormod Torf, a Norwegian historian, assures us, that the spot where Rollo embarked, in the province of Sundmoër, in Norway, and also the cables of his vessels, were still shewn in the beginning of the 17th century; the tradition of his memorable departure having been constantly delivered down without alteration for the space of seven centuries. Busching also says, that near Wiborg, in the North Jutland, there are two remarkable vallies called the great and little Norman-dale, where the Normans assembled before they set out on their foreign and distant expeditions.

From these different documents it appears, that excepting the sentence of expulsion pronounced by King Harald against Rollo, in punishment of his disobedience, there was no other cause for his expatriation and that of his followers, but their decided taste for distant and adventurous expeditions ; a taste which they preserved for a long time, even after their complete settlement in Normandy : as appears by the ardour with which they engaged in the crusades to the Holy Land, and by the successful expeditions of the Normans in Palestine, Greece, Calabria, and Sicily. It is well known how rapidly the Normans became a civilised nation, particularly after the conquest of England ; it is indeed a most remarkable circumstance, and worthy of particular observation. Scarcely emerged from barbarism, they became a model of imitation in almost every respect, both to neighbouring and distant nations. Ingulph, a very interesting historian, who was brought up in the court of Edward the Confessor, says, that his nation abandoned their English customs, in order to adopt those

of the Normans ; and that people of rank spoke
their language, which was a mixture of Danish and
French ; the Danish language in the time of Rollo,
being the common tongue of all the northern
nations.

It is related by other historians, that Rollo, after
having pirated for some time in the North Seas, and
seeing no hope of an advantageous settlement in
any part of the island of Great Britain, pretended
to his followers that he had a supernatural dream,
which promised him a glorious fortune in France,
which was the more readily believed by them from
the known weakness of the government of that
kingdom, and from the confusion in which it was
involved. Rollo, therefore, made for the coast
of France, and sailing up the Seine to the town of
Rouen, capital of the province then called Neustria, he took possession of it, and making it his
magazine of arms, advanced up to Paris, and besieged it in due form.

Charles the Simple, King of France, in order to
purchase peace, consented to give his daughter
Gisela in marriage to Rollo, together with the kingdom of Neustria, since called Normandy, as her
marriage portion, on condition that Rollo would
do homage to him as his sovereign, and would embrace the Christian religion. Rollo accepted the
terms, with the addition that Brittany also should
form a part of his dominions in case he could conquer it. He was soon after baptised by the name
of Robert, and assumed the title of the Duke of
Normandy.

A circumstance occurred, when Rollo was introduced to the French king, in order to conclude this extraordinary treaty, which shews as well the independent spirit of the Normans, as the contempt in which they held the king. Rollo being admitted with his principal followers into the royal presence, was desired to kneel, and kiss the king's foot. But this he peremptorily refused, saying, he would never kiss the foot of any man. At length, however, to get rid of the entreaties of the French bishops and nobles, he ordered one of the officers of his suite to do it for him, who taking hold of the foot, brought it to his mouth, and kissed it in a standing posture, which made the king fall backwards from his throne, and excited the laughter of all present.

Rollo being settled in his new dominions, caused all his followers to be instructed in the Christian religion, and to be baptised ; and was afterwards as much distinguished by his wisdom and justice, as he had formerly been by his intrepidity and valour. He is supposed to have established the court of justice, at first called " L'Echiquier de Normandie ;" and after Normandy was reunited to the crown of France, " Le Parlement de Rouen," which was always the next in dignity and consequence to the parliament of Paris. Rollo also ordained, that none of his subjects, however mean, who should invoke his name on any occasion, should be denied the assistance of the law, or be punished without a trial. It is probable that this invocation of the name of Rollo, consisted at first in crying out " Ha, Hrolff," which was afterwards frenchified into " Haro," and continued as a special privilege of the Normans, under the name of " Clameur de Haro," and " Charte Normande," down to the time of the French Revolution.

Rollo had no children by his wife Gisela, daughter of Charles the Simple ; and upon her death, he married Popa, or Popœa, daughter of Berenger, Count of Bayeux, whom he had carried off by force on his first arrival in Normandy, and by whom he had a son. On his marriage with the daughter of the French king, he had repudiated Popœa, but by his second marriage he legitimated her son, whom he named William, and appointed him his successor in the dukedom of Normandy. In the year 927, he resigned his dominions to him, and lived five years afterwards, as the time of his death is fixed by the principal Norman historians, in the year 932. If the dates of the birth and death of Rollo are exact 843—932, this venerable patriarch of so many kings and princes, was 89 years old at the time of his death, a greater age than has ever been attained by any of his posterity. Rollo was buried in the cathedral church of Rouen, where his monument is still to be seen.

WILLIAM I.

SURNAMED LONGSWORD,

SECOND DUKE OF NORMANDY.

═══

William, the successor of Rollo, was surnamed Longsword, from a sword of extraordinary length, which was presented to him at the ceremony of his coronation, and which he afterwards wore. He was a brave and pious man, and an excellent prince, but governed the Normans only ten years after the death of Rollo, when he met with a very tragical end; for having gone into a small island in the river Somme, near Amiens, in order to meet Arnulph, Count of Flanders, to conclude a treaty with him, he was treacherously assassinated by his orders, in the year 942. William I. married Sprota, daughter of Herbert, Count of Senlis, by whom he had a son and successor called Richard.

RICHARD I.

SURNAMED SANS-PEUR,

THIRD DUKE OF NORMANDY.

Richard, third Duke of Normandy, was only
ten years old when he succeeded his father, and
the King of France taking advantage of his tender
age, thought it a favourable opportunity for re-
uniting Normandy to the dominion of the French
crown. With this view, he went to Rouen soon
after the assassination of Duke William, and found
means to carry off the young duke, under pretence
of protecting him from his enemies, and superin-
tending his education. However, by the dexte-
rity of Osmond, his governor, Richard contrived
in a short time to make his escape. The French
king pursued him into Normandy, but was defeated and taken prisoner by Aigrold, King of Denmark, whom the Normans had invited to the assistance of their young duke; nor was he set at
liberty, till he signed a solemn engagement not to
molest Richard in the enjoyment of his duchy;
and was moreover obliged to deliver up his two
sons, and some of his nobles, as hostages for his
future conduct. This treaty was chiefly managed
through the mediation of Hugh the Great, Duke
of Paris; who was so much pleased with the young
Duke of Normandy, that he betrothed to him his

daughter Emma, then only eight years of age, whom he afterwards married. Some years after, Hugh the Great being on his death bed, appointed Richard, guardian to his son Hugh Capet, a trust which he faithfully executed, and moreover greatly contributed by his exertions to the elevation of Hugh Capet to the throne of France.

Richard, Duke of Normandy, was engaged in perpetual wars, and displayed on all occasions so much personal courage, that he obtained the name of " Sans Peur :" but his internal government was just and mild, and he was greatly beloved by his subjects.

He had no children by the Princess Emma, sister of Hugh Capet; but after her death, he married Gunnor, a Norman lady, by whom he had Richard, his successor in the dukedom of Normandy, William, Count of Eu, ancestor of the Clifford family, and several other children. Richard Sans Peur died in great sentiments of piety, at the abbey of Fécamp, in Normandy, in the year 996, and was buried in the abbey church at that place.

The lives and exploits of the three first Dukes of Normandy, Rollo, William, and Richard, were celebrated in three separate poems, by Robert Wace, who was a native of Jersey, and flourished in the reign of Henry II. King of England. The first of these poems, entitled " Roman du Rhou," was composed about the year 1160, and was highly esteemed. They are all three preserved in manuscript in the king's library, at Paris. Wace af-

terwards wrote a history of the following Dukes
of Normandy, which is carried down to the sixth
year of the reign of Henry I. in a poem containing
12,000 verses, which is preserved in the British
Museum.

WILLIAM, COUNT OF EU.

Richard Sans Peur, having appointed his eldest
son Richard, afterwards surnamed the Good, to
succeed him in the duchy of Normandy, made
him promise on his death-bed, to make a handsome provision for his brothers. Richard was not
neglectful of this paternal injunction, and immediately on his father's death, he conferred the
county of Eu on his brother Godfrey, and the
county of Hyemes, on his brother William. But
the conduct of William unfortunately did not cor-
respond with this fraternal kindness. Being led
astray by some wicked companions, he refused to
do homage to Richard, his brother and lawful sovereign ; and withdrawing himself from his allegiance, actually levied war against him. Duke
Richard, after having repeatedly sent messengers
to him to no purpose, in order to bring him back
to a proper sense of his duty, at length besieged
him in his castle of Hyemes ; and having taken
him prisoner, confined him in the tower at Rouen,

in the year 998, where he remained in close confinement for the space of five years. At the end of this period, William contrived to let himself down from a high window of the tower, by means of a rope, which one of his friends conveyed to him in a bottle, and thus made his escape, with an intention to take refuge in some foreign court. But being diligently pursued, he was obliged to lie hid in the day-time, and travel only by night, till having reflected on his unfortunate situation, he at length came to a resolution rather to trust to the mercy of his brother, than to seek an inglorious refuge as a miserable dependant and exile among strangers. With this intention he threw himself in the duke's way, while he was taking the diversion of hunting in the forest of Vernon, and prostrating himself on the ground implored his forgiveness. Duke Richard, moved with compassion, immediately ordered him to rise ; and having learnt from his own mouth the particulars of his escape, he not only forgave him his past errors, but cherished him for ever after with all the affection of a brother. Though he never restored to him the county of Hyemes, which he had justly forfeited, yet on the death of Gislebert, son of his brother Godfrey, he made over to William the county of Eu, and gave him in marriage a very beautiful young lady, called Asseline, or Esseline, the daughter of Count Turchetil, and niece of Toroulf, of Pontaudemer, who were two of the greatest noblemen in all Normandy.

William, being thus restored to honour and consideration, settled himself at Eu, the capital of his new county, and erected there a spacious castle, which was long the residence of his direct descendants, and of which some remains are still to be seen. He also gave an example of piety, according to the customs of those times, in which he was frequently imitated by his posterity both in Normandy and England. In concert with his wife Esseline, who was an heiress, and was called " La Dame D'Auge," he founded a Benedictine abbey, at St. Pierre sur Dive, about the year 1040; and also the church of Our Lady, at Eu. He appears to have died before 1050, having survived his brother Richard the Good, who was grandfather of William the Conqueror.

William Count of Eu, had by his wife Esseline, four sons : Robert, his successor, who founded the Benedictine abbey of Treport, and accompanied William the Conqueror into England ; William, who was Count of Soissons ; Hugh, Bishop of Liseux, in Normandy ; and Ponts, who also went over to England at the time of the Conquest, where he settled, and was ancestor of the illustrious family of the name of Clifford.

PONTS.

I have already explained in another place the probable origin of the name of Ponts, and have also stated, that in the survey of England called Doomsday-book, which was executed in the reign of William the Conqueror, three sons of Ponts are named as possessors of several manors and lordships in different parts of the kingdom. Of Ponts himself, it seems that little is known. Among the Harleian manuscripts in the British Museum, is a paper marked No. 154, and entitled " Notes of old Mr. Clifford of Frampton, taken in 1602." These notes relate to the Clifford family, and were probably drawn up by the writer from authentic documents in his possession. Of Ponts and his sons, he gives the following information :

" Pontius was a noble in Normandy, at the time of the Conqueror. His arms are yet extant on the stonework of the porch of the great church at Rouen. He had issue by *Basilia* his wife, four sons :

1. Richard.

2. Osbern, Lord of Longeneye, in Gloucestershire, which he gave to the priory of Great Malvern, in Worcestershire; where he died.

3. Drogo, or Dru, Lord of Frampton, who left the same to his brother Richard.

4. Walter, Lord of Lea, in the forest of Deane."

I

It appears also by Domesday-book, that Drogo Fitz-ponts at that time held Frampton, and part of Leech, in Gloucestershire ; and moreover, six manors in Herefordshire, four in Wiltshire, and the same number in Worcestershire : And that his brother Walter held the manor of Eton, in Berkshire, (whereof he gave three hides to Westminster Abbey, for the health of his soul,) together with three manors in Oxfordshire, and part of Leech in Gloucestershire.

With respect to Osbern Fitz-Ponts, the second son of Ponts, it appears from a grant of King Henry I. to the priory of Malvern, dated in the year 1127, that Longeney, in Gloucestershire, was given to Osbern by William the Conqueror : and that some years after, he resigned it again into the king's hands, in his royal presence, at Winchester, in order that it might be made over to the priory with more security and without dispute. Moreover, in Dugdale's Monasticon, we find " Osbernus Pontium, et Ricardus Pontium, benefactores Prioratûs de Malverne Major."

What were the arms of Ponts, which were carved on the porch of the cathedral at Rouen, I have not discovered ; but in " Nash's History of Worcestershire," the following description is given of the seal which was used by his son Osbern. It represents a man in a helmet, and coat of mail, but without any offensive weapon, holding a cross in his right hand, and seated on a horse caparisoned, but without a bridle. The rider's knees are protected by something resembling a Scotch fillybeg, and which like that, seems to be *chequered.* Round the circumference is written :—" Sigillum Osberni filii Pontii."

RICHARD FITZ-PONTS.

The line of the family was continued by Richard Fitz-Ponts, who seems to have inherited almost all the property of his brothers Drogo and Walter. He had also large possessions in Wales, which were increased by very considerable donations from King Henry I. about the year 1113. Among them was the castle of Landovery, in the heart of Caermarthensire, which was attacked in the year 1116, by Griffith ap Rees, one of the Welch kings, who attempted to take it by surprise, and burn it to the ground; but Meredith ap Caradoc, who had been appointed lieutenant of the castle by Fitz-Ponts, during his absence, defended it manfully, and forced Griffith to retire with considerable loss.

Richard Fitz-Ponts, who was otherwise called de Pons, was a considerable benefactor to the priory of Malvern, on which he bestowed several lands and tithes, with the consent of his wife and eldest son. By his wife, whose name was Matilda, he had three sons :

1. Simon, founder of Clifford priory, in Here-

I 2

fordshire, and who in an ancient deed is styled
" Dominus de Clifford."

2. Walter, the first who assumed the name of
Clifford.

3. Richard.

WALTER FITZ–PONTS,

SURNAMED DE CLIFFORD OF CLIFFORD-CASTLE,

IN THE

COUNTY OF HEREFORD.

Walter Fitz-ponts was governor of Landovery-
castle, after his father's death, and occasionally
resided in another castle called Brynlys, situated
between Clifford and Brecon, of which one stately
tower still remains.   This castle was the scene of a
remarkable accident.   Walter Fitz-Ponts had invited to Brynlys-castle Matthew, the son of Milo,
Earl of Hereford, and was treating him with a
sumptuous entertainment, when all of a sudden
the castle took fire, and a large stone falling from
the top of the principal tower, struck Matthew on
the head, and killed him on the spot.   He was a
man of odious character, for Camden, relating this
event, says, " thus by the just judgment of heaven
was he remarkably punished for his greedy designs,
inhuman cruelty, and boundless avarice, always
usurping other men's rights."

146

In the year 1157, Roger, Earl of Clare, having obtained a grant from King Henry II. of any lands he could obtain from the Welsh, went to Cardigan, and fortified some castles in those parts. In order to make a diversion in his favour, Walter de Clifford made inroads into the territories of Rhys, Prince of Wales, and having slain many of the Welsh, and laid waste their country, he retired with considerable booty, and laden with spoil. Incensed at these hostilities, Prince Rhys sent an express to King Henry, to complain of the vexations which his subjects the Earl of Clare, and Walter de Clifford, had committed in his country. But finding that the king still put him off with only smooth words, and fair promises, he laid siege to the castle of Landovery, belonging to Walter de Clifford, and in a short time made himself master of it.

I find nothing further respecting the military exploits of Walter de Clifford, but like most of his ancestors and descendants, he was a considerable benefactor to the church. By the name of Walter, son of Richard, son of Ponts, he gave to the abbey of St. John at Hagmon, in Shropshire, his mills at Tenbury in Worcestershire; and afterwards, by the name of Walter de Clifford, he gave to the nunnery of St. John Baptist, at Godstow, in Oxfordshire, his mill at Frampton, in Gloucestershire, with a little meadow adjoining, and also a saltwork, for the health of the souls of his wife, his daughter, and his ancestors.

Walter de Clifford was possessed of very extensive property, having manors and lordships in many parts of England ; and particularly in Shropshire, Worcestershire, Gloucestershire, Herefordshire, Lincolnshire, and Wiltshire, besides great estates in Wales.

He married, as has already been stated, Margaret, daughter of Ralph de Toeni, standard-bearer of Normandy, and Lord of Clifford-castle in the county of Hereford. By this marriage, Walter de Clifford obtained possession of Clifford-castle, which was the portion of his wife ; and as it was customary in those times, for the great men of the realm to call themselves by the name of their principal estate or barony, he changed his name of Fitz-Ponts into that of De Clifford, which he transmitted to his posterity in England, being the first man on record who ever bore the name. This happened about the year 1150. By his wife Margaret de Toeni, Walter de Clifford had five sons, and two daughters :

1. Walter, his heir, and successor in the barony of Clifford, who was the second Lord Clifford, of Clifford-castle, in the county of Hereford.

2. Richard de Clifford, Lord of Frampton, in Gloucestershire.

3. Roger.

4. Simon.

5. Hugh.

The three last died without issue. Of the daughters, Lucy, the youngest, was married to Lord Say, Baron of Richard's-castle, in the county of Hereford : the eldest was Rosamund Clifford, so much celebrated in English history, and in ancient tales, and ballads, by the name of " Fair Rosamund."

The name of Fair Rosamund is familiar to every reader, but it is difficult to form a just opinion on the facts which have been transmitted down to us concerning her ; for though they have certainly some foundation in truth, they often wear the appearance of fiction and romance. It is pretended that king Henry II. built a bower or labyrinth for her, near his palace at Woodstock, in Oxfordshire, which was full of intricate passages and windings, in order to screen her from the jealousy and resentment of Eleanor his queen ; who, however, found her out by means of a clue of silk, and compelled her to swallow poison. But the old chroniclers, Brompton, Higden, and Knighton, say, she died a natural death. According to Maitland, in his " History of London," she had also a mansion in that city ; for he says, " Upon Paul's Wharf Hill, within a great gate, and next to Doctors' Commons, were many fair tenements, which, in their leases made from the dean and chapter, went by the name of " Camera Dianæ," that is Diana's Chamber; so denominated from a spacious building, which in the time of Henry II. stood where they were. In this camera, or arched and vaulted structure full of intricate ways and windings, this Henry kept, or was supposed to have kept, that jewel of his heart, " Fair Rosamund ;" she, whom at Woodstock he called Rosa Mundi, and here by the name of Diana, and hence had this house that title."

King Henry also made her a present of a beautiful casket, or cabinet, of admirable workmanship, on which were represented the struggles of wrestlers, the motions of animals, the flight of birds, and the leaping of fishes; all so wonderfully contrived, that these different objects seemed to move of themselves without being touched. According to Leland, this precious casket was preserved ·in Godstow nunnery, where Rosamund was buried, long after her decease.

Hearne, the antiquary, appears to have felt a particular affection for the memory of Fair Rosamund. He has devoted some pages to her history, in his supplement to the second volume of Leland's Itinerary ; and in his edition of the History of England, by " Gulielmus Neubrigiensis," he has inserted a long account of her ; which, as it contains many curious and interesting particulars not elsewhere to be found, I shall here transcribe for the entertainment and satisfaction of the reader.

A DISCOURSE ABOUT

FAIR ROSAMUND,

AND THE

NUNNERY OF GODSTOW,

WRITTEN IN THE YEAR 1718.

It is well known, that Rosamund Clifford is reported to have been the mistress of King Henry the Second, a prince of very great virtues; who, as he was naturally inclined to an immoderate love of women, so he could not resist the charms of this admirable young lady, who is said to have been the masterpiece of nature, and the most complete beauty of that age. I shall not here amass together all that is transmitted to us about her; that would be only to confound and perplex the reader : but shall content myself with what Stow has written concerning her, and with some short observations that I have made myself. The passage of Stow is in these words :

" Rosamund, the fayre daughter of Walter, Lord Clifford, concubine to Henry the Second, poisoned by Queene Elinor, as some thought, dying A.D. 1177, at Woodstocke, where King Henry had made for her a house of a wonderfull working, so that no man or woman might come to her but he that was instructed by the king, or such as were right secret with him touching the matter. This

house, according to some, was named Labyrin-
thus, or Dedalus worke, which was thought to be a
house wrought like unto a knot in a garden, called
a maze ; but it was commonly said, that lastly the
queene came to her by a clew of thredde, or silke,
and so dealt with her that she lived not long after,
but when she was dead, she was buried at Godstow, in a house of nunnes, beside Oxford, with
these verses upon her tombe :

Hic jacet in tumba, Rosa mundi, non rosa munda,
Non redolet, sed olet, quæ redolere solet.

The rose of the world, but not the cleane flowre,
Is now here graved, to whom beauty was lent ;
In this grave full darke now is her bowre,
Who in her life was sweete and redolent."

This beautiful lady's father, Lord Clifford, having
been a great friend to this nunnery, and she having
spent part of her time among the nuns, who during
the innocent part of her life were mightily delighted
with her conversation, for her parts were equal to her
beauty, no one will wonder that after her death,
her body was conveyed hither, and buried in one of
the chief parts of the church; especially since she
herself was likewise a considerable benefactress to
the place. History informs us, that her body was
laid in the middle of the quire, and that a very
handsome tomb was erected to her memory, with
very fine lights all about it constantly burning.
King Henry himself had also a particular affection
for the place, as well as for this most accomplished
lady. No scruples therefore hindered the abbess

and nuns from permitting her to be laid in so sacred a part of the church, especially since there was a very handsome gratuity left by her to pray for her after her death. But after her body had continued in this manner for about fourteen years, Hugh, Bishop of Lincoln, caused it to be removed, as is noted by Stow, who hath left us the following account of this transaction :

" Hugh, Byshop of Loncolne, came an. 1191, to the abbey of nunnes, called Godstow, betweene Oxford and Woodstocke, and when he had entered the church to pray, he saw a tombe in the middle of the quire, covered with a pall of silke, and set about with lights of waxe. And demanding whose tombe it was, he was answered that it was the tombe of Rosamund, that was sometime Lemman to Henry the Second, King of England, who for the love of her had done much good to that church. Then, quoth the bishop, take her out of this place, and bury her without the church."

The body being thus removed by the command of the bishop, let us now follow it out of the church, and observe the conduct of the nuns upon that occasion. The bishop's injunction was of that force, that they did not presume to act contrary to it ; and for this reason they did not venture afterwards to restore the body to its former place. But gratitude to herself, as well as to her father, and respect to the memory of King Henry the Second, who for her sake, had done extraordinary things for this nunnery, obliged them to take particular care of the body, so as to cause it to be buried in holy ground. Besides, I do not see any reason to think, that she did not die a true penitent. For which cause, these chaste nuns, who were famous for their continence, might judge it altogether proper to shew the greater regard to one, who before she suffered herself to be tempted, and drawn aside, by the allurements of King Henry, had been, as it were, a constant companion with them. Though, therefore, after her removal, there were not the same ornaments about her as before, yet the nuns inclosed the bones in a perfumed leather bag, which they afterwards inclosed in a leaden coffin, over which a tomb different from the former was laid, being a fair large stone in form of a coffin, agreeable to those times, on which was put this inscription:

Tumba Rosamundæ.

Thus it continued till about the time of the dissolution of monasteries: when it was taken up as we are told by Leland, in these words: " Rosamunde's tumbe at Godstow nunnery was taken up a late ; it is a stone with this inscription : *Tumba Rosamundæ.*"

Her bones were closid in lede, and withyn that in ledder. When it was openid there was a very swete smell came owt of it. There is a crosse hard by Godestowe with this inscription:

> " Qui ment hàe, oret, signumque salutis adoret,
> Utque tibi detur requies, Rosamundæ precetur."

Without doubt it will be expected, that I should now signify in what place the body was buried, after it was taken up. And this I shall do very freely.

It seems therefore to me, that it was buried either in the chapter-house, or in the cloisters. Indeed I think it was rather in the former than in the latter, where the nuns themselves, as I take it, were buried. And this notion I think sufficiently confirmed by Ranulph Higden, who tells us expressly, that it was in " capitulo monialium." Which word " capitulum" is translated " Chapter-house" by Grafton. Nor did the bishop prohibit her frombeinglaid in the chapter-house. Hoveden tells us he ordered her to be removed out of the church and be buried with the rest, " Anno Domini," saith he, " MCXCI. Hugo Lincolniensis episcopus, faciens visitationes suas per domos religiosorum in suâ diœcesi, venit ad abbatiam sanctimonialium de Godstowe, quæ est inter Oxonium et Wodestoc. Et cum intrasset ecclesiam ut oraret, vidit tumbam in medio chori ante altare, sericis pannis velutam, et lampadibus et cereis circumdatam : et quœsivit cujus esset tumba, et dictum est ei, illam esse tumbam Rosamundæ, quæ quondam extiterat amica Henrici regis Angliæ, filii Matildis imperatricis, et quod ipse pro amore ipsius multa bona ecclesiæ illi fecerat. Et respondit episcopus, tollite eam hinc, et sepelite eam extra ecclesiam cum ceteris. Et factum est ita."

I have produced this passage at large, because it is proper to compare it with the passage extracted above out of Stowe's Annals. The words *cum ceteris*, with the rest, seem to me to be understood of the nuns. Now if any should question the probability of the nuns being buried in the chapter-house, I shall only reply that it is very certain that it was usual to do so in other places. Upon occasion of which, I cannot but relate what a very worthy friend lately informed me of. He said, that he was at the nunnery of Lacock, in Wilts, in September 1712, and that a woman showing him the house there, brought him into the chapter-house, which as well as the treasury, which is a sort of stone tower, and the kitchen, where is to be seen the nuns' old boiler, is still standing, where she told him many lay buried, and putting by the mould, she took a scull out of a stone coffin, within half a foot of the surface of the earth, and gave it him to look at. He asked the woman whether the tradition of the place gave an account of any who there lay buried; but all the answer she could give him was, that that house had formerly been a nunnery, and the nuns lay there all buried; which he the more easily believed, because he knew it to be a common thing even now a days, for monks to bury in their chapter-houses. Nay, all religious, excepting prelates, are either buried there, or in the cloisters. Besides, he knew that it was the custom here in England likewise; but I shall now return to Rosamund.

And here, I suppose, it will be asked, what became of her tomb, upon its being taken up, at the dissolution of monasteries? To which I wish I could give such an answer as might clear those that took it up from the guilt of sacrilege. But, indeed, the person that has left an account of this upon record, was a man of that credit, that there

is no room for any dispute about that point. For
the famous Mr. Thomas Allen, of Gloucester-hall,
now Worcester College, who died an. 1632, in the
90th year of his age, hath told us in a MS. note,
that " the tomb-stone of Rosamund Clifford was
taken up at Godstowe, and broken into pieces,
and that upon it there were enterchangable weav-
ings, drawn out, and decked with roses, red and
green, and the picture of the cup, out of which
she drank the poison, given her by the queen,
carved in stone."

In my Appendix to the second volume of Leland's
Itinerary, I have showed that Rosamund died a natural death. I know that the vulgar accounts make
her to have been poisoned. And perhaps some
may think, the figure of the cup taken notice of
by Mr. Allen, to be a sufficient confirmation of
those accounts. But for my own part, I rely rather upon the authority of those authentic historians that have asserted the contrary ; and 'tis probable that the nuns were imposed upon, so as to
think she was really poisoned. And the story
might be spread the more industriously, on purpose to bring the greater odium on Queen Eleanor,
who had certainly been very harsh to Rosamund.
Her jealousy being very plain to the king himself,
what could he do in this case but contrive, that she
might be secured by all means possible, from the violent atttempts that might be made upon her life by
the queen ? The best method that could be thought
of, was to screen her from attacks, by confining her
to some safe place, yet so as she should have all the

pleasures that otherwise could be desired. Farnham-castle in Surrey, was one while her close retirement. But this not being judged so proper as could be wished, he at length conveyed her to Woodstock, where in the park he caused a very curious dwelling to be made for her, in the nature of a labyrinth, which consisted of such strange intricate windings, the best and most subtle artists being employed, with so many different ways, that it was not possible for any to find her, unless either the king himself, or such as carried the key of his secrecy, directed to the place. But notwithstanding all this caution, and cunning, the king himself proved his own enemy. For having drawn a small silken twine after him with his foot, (which twine was the guide to the place of her abode,) even into the presence of his queen, she, having by this accident obtained what she earnestly desired, dissembled the matter so cunningly, that no suspicion appeared ; and the king being suddenly called over to France, where he met with very great troubles, the queen, by the help of that silken thread, found out Rosamund ; and with menaces, and furious expostulations, so frightened her, that she fell into convulsions : and although all proper remedies were used to recover her former sprightliness and vigour, yet she died not long after, being unable to brook the severe language she had received from the angry queen ; who, however, must not be supposed to have wrought her death by poison. Rough language was sufficient in this case, especially when used by one of her quality to a young lady, who had never met with any such severity ; and was of such an unparalleled good nature, which was of no small advantage to the charms of her beauty, that she would necessarily sink under any other pleasures than those that were gentle, and agreeable to that soft way of living into which she had entered, and from which she expected as much satisfaction as such a kind of life could afford.

On the north-west side of the remains of the old manor-house of Woodstock is a pool, that is commonly called *Rosamund's Pool*, or *Rosamund's Well*, being the same in which she used to bathe herself. And there is much such another at Godstow, in which she, as well as the nuns were wont to bathe, when she resided in the nunnery. Just by the pool at Woodstock, are seen the foundations of a large building, which, I believe, was the very same building that was contrived for Rosamund. I have often viewed the ruins of this building with some considerable pleasure and delight ; as I have likewise what is now remaining of the old manor-house, which was one of the most considerable palaces in old time that our kings had.

Some have surmised that the tesselated pavement, lately found at Stansfield, with the figure of " Apollo Sagittarius" upon it, and which was as fine almost as any known, did once belong to this apartment of Rosamund, commonly called *Rosamund's Bower*. But I see no reason to ground the conjecture upon ; though I am ready enough to

K

allow, that Rosamund had liberty of going to Stansfield, and other neighbouring places of recreation, provided it were done so as to conceal herself from the queen, and upon such occasions,
she might make use of any room in which there
lay such a kind of pavement.

From the privilege granted her of going to such
neighbouring places, for this was what her health
required, and the king could not deny it to one
on whom his heart was fixed, I am inclined to
think that the common stories arose, that there was
a passage under ground, from Woodstock to
Godstow, and another from Godstow to St. Peter's
church, in Oxford. Be this as it will, I am apt to
think, that one reason which made many, and
the nuns among the rest believe, that Rosamund
was poisoned, was this ; namely, that immediately
upon her death mournful songs were made, and a
narrative given in them of the occasion of her
death. As her frailty was represented in them, so
the queen's resentments were likewise artfully described ; and to conclude the story the more plausi-
bly, the authors said she was taken off by poison.

As soon as these songs were spread about,
which was done very cautiously, it being difficult
in those times to disperse things of this nature, new
improvements were made, and the nuns of Godstow, who had a great respect for the king, and
for this beautiful young lady, were soon persuaded
that this was her fate ; and they often lamented it
among themselves, as well as among her relatives

and others that came to visit them, and to see the tomb after it was erected.

The songs and mournful dities that are now handed about, such as that in the " Garland of Good-Will," as well as the vulgar narratives upon the same subject, are, in divers respects, different from the original songs and relations that were published soon after her death. For which reason it were to be wished that we had the stories exactly now remai.ing as they were delivered then. But this we must not expect, the old accounts having been quite destroyed upon the appearance of such as were done in a more modern dress, and improved with many additions; and this way of alteration is what happened to many old English pieces.

As I take it, one principal ground for raising the story about Rosamund's being poisoned, was to prevent and deter others from committing the same fault. It was judged, that if such a fate, as being taken away by poison, were mentioned in the accounts of Rosamund, it would frighten other young ladies from engaging in the same course of life, particularly such as were equally eminent for their birth, beauty, and other accomplishments. Therefore the story was set out with all the advantages the keenest inventions could contrive, and it was not looked upon as culpable to falsify in a matter where so good an end was proposed. For the same season it was, unless I am mistaken, that a very ridiculous story was raised about King Henry the Second's visiting

K 2

her body, upon his return from beyond sea, which
I shall tell in the same manner as I find it published in a very rare and uncommon book, entitled
" Dives et Pauper," being an Exposition on the Ten
Commandments, printed at London, in 4to. by
Richard Pynson, an. 1493." The words occur in
the sixth precept, or commandment, chap. 14,
thus: " We rede that in Englonde was a king
that had a concubyne, whose name was Rose, and
for hyr greate bewte he cleped hir Rose amound,
Rosa mundi, that is to saye, Rose of the worlde.
For him thought that she passed al wymen in
bewtye. It bifel that she died, and was buried
whyle the kynge was absent. And whanne he cam
ayen for grete love that he had to hyr, he wolde
se the body in the grave. And whanne the grave
was openned, there sate an orrible tode upon hir
breaste, and a foule adder begirt hir body about in
the midle. And she stank so that the kyng, ne
non other might stonde to se that orryble sight.
Thanne the kynge dyde shutte ayen the grave,
and dyde wryte these two veersis upon ye grave:

Hic jacet in tumbâ, etc."

To shew the greater respect to Rosamund, King
Henry II. caused a cross to be set up in every
place where her body rested between Woodstock
and Godstow. I cannot tell the exact number,
but I suppose it rested pretty often, and that considerable gifts were made to the poor at each place.
This is certain, that there was a fair cross set up by
Toll-bridge, which is the bigger of the bridges
that conduct us to Godstow, and on the cross were

put those verses I have inserted above from Leland.

After Rosamund had given herself up to the embraces of King Henry, upon her coming to Godstow, for she went thither frequently, the nuns, who admired her conversation, as indeed all did that happened at any time to be with her, used to expostulate with her about her way of life: to which she always returned very pretty, though by no means satisfactory answers. These nuns being always famous for their chastity, for even at the dissolution, the most malicious adversaries had no reason to object the contrary, they could not be put off with such arguments as were drawn barely from present pleasures. They looked further than this life, and well knew, that there was something more substantial to be sought after. Neither was Rosamund herself unacquainted with such kind of reasoning, her noble father having given her an education as was every way suitable to the great and good character which he bore. Neither did he at all countenance any of the vanities that afterwards sullied and stained the innocent part of her life. On the contrary, they proved a grief to him, as he often declared to his friends. As the nuns were once conversing with her, and talking of heaven and hell, and the danger she was in of having her share of the latter, without a sincere and hearty repentance, she replied, " that though she was a sinner she should be saved." " How shall we know that ?" said one of them. " Why," said she, " if that tree, (pointing to one that had then green leaves thereon) be turned into stone after my death, then shall I have life among the saints of heaven." The same answer she returned also at several other times, when the same kind of discourse was started. And it is said, that within a few years after, this thing came to pass, and the stone was commonly shewn to passengers at Godstow, even till the house was dissolved.

This thing, though rarely spoken of now, yet some years ago, was the common discourse, especially when any stangers came out of curiosity to see Godstow. Not many years since, a stone was also shown at Woodstock, which they called ROSAMUND's STONE, but then it was different from this at Godstow, and was kept for no other reason but to get money from such as came to Woodstock, a place so much celebrated on many accounts in our history. But now, though there be no stone shewn at this time at Godstow, yet there is still a tree at Lower Wolvercote, which goes by the name of ROSAMUND's TREE ; as there was another before which bore the same name, being planted as is supposed, in the very same place where the tree grew, which is reported to have been turned into stone.

Many ladies have been famous for painting, and fine writing, and works of this nature were very often done by the nuns. Perhaps, Fair Rosamund herself, who conversed so much with them, might sometimes practice these arts ; for I am apt to think she wrote a very neat hand, and that might be one recommendation of her to the nuns, who were delighted with those that excelled in such accomplishments.

There is one thing which makes me think that Rosamund was skilled in these fine arts, and that is, that we are assured she was excellent at needle-work, in which few ever surpassed her. 'Twas upon that, as well as other accounts, that King Henry presented her with a cabinet so delicately adorned with variety of figures. Her method of working, in every part, answered her uncommon beauty ; and therefore, what was performed by her was kept with very great care. Without doubt, there was much of it at Godstow, but the particulars are lost.

It were to be wished we had as good inventories of this as we have of some other religious houses. However, notwithstanding this defect, I find, that at Bildwas Abbey, in Shropshire, was for several ages religiously kept, a *cope* of this exquisite lady's needle-work, about the skirts whereof were these words : ROSAMUNDA CLIFFORD PROPRIIS MANIBUS ME FECIT. " Rosamund Clifford made me with her own hands." But I take it for granted, this cope was not used, but kept and shown as a curiosity in the vestry. This art was also a qualification which recommended her to the nuns ; and there was an emulation among them, who should come nearest to what Rosamund wrought ; what she did being proposed as a pattern for the rest.

But whether she either painted, or wrote finely or not, there is however no doubt, but if we had remains of either, a very great price would be set upon them, and indeed perhaps a much greater, than would be put upon any thing of that kind, done either by her paramour, King Henry II. or his queen, Eleanor. For, though in her life time, any thing by royal hands would be reckoned superior, yet it so happens, that we sometimes value things done by persons of most exquisite beauty, much more after their deaths, than we did before; especially if they have been as eminent as Fair Rosamund, who was the most renowned royal mistress, that ever was in this kingdom, Jane Shore herself not excepted, whose beauty does not seem to have equalled that of Rosamund in all respects. Now the best way to discover Rsosamund's beauty, is by considering the person of Jane Shore, who is thus described by the famous Michael Drayton. " Her stature was mean, her hair of a darke yellow, her face round and full, her eye gray, delicate harmony being betwixt each part's proportion, and each proportion's colour, her body fat, white and smoothe, her countenance cheerefull, and like to her condition." This agrees with what Sir Thomas More, in whose time she was alive, though poor and aged, had observed of her before. From a nice comparison of the accounts left to posterity, I think it will be clear that Fair Rosamand's beauty was more consummate than Jane Shore's; and that her stature was altogether agreeable, and by no means too small. But then it must be confessed that there are no authentic pictures of Rosamund extant, as there are of Jane Shore, which if there were, the description given of her might,

perhaps, be rendered more compleat than we find
in any of our writers.

It is a common report among some, that the nuns
of Godstow were so confined, as to be hindered
from any kind of recreation; but there is no ground
for this. Godstow itself indeed wanted nothing
that was requisite for pleasure. Here were fine
recesses and delicate walks; but then even the
most exquisite things of this kind by degrees prove
tiresome unless attended with variety. For that
reason the nuns were permitted to go to neighbouring places, as well as to places of a more remote distance, on purpose to prevent the ill consequences of a too confined life : and at such times,
they omitted no kind of mirth that was innocent.
One of the places where the nuns used to recreate
themselves was at Middley, or Medley, a large
house between Godstow, and Oxford. Being in
the midway, it thence received the name. It belonged to Godstow, being given to the nunnery in
King Henry the Second's time, by Robert de Wit-
ham, who had three daughters that were nuns at
Godstow. The Withams were persons of great
note and distinction ; and Rosamund, who was
well acquainted in the family, received signal favours from it. She became acquainted there by
her interest with the nuns at Godstow ; and the
same acquaintance made the family respected by
King Henry the Second. 'Twas customary for Rosamund to go to Medley with the nuns, and much
mirth passed on such occasions, the place being
very pleasantly situated just by the river, and care

being taken that no disturbance should be given to them whenever they had a mind to solace themselves here. There was the more need for preventing such disturbances, because of the great concourse of people who came from Oxford and other places to divert themselves here, it being then celebrated for its pleasantness, as it has been since; whence 'tis that George Withers writes thus in a love sonnet, printed in the year 1620.

> In summer time to Medley
> My love and I would go
> The boatmen there stood ready
> My love and I to rowe:
> For creame there would we call
> For cakes for pruines too,
> But now alas she's left me
> Falero, lero, loo.

I might take notice of other places where the nuns of Godstow used to recreate themselves, but this would be beside my design. Omitting therefore, what might be remembered upon that subject, I shall retire back to Godstow, and for the further reputation of the nuns there, shall observe, they spent a great part of their time in reading good books. There was a common library for their use well furnished with books, many of which were English, and divers of them historical. The lives of holy men and women, especially the latter, were curiously written on vellum, and many illuminations appeared throughout, so as to draw the nuns more easily to follow their example. And for the same end several sacred stories were painted in the church; so that there was much painting at Godstow, and some of it, I believe was extraordinary in its kind. As the nuns delighted in good painting, so we must needs think they took care to procure the best artists. It is very probable that Rosamund's name was painted in several places, at least till such time as her body was removed out of the quire. For without doubt their benefactors were all recorded, and therefore we must suppose that many of their names occurred in the windows, which was very laudable; and there are still remains of old painting on the walls of the chapel at Godstow, which will, in some measure, confirm what I have observed.

I shall now proceed to inform the reader, that coffins, and fragments of monumental stones, are still found in the present ruins of Godstow, and many have been taken up within the precincts of the nunnery, which, I believe, lay formerly in the the church, or the chapter-house, or else in the cloisters. I lately saw part of an old stone coffin, which had been about two yards and a quarter in length, dug up at Godstow, at a little distance from the remains of the tower of the nunnery church. Many bones were found with it, and the teeth were very good and firm. The bones seem to have been those of some lady, either an abbess or a nun. But according to the account of Mr. Francis Vernon, in his " Oxonium Poema," they were the bones of Fair Rosamund herself, to whom also the coffin belonged. The meadow in which it was found is called the church-yard, because the church, and some cloisters, and even the chapter-house stood on it. Many other stone coffins have also been found in it, and 'tis commonly said, that Rosamund's coffin was really dug up in the same, which will justify the observation of Mr. Vernon, in whose poem above-mentioned, are the following lines, in commemoration of Fair Rosamund.

—— Hic quondam, si non et perfida fama,
Dædaleos flexus, et multiplicem labyrinthem
Cercuit et regi placuit Rosamunda procanti.
Cuireferunt, motam thalamo super, Heleonoram,
Lethiferas mississe dapes, et triste venenum.
Defunctum tandem vitâ, atque exangue cadaver,
Godstovii nemus, et riguos devenit in hortos.
Hic infelices obitus, vitamque peractam,
Fleverunt, multumque piæ gemuere sorores.
Sedsi scire cupis quæ jam post fata supersunt
Relliquiæ, et tantæ famam non negligis umbræ,
I pete quod ponti junctum est invisere pratum :
Hic, licet obscurum lappis, et gramine tectum,
Marmoreum invenies et nostrâ ætate sepulchrum.
Quod quoniam mutum est, titulo nec cernitur ullo,
Eia age, nos memores tumulo incribamus honores.

Hic ego marmoro jaceo Rosamunda sepulchro,
Mollius at quondam regalis flamma jacebam.
Qui tamen extinctæ quæris vestigia flammæ,
Hic fumos tantum, et cineres spectabis inanes.

Such is the account of Fair Rosamund, by Hearne ; which I shall conclude with the following translation of the Latin verses, which he has quoted from Mr. Vernon.

At Woodstock once, if ancient tales say true,
A wondrous Bower in verdant mazes grew ;
A winding labyrinth, with endless ways,
Like that which Dedalus in Crete did raise.

Here, in soft shades, and arbours ever green,
Safe from the vengeance of his jealous queen,
Fair Rosamund, with every beauty graced,
Was by King Henry, her lover, placed.
But all his tender caution fruitless proved ;
The queen by jealousy relentless moved,
Gaining possession of the fatal clue,
Furious to Rosamund, through the labyrinth flew ;
Then, with keen words, a deadly poison gave,
Which brought her soon to an untimely grave.

Her lifeless corps to Godstow's groves conveyed,
Within their cloisters by the nuns was laid,
Those pious sisters long wept o'er her tomb,
Lamenting her sad fate, and melancholy doom.

But if by curious inquiry led,
You'd trace the mouldering relics of the dead,
If touched by Rosamund's romantic flame,
You're not indifferent to so great a name,
To yonder flowery mead, whose verdant side
Adjoins the bridge, your eager footsteps guide.
There, though with weeds the marble's overgrown,
You still may find her monumental stone.
On which, as no inscription can be traced,
For every vestige seems by time effaced,
Let us, whose thoughts with ancient ardour glow,
This humble tribute of our Muse bestow.

Here, in this marble tomb inclosed, I lie,
Fair Rosamund, whose name will never die.
With ardent passion by a king beloved,
Alive, in pleasure and in pomp I moved.
But of my former state here all you see,
A heap of dust alone remains of me.

171

Henry the second, and his sons Richard and John, were great benefactors to the nunnery at Godstow, and also to the Clifford family, and their connexions, for the sake of Fair Rosamund. Her father and mother were buried there, and an annual service was always performed for the repose of their souls.

Rosamund had by King Henry, two sons : William, surnamed " Longspée," and Geoffrey, who was born in the year 1159. Her connexion with the king, therefore, must have begun some years before that period ; and as she died in the year 1177, their intimacy appears to have lasted about twenty years ; nor could Rosamund have been very young at the time of her death.

William Longspée, Rosamund's eldest son, married Ela, sole daughter and heir of William Fitzpatrick, Earl of Salisbury, through the interest of his half brother King Richard I. who after his marriage, conferred the title of Earl of Salisbury upon him

Longespée was governor of Dover-castle, and sailing with Richard, Earl of Cornwall, his nephew, into Gascony, in the beginning of Henry the Third's reign, recovered Poitiers, which had been lost by King John ; but on his return to England, he was cast on the shore of Cornwall, and narrowly escaped being shipwrecked. He died shortly after, in the year 1227, not without suspicion of being poisoned by Hubert de Burgh, Earl of Kent, and chief justice of England. He was buried in Salisbury

cathedral, where his monument is still to be
seen.

William Longespée, his son, rendered himself
famous by the feats of valour he performed in the
Holy Land, where he was slain, fighting against
the Saracens, 1250. By his wife Idonea, he left
a son called also William Longespée, who was
great grandson of Henry and Rosamund; and
who married as I have mentioned before, his cousin Matilda de Clifford, only daughter and heiress
of Walter de Clifford, and great grand-daughter of
Walter, Lord de Clifford, of Clifford-castle, Rosamund's father. Matilda inherited Clifford-castle,
and had by her husband, William Longespée,
only one daughter named Margaret, who married
Henry de Lacy, Earl of Lincoln. It was thus, that
a descendant of Fair Rosamund came to inherit
the original property of the Clifford family, and
the very spot from which they derived their name.

Geoffrey, the second son of Henry and Rosamund, was, when very young, made archdeacon
of Lincoln; and in the year 1182, when only 23
years of age, was elected bishop of that see, and
held it seven years without consecration, when he
resigned it into the hands of the king his father.
At the same time he was appointed chancellor of
England; and in the year 1191, was advanced to
the archbishopric of York, which see he governed
with singular approbation. In the reign of King
John, he underwent many difficulties by opposing
that tyrannical monarch, who at length seized his

whole estate, and forced him to retire into banishment till his death, which happened five years afterwards at Grosmont, in Normandy, in the year 1212.

I have stated above, that Walter de Clifford of Clifford-castle, had two sons, Walter, his heir, and Richard. To Richard he gave the manor of Frampton in Gloucestershire ; and it continued with his decendants in a direct male line for 15 or 16 descents; till at length it fell to a daughter, who died without issue towards the latter end of the 15th century. The manor then went out of the Clifford family ; but the principal seat, and divers lands in Frampton, remained with a younger branch of the same name, and descended to John Clifford, Esq. who died in the year 1684, leaving three daughters, of whom the eldest married Nathan Clutterbuck, Esq. and suceeded to the estate of Frampton. Richard Clutterbuck, his descendant, built a handsome house at Frampton, in the year 1731, on the scite of the ancient mansion of the Cliffords; and devised it together with his estate to Nathanial Winchcomb, Esq. who assumed the name of Clifford. In this house is a portrait of Fair Rosamund, but somewhat different from that described by Hearne.

The parish of Frampton contains 2,300 acres of land, and the village is one of the neatest and pleasantest in the county of Gloucester. The ground on which some of the houses are built was formerly called Rosamund's Green. In the church is a tomb, on which are two recumbent figures in freestone, under arcades, representing a crusader and his lady, supposed to be of the Clifford family.

This branch of the family resided at Frethorn, in the county of Gloucester, where was an old house, in which Fair Rosamund was said to have been born. James Clifford, Esq. who was a gentleman of the Privy Chamber, erected a new house there, for the reception of Queen Elizabeth, in her progress to Bristol, in the year 1574. It stood on the banks of the Severn, and is described by Sir Robert Atkins, in his History of Gloucestershire, as a pleasant large stone house, with a prospect over the river, and remarkable for a grand staircase, and a turret of freestone, and two noble chimney-pieces finely carved in stone; one of them dated 1598, with the Clifford arms. It was demolished in the year 1750; but a house is still shown at Frethorn, which is said to have been the residence of Walter, first Lord Clifford.

L

WALTER DE CLIFFORD,

SECOND LORD CLIFFORD,

Of Clifford-castle in the county of Hereford.

———

The Clifford family being thus established in the county of Hereford, on the borders of Wales, soon became famous both for their deeds of valour, and their acts of piety. I have already related the valorous enterprises of the first Lord Clifford. His son and heir, Walter, second Lord Clifford of Clifford-castle, was particularly remarkable for his piety, and his munificent donations to monasteries and churches.

He married Agnes, sole daughter and heir to Roger de Cundy, of Covenby and Glentham, in the county of Lincoln, by Alice his wife, Lady of Horn-castle in that county, sole daughter and heir to William de Cheny, Lord of Covenby and Glentham, in the time of William the Conqueror.

During the reign of King John, he was several times sheriff of Herefordshire; and with the consent of Agnes his wife, confirmed to the convent of the Virgin Mary at Barlings, in Lincolnshire, certain lands in Covenby and Glentham, which they had purchased of her. He made several donations also to the Gilbertines at Broadholm, in the county of Nottingham.

Agnes died before her husband: and by her last

will made with his consent, she bequeathed considerable sums to the church, and to different
religious establishments, as appears by the following list extracted from it:

To the convent of the Holy Trinity
    at Canterbury, *her body*, with land
    in the neighbouring town of
    Wickham, of the value of ...... 100 shillings
To the churches of St. Augustine and
    St. Gregory, in Canterbury, each 40 sh.
To St. Sepulchre................ 20 —
To the five hospitals in Canterbury. $5\frac{1}{2}$ marks
To every *hermit* there........... 12 d.
To three maidens to be married, with
    the obligation of observing three
    anniversaries for her soul....... 30 sh.
To the making of an aisle in the
    church of St. Andrew, at Wick-
    ham ; and also an altar in honour
    of All Saints................. 10 marks
To the church of St. Radigund,
    with an order for five *trentalls* to
    be said for her soul........... 20 sh.
To the church of Hollege......... 1 mark
To every parish church in Canter-
    bury......................... 1 sh.
To the cathedral church of St. Ethel-
    bert, Hereford............... 40 sh.
To Clifford Priory, for vestments and
    a cope, and to the fabric of the
    church..................... 40 sh.

L 2

To that of Haghmon in Shropshire one vestment, and........ 40 sh.

To Wentworth church........... 2 marks

To the hospital of St. Wulstan at Worcester, she
left *one silk matteris*.

For the education of her daughter Basilia, twenty
marks.

To her mother, and each of her sons and daughters, a gold ring.

For the fulfilling of this her will, she purchased
of Walter Lord Clifford, her husband, for one
year after her decease, the whole income of the manor of Covenby, and the value of half her chattels.

Walter, second Lord Clifford of Clifford-castle,
departed this life about the year 1223. The place
of his interment is not known; but by records it
is evident, that the Cliffords of Clifford-castle were
great benefactors to the monasteries of Aconbury
and Dore, in the county of Hereford, and probably he was interred in one of those places, or in
Clifford Priory, founded by Simon de Clifford, his
uncle.

WALTER,

THIRD AND LAST

LORD CLIFFORD,

OF CLIFFORD-CASTLE.

Walter, third Lord Clifford, was constituted governor of the castles of Caermarthen, and Cardigan, by Henry III. Some years after he made a truce, on the king's part, with Llewellyn, Prince of Wales, for one year, which was afterwards prolonged. In the same year, upon the death of Roger his younger brother, he gave 100*l.* fine to the king for the wardship and marriage of his heir. But in the year 1232, adhering to Richard Marshall, Earl of Pembroke, and other great barons, in the unhappy difference which took place between the king and them, he was outlawed, and his lands seized; and the king issued his mandate to the sheriff of Shropshire, to take into his hands the manor of Corfham, with all the corn and cattle there found; and also to the sheriff of Kent, to seize all the lands of the said Walter, in that county. But he soon after made his peace with his sovereign; and the year following, his castle of Clifford, which he had put into the king's hands as a pledge for his loyalty, was restored to him.

Walter de Clifford, John Fitzalan, Ralph de Mortimer, and John de Monmouth, were the four Lords Marchers of the Marches of Wales : and at the coronation of Queen Eleanor, wife of Henry III. they pleaded their right to carry the canopy over the king and queen ; but the barons of the Cinque Ports asserted it to be their right, as also to sit that day at the royal table, on the right hand of the king, and the claim of the latter was allowed.

The same year, a tilting match being appointed to be held at Sherborne, between the esquires of this Walter de Clifford, and Henry Fitz-Matthew; and the king receiving information that Clifford and Fitz-Matthew, concerned themselves seriously therein, he forbade it to take place, to prevent the effusion of blood.

As for his works of piety, this Lord de Clifford, by deed, gave to the convent of St. Mary at Dore, Nanteglas, with the appurtenances, (a considerable territory, says Dugdale) and by another deed, confirmed to them all the lands and tenements which they held of him and his ancestors in Cantrescliff. To the canons of Hagmon in Shropshire, he gave his mills at Culmington and Sinchine, half a virgate of land in Sinchine, and a messuage He granted to the nunnery of the Virgin Mary at Aconbury, for his soul, and the souls of Margaret his wife, and Maud his daughter, certain lands in Corfham. To the priory of Clifford he gave, for the souls of Walter his father, Agnes his mother, and Isabel his first wife, a mark sterling yearly for ever, out of certain lands expressed in the grant.

Isabel was his first wife, by whom he had no issue ; his second wife was Margaret, daughter to Llewelyn Prince of Wales, by whom he had Maud, his only daughter and heir, who married with the king's consent, her cousin William Longespée, third Earl of Salisbury of that name. Their only daughter and heir Margaret Longespée, inherited Clifford-castle, and great estates, which she brought in marriage to Hugh de Lacy, Earl of Lincoln, as I have mentioned above.

After the death of Walter de Clifford, Margaret his widow was married to Sir John Gifford of Brimsfield in Gloucestershire ; but some time after, she made a grievous complaint to the king, that Sir John Gifford had taken her by force from her manor-house at Caneford, and carried her to his castle at Brimsfield, and there kept her in restraint. He, being thereupon sent for by the king, and told what was informed against him, denied the charge, saying that he took her not thence against her will ; and tendered to the king a fine of three hundred marks for marrying her without his royal licence : which the king accepted, upon condition that she made no further complaint.

Walter, third Lord Clifford, died in the year 1264 ; and in the same year, Margaret his widow, by her deed dated at Ross in the county of Hereford, appointed her heart to be buried in the priory of Aconbury near Hereford, and gave to the convent fifteen marks, to be paid immediately after her

decease out of her goods. After her marriage with
Sir John Gifford, she with his consent, gave to the
canons of Barlings in Lincolnshire, her lordships
of Covenby and Glentham. She died in the eleventh year of the reign of that great King Edward
the First, and was buried in Aconbury church,
were her monument is still to be seen. It is an
altar-tomb, now much defaced. On the table is
carved a tree, or cross, very elegantly decorated
with foliage. From the branches hang two escut-
cheons : one, chequey, for Clifford ; the other a
lion rampant, with a forked tail, for Wales. Round
the verge is an inscription in Gothic letters, of
which only the following words can be deciphered :

**CI GIST DAME MARKARYD DE....COM....
....OGER DE CLIFFORD. PRIEZ PUR....**

Walter, third Lord Clifford, having died without male issue, and leaving an only daughter as
above-mentioned, the line of the Cliffords was preserved by his brother Roger, who married a great
heiress, Sibilla, widow of Robert Lord Tregoz,
and daughter and coheir of Robert de Ewyas, a
powerful baron in Herefordshire. But he died
before his brother, and by the advice of his wife,
appointed his body to be buried in the abbey of
Dore ; in consideration of which he confirmed to
the monks of that convent, all the lands granted to
them by William de Ewyas, his wife's ancestor, of
which he himself had questioned the title. In the

church at Dore, is still preserved a very ancient monument, on which is the mutilated figure of a knight, in a recumbent posture, completely armed, with a shield on his left arm. Mr. Duncombe, the learned historian of Herefordshire, who is rector of Dore, says the tradition of the place has always called it the tomb of Lord Clifford.

ROGER DE CLIFFORD.

In a history of the Clifford family, this Roger de Clifford deserves particular notice; since it was from him, that all the following barons of his name, and all the collateral branches (excepting the Cliffords of Frampton above-mentioned) whether extinct, or now existing, were descended. Besides the great possessions which he obtained by his wife Sybilla de Ewyas, his father Walter, second Lord Clifford, had settled on him the great manor of Tenbury, in Worcestershire, and the manor of Bruges in the county of Hereford. This was done with the consent of Agnes his wife, and of Walter his eldest son, third Lord Clifford; and the grant was afterwards confirmed by Matilda de Clifford, niece to Roger, and heiress of Clifford-castle.

The manor of Tenbury remained with the descendants of Roger de Clifford, till it was finally alienated by Henry Lord Clifford, of Westmorland, second Earl of Cumberland, in the reign of Henry VIII. as I have shewn above, Part 1, p. 26.

Roger de Clifford was much employed by King Henry III. in his wars both in France, and on the borders of Wales; but the chief troubles of that king, during the whole of his long reign, arose from the rebellious dispositions of his principal barons. According to the example of his father King John, Henry III. had always recourse in his difficulties to the protection and mediation of the Pope; and he seems to have considered the influence of Walter and Roger de Clifford of so much consequence in the beginning of his reign, that he wrote a letter to the pope, requesting his holiness to write to them to persevere in their loyalty to him. This letter is to be found in Rymer's " Fœdera," and begins as follows :

Litera ad Papam de Statu Regni. 8 *Henry* 3.

DOMINO PAPÆ SÁLUTEM.

Scribere velitis Waltero de Clifford, Rogero de Clifford, etc. firmiter injungentes, ut agenda nostra solitâ diligentiâ promoveant, et nobis semper viriliter assistant ; quos etiam de inceptis diligentiæ et fidelitatis suæ laudabilibus commendare velitis.

A Letter to the Pope on the state of the Realm.
8 *Henry* 3.

To our Lord the Pope, Greeting.

Be pleased to write unto Walter, and Roger de

Clifford, firmly enjoining them to promote our affairs with their accustomed diligence, and always to stand by us manfully: and be pleased moreover to commend them for the laudable proofs of diligence and fidelity which they have already shown.

Roger de Clifford, however, did not live long enough to be of much service to King Henry III. for he died young, in the year 1231; having obtained from the king a few years before, a grant of the marriage of Hawise, widow of John de Bottrel, and probably a great heiress, in favour of Roger his son and heir.

Roger de Clifford was a considerable benefactor to several religious houses.

SIR ROGER DE CLIFFORD,
KNIGHT,
FOURTH LORD CLIFFORD.

=====

On the death of Roger de Clifford, his only son
and heir being a minor, the custody of his lands,
and the wardship of his person, were granted to his
uncle, Walter Lord Clifford, on whose death, in
the year 1264, he became the fourth Lord Clifford,
though he did not succeed to the inheritance of
Clifford-castle, from which the name and barony of
Clifford were originally derived, nor to the ancient property of the Cliffords in the county of
Hereford, which, as the reader has seen above, devolved to Matilda de Clifford, his cousin, the wife
of Henry de Lacy, Earl of Lincoln.

For the sake of perspicuity therefore, I shall
call him throughout Sir Roger de Clifford; as the
modern title of lord was unknown in those days,
and can only be attributed to him, in order to show,
that through him the line was continued; and that
from him the later barons and earls of the family
were descended.

In the 27th year of King Henry III. Sir Roger de
Clifford attended the king at Hereford with horse
and arms, to restrain the incursions of the Welsh.

But that very year being made governor of the castles of Marlborough and Luggershall, in the county of Wilts, he fell from his allegiance, and joined the rebellious barons, on pretence of asserting the laws and liberties of the people ; on which occasion, doing much mischief by sacrilegious acts and otherwise, he was with the famous Simon de Montfort, Earl of Leicester, and others, excommunicated by Boniface, Archbishop of Canterbury.

The same year Sir Macy de Bescile, a Frenchman, being made by the king sheriff and constable of Gloucester, the barons were so offended, that they chose Sir William Tracy, a knight of that country, to the said office ; who one day keeping court in the town of Gloucester, the Frenchman, with a number of armed men, came suddenly upon him, and imprisoned him. The barons hearing of this, prevailed on Sir Roger de Clifford, to march with a great power to Gloucester, where he besieged the castle and burnt the bridge ; and entering the town, made the said Frenchman and all his company prisoners, and took the keeping of the castle upon himself. However, the year following he forsook the party of the barons, joined the king at Oxford, and from thence marched to Northampton. For his valour and success before that town he was made governor of Gloucester-castle, as also sheriff of that county : and as a further reward, the king granted him land of the value of 100 marks within the honor of Monmouth, and the inheritance of the same, by the service of one knight's fee.

Soon after, Sir Roger de Clifford marched into Wales with Roger de Mortimer and others, barons marchers, and gave battle to Prince Llewellyn, Montfort's confederate. About this time was fought the bloody battle of Lewes, between King Henry III. and the rebellious barons, headed by Montfort, Earl of Leicester; in which the king received a fatal overthrow, and was taken prisoner, along with Prince Edward his son, afterwards King Edward I. and many noblemen of the first rank. The prince was immediately separated from the king, and confined in a castle in the county of Hereford. Sir Roger de Clifford being informed of these u happy events, and feeling highly indignant that his sovereign should be carried about as a captive by one of his subjects, determined to concert a plot for setting the prince at liberty, and placing him at the head of the barons who remained faithful to him. For this purpose he sent the prince a remarkably fleet horse, and contrived to inform him, that if he could make his escape from his keepers, he would on a certain day, be stationed on a hill near the river Wye, with a considerable force to receive him. On the appointed day, the prince mounted the swift horse, under pretence of taking an airing with his keepers; and when they had rode gently for some way, he proposed to them to ride a race. To this they readily consented, when Prince Edward having let them blow and tire their horses, took off his hat, made them a bow, and told them he had now had enough of their company, and wished them good bye.

He then put spurs to his horse, and soon outstripped them all. They pursued him for some way, but the prince having crossed the Wye, soon espied the banner of Sir Roger de Clifford, who advanced to his assistance, and conveyed him to a place of safety.

This lucky event was soon followed by the decisive battle of Evesham, in the year 1265, in which Prince Edward was completely victorious. The king was set free, Montfort was slain, and the power of the rebellious barons utterly overthrown.

In consideration of these great and signal services which he had rendered to his sovereign in his greatest distresses, Sir Roger de Clifford obtained the custody of the lands of Robert de Vipont, a great northern baron, who was killed at Evesham, on the side of the rebels; and he was moreover appointed justice of all the king's forests south of the river Trent.

In 53 Henry 3, Sir Roger de Clifford was constituted one of the itinerant justices for the counties of Rutland, Surrey, Southampton, Dorset, Somerset and Gloucester; and the same year, was one of the guarantees for Robert de Ferrers, Earl of Derby, who was involved in the rebellion of the barons; but whose lands were restored to him on condition of his paying on a given day, the sum of 50,000*l.* to Edmund Earl of Lancaster, the king's son. It is well known, that in consequence of the inability of the Earl of Derby to bring forward the said sum at the appointed time, these lands came into the possession of Edmund, and afterwards devolved to the crown; and now constitute that vast property known by the name of the Duchy of Lancaster.

In the following year, Sir Roger de Clifford was induced by his warlike spirit to engage in a crusade to the Holy Land. Ottoboni, the pope's legate, signed him with the cross for that purpose, together with Prince Edward, and Edmund, the king's sons ; whom he accompanied to Palestine, along with John de Vescy, Thomas de Clare, Otho de Grandison, Robert le Bruce, John de Verdon, and others of great note.

On his return home, two years after, in the first year of the reign of Edward I. he was present with Philip, Count of Savoy and Burgundy, and others, when William, Lord of Toron on the Rhine, did homage to King Edward I. at the castle of St. George, near Beaufort in France.

Sir Roger de Clifford, having lost his wife Hawise, now paid his addresses to the Countess of Lorraine, whom he met in this castle of St. George, where he married her, with great solemnity, after having settled upon her his manor of Weverham in Cheshire.

His eldest son, who was also called Roger, being now grown up to years of maturity, and distinguishing himself like his father by his feats of arms, it appears, that, as titles of nobility were not known in these early times, Sir Roger de Clifford was distinguished by the appellation of Roger de Clifford the Elder. He continued to be employed in several offices of high trust and honor by King Edward the First ; who in the second year of his

reign sent him as ambassador into France ; and a
few years after appointed him one of the justices of
his forests in Hampshire, and justiciary of all Wales.
He was also commissioned to examine into, and to
hear and reform all wrongs done in those parts, contrary to the peace concluded between the king and
Llewellyn Prince of Wales, and to rectify every
thing according to that treaty.

In this employment, itis said, he was somewhat
oppressive, and created himself many enemies ; so
that he was surprised on Palm Sunday, in his castle of Hawardin, in Flintshire, by David, brother
of Llewellyn, who forgetting the great favours and
services formerly done him by King Edward, had
stirred up almost all Wales to take up arms.   This
coming to the king's ear, he sent a force into those
parts, and laid siege to Rothelan-castle ; but in a
skirmish with the Welsh, Roger, son to Roger de
Clifford, was unfortunately slain, on St. Leonard's
Day, betwixt Snowdon and Anglesey, as he was
inadvertently passing Newydd-bridge, over the river
Conway. This fatal event not only greatly afflicted
the king, but provoked him to raise a considerable number of forces, with whom he marched into
Plas, took the isle of Anglesey, and drove his
enemies back to the mountains.|

Sir Roger de Clifford survived this melancholy
loss of his valiant son about five years ; and died
at an advanced age, full of renown and glory, in
the year 1285.

It appears that besides his great estates in England, he had also some landed property in Ire-

M

land, for by a deed dated at Rochelle, in France, the morrow after Valentine's Day, 2 Edw. 1, he, together with the Countess of Lorrain, his wife, sold to Queen Eleanor, the manor of Ratouthe in that country, for the sum of 500*l.* sterling.

It is observed by Collins, (Supplement to the Peerage, vol. 2, p. 416) that Sir Roger de Clifford, and his son, were both of them chief commanders for twenty years successively, in the wars in England, Scotland, Ireland, Wales, and France, during the reigns of Henry III. and Edward I. as appears by the grants of those sovereigns conferred upon them both.

III.

OF THE ORIGIN AND ANTIQUITY

OF THE

CLIFFORD FAMILY.

IN THE

COUNTY OF WESTMORLAND.

———

In the preceding sections of this part of my work, I have shewn what was the origin of the name of Clifford; and how the Clifford family, descended from the Counts of Eu, and the Dukes of Normandy, came to change their first name Ponts, for that of Clifford; and being settled at Clifford-castle, in the county of Hereford, became possessed of very considerable domains in that, and the neighbouring counties. I have also related how, after the third generation, Walter, third Lord Clifford, having an only daughter, she became the heiress of Clifford-castle, and of the lordships and manors annexed to it; and consequently, that it ceased to be the property and reidence of the male line of the Clifford family. I have shewn that the male line of the family was continued by Roger de

M 2

Clifford, younger brother of Walter, third and last Lord Clifford, of Clifford-castle ; and it now remains for me to explain how his descendants, having removed their residence from the county of Hereford, came to establish in the county of Westmorland, where they flourished for many centuries, with great splendour and honour.

Robert de Vipont, Lord of Vipont in Normandy, came over to England with William the Conqueror, or soon after. Robert de Vipont his descendant, was with King John at the battle of Mirabel, in France, in the year 1202, in which the French and Poitevins were completely defeated, and a great number of prisoners were taken. They were all placed under the care of Robert de Vipont, and among them was the unfortunate Arthur, Earl of Britanny, nephew to King John, by whom he was afterwards barbarously murdered.

In reward of the services of Robert de Vipont, on this occasion, he first had a grant from King John of the castles of Appleby, and Brough, with the whole bailiwick of Westmorland, to hold during pleasure. The following year he had another grant of the same, together with the services of all those who held not by military services, to hold to him and his heirs, (by the wife he then had) by the service of four knights' fees for all services : Provided, he should not commit waste in the woods of Whinfell, nor hunt therein during the king's life, unless he were there himself in person : and saving to the king and his heirs all pleas of the crown.

In this grant were included the following castles and manors : Appleby, Brough, Staynemore, Flaxbrigg Park, Sowerby, Winton, Kirby-Stephen, Mallerstang, Pendragon, Langton, Meabourne-Regis, Brougham-castle, Kirby-Store, Mauds-Meaborne, and Temple-Sowerby, together with the forests, or rather the chases of Whinfell, and Mallerstang.

All these, together with the hereditary sheriffwick, and the services of the tenants of forty-five other lordships, (who held by a service called Cornage, or Horngelt) made up this great and extensive barony, bestowed by King John on Robert de Vipont.

He continued in great favour with his sovereign, and Mathew Paris ranks him among that king's wicked counsellors ; an appellation which he deserved, as he stood by him, against the other barons of England, when they forced him to sign the Magna Charta, or great charter of liberties.

Robert de Vipont had married Idonea, the daughter and heiress of John de Buly, a powerful baron, and lord of the manor of Tickhill, in the county of York : on whose death he succeeded to his whole inheritance.

Robert de Vipont died in the year 1227, leaving a son John, who left a son Robert, who married Isabel, daughter of John Fitz-Geffrey, a great baron in those times.

This Robert de Vipont joined with the rebellious barons against King Henry III. and was killed, or died of his wounds, either at the battle of Lewes, or Evesham. His lands were seized by the king, and the custody of them, together with the wardship of his two daughters, Isabel and Idonea, was given to Sir Roger de Clifford, and Roger de Leyburne.

Roger de Leyburne married Idonea, and Isabel became the wife of Roger de Clifford the Younger, who, as I have related above, was killed in Wales, as he was passing a bridge over the river Conway.

King Henry III. was so satisfied with the emiservices of Sir Roger de Clifford, and his son, that on their account he gave a free pardon to the daughters of Robert de Vipont for their father's rebellion, and restored to them his lands, of which he ordered a survey to be taken, and a partition to be made between them.

Idonea, the youngest daughter, wife of Roger de Leyburne, lived to an advanced age, but finally died without issue; so that all the great estates of Robert de Vipont came at length to a descendant of Roger de Clifford, who had married Isabel the eldest daughter.

ROGER DE CLIFFORD

THE YOUNGER,

OF BROUGHAM CASTLE,

IN THE

COUNTY OF WESTMORLAND.

This martial hero was very famous for his military prowess in the barons' wars, and for his expeditions against the Welsh, towards the latter end of King Henry the Third's time, and in the beginning of the reign of King Edward the First. He was the first of his warlike family that is recorded to have died in the field of battle ; though it was the fate of his son and successor, and of many of his descendants. Being slain in the king's service, as I have before remarked, in North Wales, he was buried in the Isle of Anglesey, in a chapel where one of King John's daughters had been formerly interred.

After his marriage with Isabella de Vipont, being possessed in her right of Brougham-castle, in the county of Westmorland, he new-built and repaired a considerable part of it ; and caused a stone to be set in the wall over the door of the inner gate, on which were engraved these words : THIS MADE ROGER : by which it is thought he meant to convey a double meaning, for some conjectured that he meant to express, that it was he who built that gate, and a great part of the castle, and repaired the great tower called the *Pagan Tower;* while others supposed that he meant that this castle was *the making of him*, since he obtained it, with many other places in the same county, by his fortunate marriage.

Isabella de Vipont, his wife, was born about the year 1254, and married at fourteen or fifteen years of age, in the year 1269. She continued the wife of Roger de Clifford, for fourteen years and seven months, and was his widow eight years; for she departed this life in the year 1291, about the age of 37, and was probably buried at Shap Abbey, in Westmorland, to which she was a considerable benefactress.

In her widowhood, she sat in person, as sheriffess of the county of Westmorland, in her castle of Appleby, with the judges; in which she was imitated about four centuries after by her descendant the celebrated Lady Anne Clifford, Countess of Dorset, Pembroke, and Montgomery. A little before her death, she had long suits at law, with Edmund Plantagenet, Earl of Lancaster, the king's brother, and Gilbert de Clare, Earl of Gloucester, concerning the wardship of her only son Robert, Lord Clifford; but those causes going against her, it is conjectured that the disappointment shortened her days, as she died soon after.

This noble lady had a just title to be highly esteemed and honoured by her posterity; for it was by her that the Cliffords first obtained the great barony of Westmorland, which they held for several ages with the greatest glory and renown.

ROBERT,

FIFTH LORD CLIFFORD OF HIS NAME,

AND

FIRST LORD CLIFFORD

OF

WESTMORLAND.

The fortunate star of the house of Clifford, which had shone with so much brightness in the west of England, was now destined to rise with still greater splendour in the north. It appears, that from this period, the descendants of Walter de Clifford of Clifford-castle, began to abandon their ancient castles in the counties of Worcester and Hereford, and in Wales, and fixed their residence at Appleby, Brougham, or Skipton, or other castles in those northern parts. Nor was their translation at this conjuncture from the borders of Wales to those of Scotland, without advantage to their country.

The Welsh, about this time, were completely subdued by Edward I. and were no longer a troublesome enemy; but the Scotch continued for some
centuries after, to be a thorn in the side of the English monarchy. Nothing, therefore, could be
more advantageous to the English government, in
this respect, than the establishment at this period,
in the north of England, of a great, powerful, and
warlike family, like that of the Cliffords. And their
history shows what a bulwark they were against
their northern enemies. With the Percys on one
side, and the Cliffords on the other, England had
nothing to fear from the inroads of the Scotch,
however violent.

Robert, Lord Clifford of Westmorland, only
son of Roger de Clifford the Younger, was not
more than six or seven years old at the death of
his father. Soon after he came of age, he was one
of the peers in the parliament then held at Lincoln,
who subscribed a declaration to the pope, asserting King Edward's right to the superiority in
Scotland, wherein he styled himself Governor of
Appleby.

Two years after, being during the Scotch war at
Dunbar, he had a share in the honour of the victory obtained there, in which the Scotch lost
above 10,000 men; and was soon after appointed
commander for the King of England, in the eastern
parts of Scotland, along with Sir Henry de Percy.
While he held this employment, he carried on a
negociation with Robert Bruce, Earl of Carrick,
respecting his submission to King Edward, and the

surrender of his daughter Margery, as a hostage into his hands.

Having settled these affairs, partly by treaty and partly by force of arms, on the eastern side of Scotland, Lord Clifford resolving to give his enemies no quarter, marched to the westward, and having raised 200 men in Carlisle, and the county of Cumberland, he advanced with them and 100 *gens-d'armes*, whom he had under his command, into Annandale, in Scotland ; and the word being given *to spare none but themselves*, the foot divided in order to plunder, but the horse kept in a body, and arriving by gentle marches on the moor near Annandale, the inhabitants made a jest of their small number, calling them *dogs without tails*, as the foot did not advance with them. But an engagement ensuing, 308 of the Scotch were slain, and some were taken prisoners ; after which the English committed g reat spoil, burning whole villages and towns in those parts, and returned to Carlisle, on Christmas Eve, loaden with their plunder.

For these and other great services, Lord Clifford was that same year appointed justice of all the king's forests north of the Trent.

The year following, he was made governor of Nottingham-castle, and in the month of September, the king summoned him to meet him, on Whitsuneve next, with horse and arms, to march with him into Scotland, wherever it should be judged most proper, to suppress his enemies. Moreover, a deed dated at Carlisle, the king, in considera-

tion of the good and loyal services of this Robert
de Clifford, granted to him the famous castle of
Carlaveroc, forfeited by Herbert Maxwell, and all
the lands and tenements that were lately the property of William Douglas.

King Edward I. one of the greatest monarchs
that ever swayed the English sceptre, and an excellent judge of talent and merit, seemed to set no
bounds to the honours and rewards that he wished
to shower on Lord Clifford, nor to the confidence
he reposed in him. In the 27th year of his reign,
Lord Clifford was constituted the king's lieutenant,
and captain-general in the counties of Cumberland, Westmorland, and Lancaster, as also throughout all Annandale, and the marches of Scotland :
and at the same time was joined in commission
with the Bishop of Durham, and other great lords,
to consult about putting soldiers, in the garrisons
of that kingdom, and about guarding the marches.

The next year, he was again in the wars of Scotland, and was specially commissioned by the king
to repair with John de Britannia, and others,
to Holmcolthram Abbey, in Cumberland, when
Robert, Bishop of Glasgow, owned King Edward
to be his lawful sovereign, and swore fealty to
him by the body of our Lord, and by the " Neyte
Cross," and " Black Rode," in Scotland.

As this Robert Lord Clifford made himself highly
eminent in war, so his sovereign thought that his
counsel was not less seasonable at home ; and
thereupon summoned him by writ, bearing date
at Berwick upon Tweed, 28 Edw.I. (1299) to sit in

the parliament, which was to meet at London the second Sunday in Lent, among the barons. (It is from this summons that the female barony of De Clifford, now enjoyed by the family of Southwell, of King's-Weston, near Bristol, takes its date ; and on this account also, several genealogists call this Robert, " The first Lord Clifford." In fact, those who were lords before him, were not lords of parliament, who strictly speaking were then unknown, but barons by tenure.)

Lord Clifford was regularly summoned to all the other parliaments of this reign, and to those of Edward II.

In 34 Edw. I. in consideration of his good and laudable service, he had a grant to him and his heirs of the manor of Hart, and the borough of Hartlepool, in the bishopric of Durham, forfeited by Robert Bruce, Earl of Carrick. In which year, King Edward marching towards Scotland with a great army, sent this Robert de Clifford before him, against Robert de Bruce, who had assumed the title of King of Scotland, in derogation of the King of England. And further to reward his services, the king gave to him and his heirs, all the lands and tenements of Chistopher de Seton, forfeited by attainder, in the county of Cumberland ; together with other estates of considerable value.

Lord Clifford was sent once more into Scotland by King Edward I. when he was preparing his last expedition against that kingdom ; but being seized with a mortal illness at Brough on the Sands, where he died, he appointed Lord Clifford, Henry Lacy, Earl of Lincoln, Guy Earl of Warwick, and Aymer de Valence, Earl of Pembroke, to be counsellors to his son Prince Edward : and lying on his death-bed, he requested them to be kind to him, and to take particular care that Piers de Gaveston, the prince's favourite, should not return any more into England to debauch him.

Being now considered as one of the most powerful men in the realm, King Edward II. constituted Lord Clifford Earl Marshal of England. The same year, being at Boulogne in France, he joined with that great prelate, Anthony Beke, Bishop of Durham, and with the Earls of Lincoln, Warren, and Pembroke, and the Lords Tibetot, Gray, and Botetourt, in an association by a special instrument under his own seal, whereby they engaged themselves to support the honour and dignity of the king with their lives and fortunes.

Lord Clifford had been summoned to the first parliament of Edward II. in order to confer with the king concerning the funeral of his father ; and he was now summoned again to attend the solemnity of his marriage and coronation, and for other important affairs.

This year also, being appointed warden of the marches of Scotland, he was afterwards named captain-general, and governor of the whole realm, with power to grant protection to all those who should submit to King Edward's authority : to which, was afterwards added a commission, empowering him as the king's lieutenant in Scotland, to maintain 100 horse, and 300 foot in his retinue.

King Edward II. was not unmindful of the signal services of Lord Clifford, and in reward of them, he granted to him and his heirs for ever, a weekly market every Monday, at his manor of Severnstoke, in the county of Worcester, and a fair every year there, to continue for three days, on the eve, the day, and the morrow of the feast of St. Faith; but what was more important, Lord Clifford obtained a grant of the castle of Skipton, in Craven, and lands to the amount of about 400*l.* a year at that time, together with the knights' fees, and advowsons of the churches belonging to the castle. (1) At the same time, he had also a grant to him and his heirs of the vale of Douglas in Scotland, which was forfeited by the proprietor.

---

(1) The Skipton Fee, in Craven, which was granted by King Edward II. to Lord Clifford, had passed successively from the houses of Romille and Albemarle to the crown. It consists of about four and twenty towns, which owe suit and service to the court-leet of that place.

Skipton-castle, which is still standing, and is now the property of the Earl of Thanet, became the principal residence of the Clifford family for more than 300 years, and most of them were buried in the church of that town.

The Percy Fee, in Craven, also came to them afterwards, as I have related above, (Part I, p. 24.)

This great seignory, comprehending all the western part of Craven, consisted of near forty townships, many

In the following years, 4 and 5 Edw. 2, Lord Clifford made two expeditions into Scotland, and advanced as far as Roxburgh to attack the Scotch ; and, an act of parliament having been pa ssed, called the " Act of Redemption," whereby the nobility were empowered to take into their hands, for the king's use, divers castles, lands, and tenements, among which were the castle and manor of Skipton, so highly was Lord Clifford in esteem and favour, for his great and manifold services, that notwithstanding the act, his castle and manor were exempted.

But affairs were soon to take another turn between Lord Clifford and his sovereign. Notwithstanding the honours and favours bestowed upon him by King Edward II. Lord Clifford could not forget the dying injunctions of his former friend and sovereign, King Edward I ; and having learnt that Peirs Gaveston, the dissolute favourite of King

---

of which are surveyed in Domesday-book, under the title of " Terra Wil' de Perci."

In point of manorial and forest rights, this was an acquisition to the Clifford family, far beyond its pecuniary value, which, with a few exceptions, consisted in reserved rents alone. But it almost completed the power and influence of the Cliffords in Craven ; for the bailiwick of Staincliff, with all escheats, and other rights, incident to it, had alrealy been granted by King Henry VI. to Thomas Lord Clifford, which was confirmed by James I. to Francis, Earl of Cumberland, and is still continued in his noble descendant, the Duke of Devonshire.—(See Whitaker's History of Craven, p. 11, etc.)

Edward, had returned to England, and had fortified himself in Scarborough-castle, Lord Clifford immediately formed an association with the Earls of Surrey and Pembroke, and Henry de Percy ; and having raised a sufficient force laid siege to the place. King Edward, a weak prince, immediately commanded Lord Clifford to raise the siege on forfeiture of his life and estate ; but he persisted in his design, and soon after entered the town in a hostile manner. Upon this the king sailed from Tinmouth to Scarborough, to relieve his favourite, when Lord Clifford retired ; but the king being suddenly called into Warwickshire, and leaving Gaveston in Scarborough-castle, Lord Clifford returned directly to the siege, and having raised fresh forces, kept the garrison in such continual alarm, that the unfortunate favourite, harrased out, and seeing no hope of succour, yielded at discretion, promising to stand by the judgment of the barons. Lord Clifford and his associates were not long in condemning him to death, and had the sentence immediately put in execution.

King Edward was highly indignant at these violent proceedings of Lord Clifford and his friends, but finding that most of the powerful barons of the realm took their part, he was obliged to come to terms with them ; and therefore, at the request of the Cardinal of St. Prisca, and the Archbishop of Poitiers, the pope's envoys, in order to restore peace and tranquillity to the kingdom, he consented to enter into a treaty with Lord Clifford and his associates, which was to be settled in London,

N

but none of the commissioners were to appear in that city with any retinue of horse, nor to lodge in it, for fear of further disturbance. The king having promised his protection, and granted letters of safe conduct to Lord Clifford, his domestics and adherents, the treaty was made in the presence of the pope's legates, and some other great personages; the substance of which I shall here insert, as little notice is taken of it by any of our historians:

" This is the treaty of peace, made and concluded before Arnold, Cardinal of St. Prisca, Arnold, Bishop of Poitiers, the pope's envoys, Lewis of France Count d'Evreux, etc. by Robert de Clifford, etc. sent to London, with full power to treat on the behalf of the Earls of Lancaster and Warwick; and by the Earl of Pembroke, etc. on the king's behalf.

" First, the said earls and barons shall come before the king upon their knees, in Westminster-Hall, and humble themselves, and swear, if he require it, That what they did was not evilly intended against him, begging forgiveness, and to be restored to his favour.

" Second, whatever they took on the said Gaveston's account, as jewels and other things, they shall surrender at St. Albans, on St. Hilary's Day next, where the king will send persons to receive them.

" Third, that in the next parliament, security shall be given, that no person shall be called to account, or molested for the death of Piers de Gaveston.

" Fourth, the said deputies promise, that when matters are reconciled, they, in parliament with

208

their peers, will do their utmost endeavours that the king shall have sufficient aid from the kingdom, for the war in Scotland.

" Fifth, that all persons shall have liberty to pass and repass, to transact their affairs, without impediment or molestation.

" The safe conduct to last till Whitsunday next.

" This was made the Wednesday before Christmas, in the said cardinal's chamber at London, 1312, 6 Edw. 2."

The February following, the king, in a declaration from Windsor, acknowledged that he had received from Robert de Clifford, the jewels, horses, etc. late belonging to Piers de Gaveston : and the same year, Lord Clifford, the better to discharge all persons concerned in the death of the favourite, procured an act of parliament, " That none should be called to account for it ;" which having passed, he and others the next day, solemnly received the king's pardon.

This important affair being thus happily concluded, Lord Clifford made all the preparations in his power to carry on the war with Scotland ; and having advanced with the English forces to Bannockburn, near Stirling, where he was met by the Scotch, after a desperate battle, he was there unfortunately slain, with the flower of the English nobility, in the greatest overthrow which the English ever received, on the 25th of June, in the year 1314. Gilbert de Clare, Earl of Gloucester, cousin-german to Lord Clifford's wife, was also killed by his side ; and their bodies having

N 2

been discovered among the slain, were honourably sent by the King of Scots to King Edward II. then at Berwick upon Tweed, to be interred at his pleasure. It is presumed that the body of Lord Clifford was entombed in Shapp Abbey, in Westmorland, where several of his ancestors and succesors were laid.

Thus perished at the age of forty, in the vigour of life, Robert, first Lord Clifford of Westmorland ; who, when we consider his birth and descent, and his vast possessions, his active and martial life, his warlike enterprises, and deeds of arms, the high offices and commands that were entrusted to him, and the exalted dignities and honours conferred upon him by two successive sovereigns, with the powerful influence he possessed both in council and parliament, and in all state affairs, must be allowed to have been the most shining character in England, during the period in which he flourished. Such a hero was fit to be the head and chief of his noble race, and the bright example of his illustrious descendants ; and to their honour it may be asserted, that to the last they were all worthy of him.

Robert Lord Clifford married Matilda, daughter and coheir of Thomas de Clare, steward of the forest of Essex, and second son of Richard, Earl of Gloucester, hereditary steward, and lord of the honour of Clare, in the district of Thomond, in Ireland. He had issue by her two sons, Roger, and Robert, and one daughter, Idonea, who married Henry Lord Percy, and was great grandmother to Henry Percy, first Earl of Northumberland.

This noble lady had much land of inheritance in Ireland. Her mother's father was Maurice, lord justice of Ireland, who married Emily Longespée, daughter of the Earl of Salisbury, grandson of Fair Rosamund.

OF THE DESCENDANTS

O F

ROBERT,

FIRST LORD CLIFFORD

O F

WESTMORLAND.

Robert Lord Clifford was succeeded by his eldest son Roger, whose life was short, and his end unfortunate. He was eminent for his military talents during the life-time of his father, but after his death, he was induced to join the party of Thomas Plantagenet, Earl of Lancaster, against the king. This Lord Clifford appears to have been of a violent temper. Being present at a consultation of some of the rebellious barons at Pomfret, when the Earl of Lancaster was advised to go to his own castle at Dunstanburgh, in Northumberland, and perceiving that he refused to comply, lest he should be suspected of holding intelligence with the Scotch, Lord Clifford drew his dagger in a great passion, and threatened to stab him on the spot if he refused to go with them. But he had reason to repent of this violence, for as they marched by Boroughbridge, they were met by the king's forces, commanded by Sir Simon Ward, sheriff of York, when Lord Clifford's party was defeated, and he being sometime after arrested, was beheaded with Lord Mowbray at York. It is said he was so regardless of the king's displeasure, that when the pursuivant served the writ upon him, in the barons' chamber, at Appleby-castle, he forced him to eat and swallow the wax that the writ was sealed with.

He was succeeded by Robert de Clifford, his brother and heir, who was also of the party of the Earl of Lancaster; but Edward II. having been deposed, a general pardon was granted by act of parliament, to all who had been in arms against him.

Lord Clifford, as proprietor of lands in Ireland, was summoned by King Edward III. to attend him to that country; but the following year, he was in the war in Scotland, and in consideration of the great expenses and losses he had sustained in the king's service, an order was sent to the king's purveyor at Berwick upon Tweed, to give him a tun of wine, and six quarters of wheat, out of the stores in that place.

Soon after this, about the year 1333, Edward de Baliol, King of Scotland, came to hunt in the forests and chases of Lord Clifford in Westmorland, and was hospitably entertained by him in his castles of Appleby and Brougham. The tradition of this royal hunt has been preserved down to the present day, as there are many spots in Westmorland relating to it that are still pointed out, and particularly a great tree in the forest of Whinfell, called the Hartshorn Tree, where the King of Scotland killed a stag.

In 8 Edw. 3, Lord Clifford was joined in commission with Ranulph de Dacre, in the government of Carlisle, and the wardenship of the adjacent marches, with power to choose able men for the security of both: and the next year, he was appointed sole warden of all the marches of Cumberland and Westmorland, and captain-general of all the forces in those parts for opposing the power of the Scotch.

In 14 Edw. 3, he gave the moiety of the village of Winderton to the canons of Haghmon in Shropshire, to whom his ancestors had been constant benefactors. The following year, he was employed by King Edward III. in the affairs of Scotland, but being seized with a mortal illness, he departed this life, at the early age of thirty-nine, in the year 1343.

Robert Lord Clifford married Isabel de Berkeley, only daughter of Maurice Lord Berkeley, of Berkeley-castle. She had a thousand pounds and fifty marks for her portion. Her wedding apparel was scarlet cloth with a brown cast, the cape being furred with the best miniver; and her brother Lord Berkeley and his lady, were apparelled in like habits for the honour of the bride. Her saddle, on which she rode to church, cost five pounds in London, a great sum in those days.

Collins, from whom this account is taken, says, " Her friends certainly were of great power, as appears by their help in procuring a licence from King Edward III. to pass fines, a thing unusual in that age, between her husband, and his great aunt Idonea de Leyburne; and also those feoffments for settling all the lands in Skipton, and a great part of the lands in Westmorland on her for life : a greater dower than ever was settled on any of the wives of the Lord Cliffords, either before or after her."

It was this Lady Clifford, who made over to the students of the law that mansion in London, which was formerly the residence of the Lord Cliffords, and is now called Clifford's Inn.

Robert Lord Clifford, had by his wife Isabel de Berkeley, three sons, Robert, Roger, and Thomas.

Robert Lord Clifford, his eldest son and heir, was but thirteen years old at the time of his father's decease, whereupon his wardship, during his minority, together with the sheriffalty of Westmorland, were committed to Ralph de Nevill, a great baron of that time, and first Earl of Westmorland. Lord Clifford was in the wars of France, in the reign of King of Edward III. and fought with

the Black Prince, at the memorable battle of Crecy.
He also accompanied him in his adventurous expe-
ditions in the south of France, and the borders of
Spain, and was present at the famous battle of
Poitiers, in the year 1357.

This Lord Clifford married his cousin-german
Eufemia de Nevill, sister of his guardian the Earl
of Westmorland. He had no issue, and is supposed to have died in France, about the age of 30,
in the year 1362.

He was succeeded by his brother Roger, who
was born in the year 1334, 8 Edward III. a year
which was remarkable for two great events in the
family: the first was the hunting visit that was made
to his father Lord Clifford, by Baliol, King of
Scotland, which I have noticed above ; and the second was the death of his father's great aunt, Idonea de Leyburne, youngest daughter and coheir of
Robert de Vipont, last heir male of the Viponts,
Lords of Westmorland. She dying without issue,
that share of their lands which she had possessed
from the time of her own father's decease till her
death, then fell to this Lord Clifford's father, Robert third Lord Clifford of Westmorland.

This Roger, who was the fifth Lord Clifford of
Westmorland, being of age, 29 Edw. 3, was in
the expedition then made into Gascony ; and the
following year, was one of those northern barons
who were commanded to repair to the marches of
Scotland to defend them against the Scotch. Three

years after, he was twice in Gascony on military service in those parts. It appears, that at this early period, complaints were made in Ireland of the practice which the proprietors of great estates there had, of dwelling in England, and spending there the income of their lands which they received from Ireland. Edward III. being sensible of this abuse, and Ireland, moreover, being in a troubled state, he published a proclamation addressed to Lord Clifford and others, signifying to them that he had commanded his son Lionel, Earl of Ulster, to march there with a body of forces, and to be attended by all persons holding lands in that country, in order to restore tranquillity, and protect the inhabitants. But before his departure, he ordered Lord Clifford to repair to London, to hold a conference with him in the parliament at Westminster.

After his return from Ireland, Lord Clifford obtained permission of the king to make a park, at Skipton, in Craven, and to inclose there 5oo acres of waste lands, together with Calder Wood. The next year, he was appointed one of the wardens of the Scotch marches. But in 42 Edw. 3, there being fresh disturbances in Ireland, Lord Clifford was commanded to go there with all the forces he could raise, and there to continue on his estate, without any excuse whatever. However, he returned to England the following year, and with the exception of two expeditions against France, in which he served, he was constantly employed by King Ed-

ward III. in the negociations and wars with Scotland,
till the end of his reign, in the last year of which,
that king appointed him warden of the Marches,
sheriff of Cumberland, and governor of Carlisle-
castle.

Lord Clifford was continued in these appoint-
ments by King Richard II. and in the 7th year of his
reign, was summoned to be at Newcastle upon Tyne,
with more than his quota of horse and arms, if possible, in order to suppress a dangerous insurrection of
Scotch. He was soon after advanced to the dignity of knight banneret, in those days, the highest
rank of chivalry, and was retained by indentnre
to serve the king in his Scottish war, as long at it
lasted.

Some years after, Lord Clifford went with the
Earl of Arundel, into Guyenne, in France, in order to reinforce the king's army in those parts ; and
having discovered as much skill and knowledge in
naval affairs as in military enterprises, he was
entrusted with a squadron of ships in order to
scour the seas, and clear them of rovers and pi-
rates, and other enemies; and having narrowly
watched and pursued them, he at length encountered a great fleet of Flemings, laden with wines
from Rochelle, whom he completely defeated,
and took several of their vessels, together with the
admiral of Flanders.

This Lord Clifford was a great repairer of his
castles and houses in the north of England, and built
the greatest part of Brougham-castle, on the east,
whereon were cut his own arms, *Chequy, a Fess*,

impaling those of his wife, Matilda de Beauchamp, which were a *Fess between six cross crosslets.*

Lord Clifford died in the year 1389, and was probably buried in Shap Abbey, in Westmorland, to which himself and his ancestors had been great benefactors.

" He was esteemed," says Collins, " the wisest and gallantest man of all the Cliffords, which appeared in keeping himself out of the broils in those troublesome times in the latter end of the reign of King Edward III. and the beginning of his successor Richard II."

———————

Sir Thomas de Clifford, youngest brother of this Roger Lord Clifford, was a knight, and had lands in Ireland, in the district of Thomond.   One of his younger sons, named Richard, was brought up to the church, and is the only instance of an ecclesiastic in the long line of this noble family.   He obtained the highest ecclesiastical preferments, and appears to have been on the point of being elected pope.   Being first made Archdeacon of Canterbury, he was in 1401 consecrated Bishop of Worcester, and appointed Lord Privy Seal.   In 1407, he was translated to the see of London; and in the year 1414 was sent to the famous council of Constance, as a delegate to represent the English church.   On this occasion, he preached a sermon in Latin before the Emperor of Germany, and the other great personages who were assembled in the town of Constance.   At this council, besides the condemnation of John Huss, and Jerom of

Prague, and the Wickliffites in England, that remarkable schism was terminated, which had so long disturbed the peace of the church, by the existence of two persons at once, who both assumed the papal dignity. The council thinking it proper that thirty persons should be added to the college of cardinals, previous to the election of a pope, the Bishop of London was one of the number; and at the same time his name was put in the list of those who were nominated for the papacy. But he himself was the first who named Cardinal Colonna, who, thereupon, the others consenting to this choice, was immediately elected sole pope, and assumed the name of Martin V.

This prelate contributed a sum of money towards the library of Baliol College; and bequeathed a thousand marks towards the support of poor scholars, at Burnell's Inn at Oxford, which thence took the name of London College. Bishop Clifford died in the year 1421, and was buried in St. Paul's cathedral, near the place where the shrine of St. Erkenwald stood, towards the south.

Roger, fifth Lord Clifford of Westmorland, married Matilda de Beauchamp, daughter of Thomas de Beauchamp, Earl of Warwick, by whom he had two daughters, and one son Thomas, sixth Lord Clifford of Westmorland, ancestor of Lord Clifford the Shepherd, and the Earls of Cumberland, and father of Sir Lewis Clifford, knight of the Garter, from whom are descended the Lords Clifford of Chudleigh, in the county of Devon, and the Cliffords of Tixall in the county of Stafford, of whom, as well as of the Earls of Cumberland, some anecdotes have been related in the First Part of this Work.—(See Part I, p. 38.)

IV.

OF THE

ARMORIAL BEARINGS

O F

CLIFFORD.

Chequy, or and azure, has always been from the earliest times the coat-armour of Clifford. (1)   The *chequer* has generally been considered as the most ancient of all heraldic bearings ; and Brydson, in his " View of Heraldry," supposes, on the authority of Ducange, and other learned antiquaries, that this coat of arms was derived from the ordinary dress of some of the Celtic nations, particularly the ancient Gauls, by whom it was termed *sagum.*

"Cluverius," says he, " describes at large the different forms and ornaments of the *sagum* worn by the Germans, representing, that it was a sort of cloak, clasped before, adorned with streaks and *chequers* of various colours, sometimes even of silver or

---

(1) See Part II. p. 130.

gold. He also in some degree adverts to those simple decorations, as forming the first armorial ensigns. The invention however of the chequer, considered as a species of ornament, is, by Pliny, expressly ascribed to the Gauls. When this cloak or sagum became a coat of arms, the same stripes and chequers were retained, and with other acquired embellishments, were converted into the permanent insignia of families and sovereign states.

A habit, adorned with chequers similiar to those mentioned by Pliny, is at this day worn as the national dress, in that part of North Britain where the Celtic language prevails.

Armorial bearings abound with different chequers corresponding to the ornaments of the sagum. Among these, the chequers in the arms of Croatia, and of the ancient Kings of Soissons, with those of the Counts of Vermandois, and Dreux, are in the common form ; but in the arms of Monaco, each has an angle pointing upwards ; and in those of Bavaria, each has an angle pointing diagonally. Such chequers compose an incredible number of armories throughout the several kingdoms of Europe."

Chequy, or and azure, was also borne in England, by the ancient Earls of Warren and Surrey, which title became extinct in the year 1347, by the death of John, the last Earl. This Earl obtained from King Edward III. a 'patent for licensing public places of entertainment ; and he obliged those to whom he granted a licence to put up his arms at their doors, which is the reason why the chequer is still so often seen at the doors of public houses. The chequer is now quartered by Howard, Duke of Norfolk, as a descendant from the Earls of Surrey.

It is well known, that the armorial bearings of ancient noble families have, at different periods, undergone many alterations. " In past ages," says Camden, " they which were descended from one stemme, reserving the principal charge, and commonly the colour of the coat, took *borders, bends, quarters, bendlets, crosslets*, or some other addition or alteration. As for example, the first Lord Clifford bore *Chequy or and azure, a bendlet gules;* which the elder brethren kept as long as they continued : a second son turned the bendlet into a bend gules, and thereon placed three *lionceaux, passant, or;* from whom the Cliffords of Frampton descended. Roger de Clifford, a second son of Walter de Clifford the Second, for the bendlet took a *fess* gules, as the Earl of Cumberland, from him descended, beareth now ; and the Cliffords of Kent, branched out of that house, took the same with a border gules."

In one of the windows of Great Malvern church, in the county of Worcester, are several coats of arms, " Chequy, or and azure, on a bend gules, three lions passant guardant, or ;" and below are several figures of benefactors with this inscription : Orate pro animabus Henrici Clyfford senescalli de Longeneye, et Elizabethæ uxoris ejus, et Jacobi Clifford amigeri, filii eorundem, et animabus parentum et benefactorum eorundem.—(See above, Part II, p. 129.)

In one of the windows of stained glass, discovered in St. Stephen's chapel, (the House of Commons) are the arms of Roger fifth Lord Clifford of
Westmorland, who died in 1389 ; they are Chequy,
or and azure, on a fess five white roses.

Crest. In the inventory of the personal effects
of Henry Lord Clifford, second Earl of Cumberland, at Skipton-castle, taken in the year 1572,
mention is made of " a red dragon looking furthe
of a white castell made of silver tissay." This, Dr.
Whitaker says, was the crest of the Clifford family. The crest borne by the first Lord Clifford of
Chudleigh, Lord High Treasurer of England, and
now that of his descendants, was " Out of a du-
cal coronet, or, a wyvern rising gules."

Supporters. These appendages to the coat of
arms are supposed to have been introduced into
heraldry by King Richard II. whose supporters were
two angels. However, the arms of his grandfather and predecessor King Edward III. have been
represented as supported by a lion and a falcon.
The supporters of the arms of the Lord Clifford of
Chudleigh, are two wyverns.

Motto. The ancient motto of the Clifford family was " *Désormais ;*" and it appears carved on
the battlement of Skipton-castle, with the date
1629. In Sandford's " Genealogical History of
the Kings of England," is a plate dedicated to the
first Lord Clifford of Chudleigh, to which his arms
are annexed with the motto *Per varios casus :*
but the motto now used by his descendants is
Semper Paratus.

O

V.

THE GENEALOGY

OF THE

CLIFFORD FAMILY,

DEDUCED FROM ROLLO, FIRST DUKE
OF NORMANDY.

———

It is a reverend thing to see an ancient building not in
decay, or a fair timber-tree sound and perfect. How
much more to behold an ancient noble family, that has
stood against the waves and weathers of Time! For
new nobility is the act of *power*, but ancient nobility is
the act of *time*. (1)

———

DIED.

I. Rollo, first Duke of Normandy........ 932
   Gisela, daughter of Charles the Simple.
   Popœa, (2) daughter of Berenger,
   Count of Bayeux.

II. William I. second Duke of Normandy... 942
   Sprota, daughter of Herbert, Count of
   Senlis.

———

(1) Bacon, Essays 14.
(2) When there were two wives, the one that had issue,
by which the line was propagated, is put in Italics.

DIED.

III. Richard I. third Duke of Normandy... 996
    Emma, sister of Hugh Capet.
    Gunnor, a Norman lady.

IV. William, Count of Eu, *his second son,*
    about...................... 1050
    Esseline, daughter of Count Turketil.

V. Ponts, about................... 1090 (3)
    Basilia.

VI. Richard Fitz-Ponts, about........... 1140
    Matilda.

VII. Walter Fitz-Ponts, assumed the name
    of De Clifford. (4)............. 1216
    Margaret de Toeni. (5)

VIII. Walter, Second Lord Clifford...... 1223
    Agnes, daughter of Roger de Cundy.

---

(3) His eldest brother, Robert, second Count of Eu, died about that time.—(Art de verifier les dates. Vol. II. Eu.)

(4) He was the father of Fair Rosamund. I conjecture, that Rosamund, who had a sister called Alicia, or Lucia, was not called so by her parents at her birth, but probably Rose, or Rosa ; and that King Henry gave her the name of Rosamnnd, because on account of her beauty and accomplishments, he declared she was *Rosa Mundi*, the rose of the world. It is curious, that her son by King Henry, who was surnamed Longespée, and afterwards was created Earl of Salisbury, was first called Earl of Rosemer, (Rose of the Sea). Fair Rosamund was cotemporary with Eloisa, the famous mistress of Abelard.

(5) Margaret de Toeni's father, hereditary standard-bearer of Normandy, was descended from Malahulc, the uncle of Rollo.

DIED.

IX. Walter, third Lord Clifford. (6)....... 1263

    Isabella.

    Margaret, daughter to Llewllyn Prince
       of Wales.

    Roger, his brother, died before him.

    Sibilla de Ewyas.

X. Roger, (7) fourth Lord Clifford, nephew
      to Walter..................... 1285

    Hawise.

XI. Roger his son, died before him.

    Isabella de Vipont.

XII. Robert, fifth Lord Clifford, grandson

---

(6) He had an only daughter by his wife Margaret,
called Matilda, who married her cousin, William Longespée, Earl of Salisbury, great grandson of Rosamund.
She inherited Clifford-castle, and had an only daughter,
Margaret, who married Henry de Lacy, Earl of Lincoln.

(7) Roger seems to have been a favourite name among
the Normans, and is celebrated by Tasso, but is now
thought so vulgar or so ugly a name in England, that it
has almost fallen into disuse. With respect to the names in
ancient pedigrees, there are two points worthy of remark.
First, that before the 13th or 14th centuries, it does not
seem to have been considered of any importance to give
children Christian names taken out of the Bible, nor even
the names of Saints. If any further proof of this were
wanting, it might be found in the names of the Kings of
France, many of whom were called Lewis, a name not
to be found in the Bible, and of which the first saint was
Lewis IX. who reigned about the middle of the 13th
century. Secondly, the practice of giving children
more than one name was quite unknown.

DIED.

of the fourth Lord. (8).......... 1314

Matilda de Clare. (9)

XIII. Roger, sixth lord................ 1321

Unmarried.

XIV. Robert his brother, (seventh lord).... 1344

Isabella de Berkeley. (10)

---

(8) This Lord Clifford was the first of his family that was regularly summoned to parliament: 28 Edw. I. a custom first introduced by that king. Here we may observe, that it is of such nobility as that of this illustrious family, that Lord Bacon speaks, when he says, that *ancient nobility is the act of time.* For this Lord Clifford was not made a lord or a baron by King Edward I. by being summoned to parliament, but he was summoned to parliament, *because he was already a Baron*, that is, one of the great men of the realm, by tenure, and descent from a long line of illustrious ancestors, who were descended from the Dukes of Normandy, whose noble origin was lost in *the night of time.* The nobility of Lord Clifford was derived from the same source as that of King Edward himself. But modern nobility, particularly during the two last centuries, has been merely the *act of power*; by letters-patent from the king, conferring the title of viscount, marquis, duke, etc. which in the days of this Lord Clifford, were wholly unknown. It is of such noblemen that the poet says—

A breath can make them as a breath has made.

(9) She was daughter of Thomas de Clare, second son of Richard de Clare, Earl of Gloucester and Hertford, who married Joan de Acre, one of the daughters of King Edward I. By her he had a son who was killed with Lord Clifford at the fatal battle of Bannockburn.

(10) It was in Berkeley-castle, still standing, the house

DIED.

XV. Robert, eighth Lord Clifford, about.. 1362
Eufemia de Nevill—(no issue).

XVI. Roger, his brother, ninth Lord Clifford......................... 1389
Matilda de Beauchamp.

XVII. Thomas, tenth Lord Clifford....... 1395
Elizabeth de Roos. (11)

XVI.I. John, eleventh Lord Clifford...... 1422
Elizabeth Percy, daughter of Hotspur

XIX. Thomas, twelfth Lord Clifford...... 1454
Joanna, daughter of Lord Dacre

XX. John, thirteenth Lord Clifford....... 1460
Margaret de Bromflete, Baroness Vescy.

XXI. Henry, fourteenth Lord Clifford, (the
Shepherd)..................... 1523

---

of her father, that Edward II. was so inhumanly murdered.

(11) She was daughter of William Lord Roos of Hamlake, one of the competitors for the crown of Scotland;
being great grandson of Robert Lord Roos, by his wife
Isabel, daughter of William, King of Scotland. Besides
their eldest son John, ancestor of the Earls of Cumber-
berland, they had two younger sons, William and Lewis.
Sir William Clifford was governor of Berwick, a place of
great importance in those days, and was in particular esteem with that magnanimous prince King Henry V. He
died without issue. His brother Sir Lewis Clifford, a knight
of the Garter, who died in the year 1404, was ances-
cestor of the Lords Clifford of Chudleigh, and of the
Cliffords of Tixall, in the county of Stafford.—(See Part I.
pp. 15, 29, 40, 43, 70, 73, 76, 97.)

Anne St. John, cousin-german to King
    Henry VII.
XXII. Henry, fifteenth Lord Clifford, first
    Earl of Cumberland............ 1542
    Lady Margaret Talbot.
    Lady Margaret Percy.
XXIII. Henry, sixteenth Lord Clifford, se-
    cond Earl of Cumberland........ 1569
    Lady Eleanor Brandon, niece to King
    Henry VIII. (12)
    Anne, daughter of Lord Dacre.
XXIV. George, seventeenth Lord Clifford,
    third Earl of Cumberland. (13)... 1605
    Lady Margaret Russel.

---

(12) Henry VIII. by his will confirmed by parliament,
settled the crown of England on the issue of this marriage, in default of issue from his own children. Their
only daughter, Lady Margaret Clifford, married the Earl
of Derby.

(13) He left an only daughter, Lady Anne Clifford, who
was Baroness de Clifford, Westmorland, and Vescy, in
her own right. The title of Earl of Cumberland, which
was derived from *an act of power*, went to her uncle.
She married the Earl of Dorset, who left only two daughters by her. The eldest married the Earl of Thanet, whose
son, on the death of his grandmother the Countess of Dorset, became Lord de Clifford. He died in 1729, leaving
five daughters, and no son, on which the ancient barony
of de Clifford was in abeyance. George II. granted it to
the third daughter, Lady Margaret Tufton, wife of Thomas
Coke, Earl of Leicester. She died without issue, when
the title again fell into abeyance, and was granted by King

DIED.

XXV. Francis, his brother, eighteenth Lord
     Clifford, fourth Earl of Cumber-
     land 1641
     Grisold, daughter of Thos. Hughes, Esq.

XXVI. Henry, nineteenth Lord Clifford,
     fifth and last Earl of Cumberland. (14). 1643
     Lady Frances Cecil.

George III. to Sir Edward Southwell, who had married
the grand-daughter of Lady Catherine Tufton, eldest
daughter of the Earl of Thanet, and sister of the Countess of Leicester above-mentioned. Which Lady Southwell, as grand-daughter of the *eldest* sister, had of course
the best claim to the title, which is now enjoyed by her
descendant, Edward Southwell, the present Lord de
Clifford.

Lady Anne Clifford, Countess of Dorset, only daughter of George, third Earl of Cumberland, from whom
the female barony of de Clifford was thus derived, was
the last survivor of her illustrious race. She died at a
great age, in her castle of Appleby, in the year 1675, exactly 500 years after the death of Fair Rosamund, from
whose father, Walter de Clifford, she was lineally descended; and to whom, in beauty, talents, and accomplishments, she was probably in no respect inferior.

(14) His only daughter Lady Elizabeth Clifford, married Richard Boyle, Earl of Cork, and fifth Earl of
Burlington; who, in 1644, was by Charles I. created
Baron Clifford of Longborongh in Yorkshire. His great
grandson, Richard, Earl of Burlington, the famous ar-
chitect, died without male issue; but his daughter married
William, third Duke of Devonshire; whose grandson, the

It may be observed, that from the death of Rollo, first Duke of Normandy, (932) to that of the last Earl of Cumberland, (1643) his lineal descendant, there elapsed a period of 711 years; during which there were 23 generations; which, dividing 711 by 23, gives as nearly as possible, 31 years for each generation; a calculation which agrees with that of Buffon, and other philosophers on this subject.

In the character of George, third Earl of Cumberland, extracted from the " Heroloogia," and inserted in the First Part of this Work, it is said, he had always in his mind a line of Homer, which is there quoted, and the sense of which is according to Cowper's translation :

> That I should outstrip always all mankind
> In worth and valour, nor the house disgrace
> Of my forefathers, heroes without peer.

The whole passage is one of the finest in Homer, (Iliad, b. vi.) and some of the lines are so expressive of the vicissitudes of noble families, and illustrate so well the character and conduct of the heroes of the race of Clifford, that I cannot do better than to quote them here, from the translation of Pope.

> Like leaves on trees, the race of man is found,
> Now green in youth, now withering on the ground.

---

present Duke, is Lord of the Percy Fee in Craven, and representative of the last male line of the Cliffords, Earls of Cumberland.

Another shoot the following spring supplies,
They fall successive, and successive rise.
So generations in their course decay,
So flourish these, when those are past away.

Hippolochus survived, from him I came,
The honoured author of my birth and name.
By his decree I sought the Trojan town,
By his instructions learn to win renown;
To stand the first in worth as in command,
To add new honours to my native land,
Before my eyes my mighty sires to place,
And emulate the glories of our race.

END OF THE SECOND PART.

COLLECTANEA CLIFFORDIANA.

PART THE THIRD:

CONTAINING

CLIFFORD;

OR, THE BATTLE OF TOWTON.

AN HISTORICAL TRAGEDY, IN FIVE ACTS.

BY ARTHUR CLIFFORD, ESQ.

CLIFFORD; A TRAGEDY.

As a perfect tragedy is *the noblest production of human nature*, so it is capable of giving the mind one of the most delightful and most improving entertainments. A virtuous man (says Seneca), struggling with misfortunes, is such a spectacle as gods might look on with pleasure, and such pleasure it is which one meets with in the representation of a well-written tragedy. Diversions of this kind wear out of our thoughts every thing that is mean and little. They cherish and cultivate that humanity which is the ornament of our nature. They soften insolence, soothe affliction, and subdue the mind to the dispensations of Providence.

It is no wonder therefore, that in all the polite nations of the world, this part of the drama has met with public encouragement. ADDISON—*Spectator*, N°. 39.

I would submit to the reader's judgment, whether the tragic poem does not demand a stronger exertion of the mental faculties, within the compass of its composition, than the epic poem. In a drama, where every thing must be in action, where characters must be strongly marked, and closely compressed, the passions all in arms, and the heart alternately seized by terror, and subdued by pity, where the diction must never sleep in detail, nor languish in description, but be lofty yet not dilated, eloquent but not loquacious, I have no conception how the human genius can be strained to greater euergy. CUMBERLAND—*Observer*, N°. 132.

Now followeth that black scene, borne up so wondrous
    high,
That but a poor dumb shew before a tragedy,
The former battles fought have seemed to this to be :
O Towton ! let the blood Palm Sunday spent on thee,
Affright the future times, when they the muse shall hear
Deliver it so to them ; and let the ashes there
Of forty thousand men, in that long quarrel slain,
Arise out of the earth, as they would live again,

To tell the manlike deeds that bloody day were wrought,
In that most fatal field, with various fortune fought.

DRAYTON—*Polyolb.—Song* xxii.

PERSONS OF THE DRAMA.

MEN.

Henry VI. of the House of Lancaster, deposed.
Edward, Prince of Wales, his only son, a boy.
Edward IV. son of Richard, Duke of York.
Earl of Warwick, friend to Edward IV.
Duke of Somerset,
Duke of Exeter,
Earl of Northumberland, Friends to
Earl of Westmoreland, Henry VI.
Lord Nevill, his son, engaged to Matilda,
Lord Clifford,
Two little boys, sons of Lord Clifford.
The mitred Abbot, of Fountains Abbey, near Ripon.
Warder of Skipton-castle, the seat of Lord Clifford.
Michael, his son.

WOMEN.

Margaret of Anjou, Queen of Henry VI.
Lady Clifford, wife of Lord Clifford.
Matilda, his sister, engaged to Lord Nevil.
Attendant on Lady Clifford.

Guards, Officers, Soldiers, Lord Clifford's Ghost,
Messenger.

SCENE.—In the three first acts, and in the last,
at Skipton-castle; in the fourth act, a field of
battle, near Towton.

CLIFFORD; A TRAGEDY.

ACT I.

SCENE I.—The Hall of an old Baronial Castle.—Enter hastily the aged Warder of the Castle in armour, with a red rose in his helmet, followed by Michael, his son.

Mich. Where in such haste, good father? Prithee stay :
Why in such anxious agitation,
Do you thus wander, restless, and alone?
Ward. I thank thee, Michael, for thy friendly care.
These woeful times, and thoughts of other days,
Press on my mind, and agitate my heart.
'Twas this day, sixty years, my noble lord,
(Whose fatal end I ever must lament)
Entrusted to my charge those massy gates ;
Whose solid, oak-ribbed sides, and ponderous bolts,
Have oft withstood the rage of savage foes,
And driven back the bloody tide of war,
Baffled, inglorious, from these time-worn towers.
Alas ! not long they held their noble master. [*Weeps.*]
Mich. Father, no more of this, you're too much moved.
Ward. No, no, it soothes my heart to dwell upon it.

Fired with the heat of youth, and love of arms,
And placing in his eye the wide-spread fame,
And exploits of his great progenitors ;
With our late sovereign, he embarked for France :
Conducting to his aid, a chosen band
Of hardy mountaineers, the flower and pride
Of Westmoreland, and Craven's rough domains.
There, by his side, in many a toilsome march,
And furious skirmish, did they win their way,
Resistless, till on Agincourt's proud plain,
They rode triumphant o'er their crest-fallen foes,
And trampled in the dust the power of France.

Mich. Immortal day for England and her sons !
Her boast and triumph to the end of time !

Ward. Oft have I heard, that in that glorious fight,
With his own hand, the gallant Clifford slew
Twelve of their bravest captains ; but alas !
Not all his valour could secure his life
Against the fated accidents of time.
For, while his beauteous lady, here at home,
Expected his return, with joyful smiles
To greet her lord, and hail him conqueror ;
He, at the siege of some strong citadel,
Was by the sudden bursting of a gun,
Deprived of life.   O fatal, dreadful stroke !

Mich. In an old book of genealogies,
I've read, that scarcely any of the Cliffords
Died in their beds at home, but mostly fell,
Fighting like heroes in the tented field.

Ward. My good lord's father, in my early youth,
Warring in Prussia, 'gainst the Infidels,
With Thomas of Woodstock, Duke of Glo'ster,
Was, in that foreign land, untimely slain.
Our late lord, as you know, scarce five years since,
In the first onset of this civil war—

O cruel, murderous, heart-sickening war!
In the first onset, at St. Alban's town,
He, with his uncle, Earl Northumberland,
And other kinsmen, miserably fell.
Thus, have I lived, in my short round of time,
To see, with these unhappy faded eyes,
Five generations of this martial race!
Three are already fallen—and much I fear—

Mich. Be comforted, good father, dry your tears.
Is not our present lord himself a host?
His very name a terror to our foes!
Has he not, like a thunderbolt from heaven,
Fallen with tenfold fury on their ranks,
Blasted, and scattered their aspiring aims,
And, in the blood of their ambitious chiefs,
Taken due vengeance for his father's death?

Ward. Vengeance, alas! which may recoil on us.

Mich. At Wakefield, first, then at that same St. Albans,
Did he not still, with his victorious sword,
Maintain the lustre of his noble name,
And with resistless, unremitting rage,
Pursue those traitors to their king and country?

Ward. Truly, he is indeed a princely chief,
My aged eyes delight to gaze upon him.

Mich. Last week, at York, as I surveyed the town,
High on the city gates, well-pleased, I saw
Decked with a paper crown, the gory head
Of that rebellious prince, Richard of York,
Whose mad ambition first stirred up this strife,
And spread the flames of discord through the realm.

Ward. O horrid sight! that was a barbarous act.

Mich. Clifford's old tower, within those ancient walls,
Seemed to revive, and smile amidst its ruins.
Gazing with pleasure on the ghastly sight,
I said within myself, so perish all,

Who tear the bosom of their native land,
And brave with impious hands the lords anointed.

Ward. Alas! my son, 'tis this excites my fears.
This unrelenting spirit of revenge,
This worse than savage treatment of each other,
Like a corroding poison in the veins,
Festering with deadly rancour through the state,
Exasperates these dire calamities,
And cuts us off from every ray of hope.
The Yorkists, furious at their late defeats,
Strain every sinew to uphold their cause.
With odious names they brand our valiant lord,
Calling him black-faced Clifford, and the butcher.
And much I fear——

Mich. Trust me, good father,
Their edgeless swords are just as dangerous,
As their loud taunts and threats——

Ward. The thought o'erwhelms me,
Should the usurper e'er collect a force,
Equal to cope with our brave northern lords;
Should he, which God forbid! e'er win the day;
No age, nor sex, no dignity of blood,
No ties of law, or nature, would avail :—
No mercy to their vanquished countrymen,
No shadow of compassion would be shown
By that hard-hearted faction to their foes;
But all would be one dismal direful scene
Of havock, bloodshed, massacre, and death.

Mich. All-pitying heaven avert such misery!

Ward. But truce to these forebodings—'tis the hour,
When with his noble guests, my lord is wont
Here in the hall, or armoury, to meet.
'Tis time we make our daily morning rounds,
Relieve the sentry, and unbar the gates.   *[Exeunt.]*

*SCENE II.—An ancient Armoury.—On each
side, figures of Knights, in complete armour,
with large black plumes of feathers.*

Enter NORTHUMBERLAND, *and* WESTMORELAND.

North. Good morrow, gentle cousin, I understand
Your faithful vassals are collecting round.
From Skiddaw, and Helvellyn, Furness Fells,
And Windermere's romantic glassy lake,
With bows and spears well armed, they pour along,
Joined with our hardy Cheviot yeomanry,
And the fierce youths, who follow valiant Clifford,
To try once more the glorious chance of arms.
    West. In truth, Northumberland, this weary war,
This impious conflict of contending kinsmen,
Pierces my heart, and overwhelms my soul.
If, like our fathers, in some generous cause—
To humble our inveterate ancient foe ;
To guard our conquests on his hostile shore ;
Or reap fresh laurels in those blood-stained fields,
The immortal plains of Crecy, and Poitiers :
Or if, with pious ardour, we did arm
Against the Infidels in Holy Land,
Which, our Fifth Henry, with his dying breath,
Commended to us all, most solemnly ;
This were a cause——
    North. I grant it, Westmoreland.
Oft do I grieve in secret o'er the times,
And sigh to think upon the deep distress,
And desolation, which on every side,
Afflict my view with horror and dismay.
But this is not a time for lamentation.

The die is cast—this young, audacious York,
Stoutly maintains his father's claims, and backed
By Warwick, and his other southern friends,
Has seized meek Henry's crown, and now usurps
As his own right the regal style and office.
While our good king, a houseless fugitive,
An exile from his palaces, and throne,
With his heroic queen, and princely boy,
In parts remote, distressed and succourless,
Implores our aid, and leans on our support.
This is a time for action, not for grief.

West. Such are the curses of a feeble reign !
Led by his flatterers, or favourites,
The weak, deluded monarch puts his trust,
In creatures, mean, and selfish, as himself.
In private ends, and slavish purposes,
The public interest forgotten sinks.
The sovereign's glory, and the nation's good,
The strength and majesty of empire,
The very independence of the state,
All, all is sacrificed to base intrigues,
To fawning traitors, and insidious villains.
Corruption, and oppression, sway the sceptre.
While from all ranks, the flames of discontent
Burst with volcanic fury o'er the land,
And bury all in undistinguished ruin.

North. Excuse me, Westmoreland, our king's mis-
            fortunes,
Arise not solely from his faults, or weakness.
Though I must ever from my heart condemn
This proud presumption of the house of York,
And ever execrate those rebel chiefs,
Who for these five years past, have torn the state,
With all the horrors of a civil war :
Yet we must own, had not our sovereign's grandsire,

Henry of Bolingbroke, with lawless force,
Deposed King Richard, and usurped his throne;
England might still, free from internal broil,
Nourish her children on her peaceful bosom.

West. O could we taste again the sweets of peace!
This civil discord is a viperous worm,
That gnaws the vitals of the commonwealth.

North. 'Tis this estranges many from our side,
While York's pretensions to the crown, are held
To have a prior claim, in truth, and justice.
Our prince is virtuous, mild, and pious;
Unfitted for the shock of these rude times;
And, till of late, with undisputed right,
Has worn, near forty years, his father's crown.

West. These facts, Northumberland, we all allow.

North. Then why consume our time in fruitless talk?
Our men are gathering round us, all prepared,
And eager for the field. I long to hear,
Whether their majesties have joined the camp,
Under his grace of Somerset, at York;
What force is there collected, and what news
Of the usurper, or his parliament,
May yet have reached our army from the south.

West. This day may possibly inform our doubts.
Meantime, I own, I feel much confidence,
In Clifford's desperate and dauntless spirit;
He smiles at swords and spears, his joy is war:
The noise and uproar of the field delight him:
Loyal and brave, by danger unappalled,
He loves the storm of battle—see, he comes.

SCENE III.

NORTHUMBERLAND, WESTMORELAND, CLIFFORD.

Cliff. All hail! my noble guests, I give you joy.
Health to our friends, and to our arms success!
This smiling morn hath brought us welcome news:
You will rejoice to hear, I've just received
A hasty message from our much-lov'd king;
By which, he graciously is pleased to tell me,
This morn, at dawn of day, it was his purpose,
From Fountains Abbey, where last night he rested,
Strait to proceed; and that, ere noon, this day,
He hoped to visit us within this castle.
The queen and prince are also with the king:
And, at his majesty's express desire,
The venerable abbot of that convent,
As far as Skipton will attend his person.
Such is the substance of the kign's dispatch.
  North. Welcome intelligence, indeed, my lord.
  Cliff. Enquiring of the messenger, I learnt,
With indefatigable zeal, the queen
Has raised a force of forty-thousand men;
Who, with his noble grace of Somerset,
Twixt York and Tadcaster have pitched their tents.
But of the foul usurper, and his train,
No certain tidings have been yet received.
  North. I think, my lord, they soon will hear of us.
  Cliff. Now, by my hopes, my ever valiant friends,
Sworn brothers in this honourable cause,
Soon may this hot, adventurous son of York
Advance to meet us, with his rebel band.

On the same spot, where with their traiterous blood,
His father and his brother stained the field,
There may he also, and his ruffian rabble,
Pay with their lives, the forfeit of their guilt.

North. Auspicious herald of unlooked-for joys,
You come, my lord, to cheer our languid hearts.
With what undaunted magnanimity
Our heroine queen maintains her royal rights!
With sixty thousand of our northern men,
Raised by her voice, obedient to her call,
Onward she marches, fearless and erect,
To hurl the proud usurper from his seat.

Cliff. And, like the flaming thunderbolts of Jove,
Our arms shall dash him from his guilty throne.
Presumptuous traitor! he our sovereign liege!
Clifford, and York, are names of deadly hate,
Which must in endless discord ever jar.
Curse on the name! the very sound distracts me.
Fury, revenge, disdain, and indignation
Storm in my breast, and burst my swelling heart.
They slew my father—vile accursed wretches!
May that ground gape, and swallow me alive,
That sees me spare but one of all the race.

North. A speedy vengeance overtake them all!
With heartfelt joy, I shall behold again
Our virtuous sovereign; his misfortunes,
His mildness, patience, and unblemished life,
Make him an object, to all feeling hearts,
Of pity, filial reverence, and love.
Our cousin, Westmoreland, with drooping thoughts,
Broods in despondency on our affairs,
And blasts our hopes with gloomy presages.

West. These joyful tidings have revived my heart,
And banished sadness from my anxious breast.

My melancholy fears are all dispersed,
And light as air I'm eager for the field.

Cliff. This sad anxiety, and deep depression,
These wavering thoughts, and sinkings of the heart,
Are but the feverish agues of the soul.
The coward, and the brave, the fool, and sage,
Are to their influence alike exposed ;
But 'tis the part of bravery, and wisdom,
Still to bear up against outrageous fortune,
And rise superior to the storms of fate.
Is this a time for sighs and soft laments ?
Were not our fathers, and our brothers slain,
In deadly conflict with those perjured rebels ?
Do not their mangled bodies still remain,
Far from the sepulchres of their ancestors,
Their death unhonoured, and their rites unpaid?
Their blood, their sacred blood calls out for vengeance.
Each gaping wound still summons us to arms.

North. Nor shall they summon us to arms in vain.

Cliff. Our names insulted, our oaths, and honour,
The safety of our friends, and families,
Our desolated country's bleeding wrongs,
And injured monarch, call aloud for vengeance.

West. And the loud call shall surely be obeyed.

Cliff. For me, my lords, whene'er in thoughtful
        mood,
Through the apartments of this spacious castle,
Pensive I walk, and ruminate the wrongs,
We all have suffered from this cursed branch,
This viper-brood of York's detested race—
The warlike portraits of my forefathers
Seem from their mouldering frames to frown upon me ;
Bid me be loyal, brave, and resolute,
And rouse my soul to unrelenting fierceness.

North. O may their spirits reign within our breasts,
And urge us on to rival their renown !

Cliff. If in this armoury alone I watch,
I startle at imaginary sounds :
Methinks these steel-clad figures couch their spears,
Clash on their hollow shields the note of war,
Or sternly nod their sable plumes around me.
Each night, when sleep has closed my weary eyes,
And tamed my angry passions to repose,
The bleeding image of my murdered father,
A ghastly vision ! stalks around my bed,
Points to his wounds, and fires my heated brain,
To madness, desperation, and revenge.
Then let not sighs, nor womanish complaints,
But fierce resolves, and curses on our foes,
Be the familiar subject of our thoughts,
And daily topic of our conversation.

Enter LORD NEVILL.

Who comes there? my Lord Nevill, is the king,
And train in sight?——

Nev. Not yet, my lord. A troop
Of horse, according to your late commands,
Is gone to meet his highness, but as yet,
There is no signal of his near approach.

Cliff. Ten thousand of our vassals, here assembled,
All well-resolved, stout, native Yorkshiremen,
Have just marched off; and with ten thousand more,
Picked chosen men, from all our northren lands,
Lord Dacre is expected every hour
To pass this way. A more heroic band,
Of valorous champions, panting for the field,
Ne'er met my eyes on the embattled plain.

B

Nev. From the Lord Dacre, there is just arrived
A messenger, who states, within this hour,
With a brave body of twelve thousand men,
His lordship passed about a mile from Skipton.
His route is onwards, strait to Tadcaster:
But ere he marches further, 'tis his wish
To have an interview with you, my father.

West. I will attend him instantly : my lord
Farewell ; I shall with loyal haste return,
To pay my duty to your royal guests.

[*Exit Westmoreland.*

SCENE IV.

NORTHUMBERLAND, CLIFFORD, NEVILL.

North. In a few days our force will be collected.
It is the greatest army, which as yet,
Has been assembled in this civil war.
With such a mighty host, and such brave spirits,
Fairly we may presume, our rightful cause,
Favoured of heaven, cannot fail to prosper.
Know you, my lord, the course, or plan of action,
His grace of Somerset intends to follow?

Cliff. I have received no late intelligence ;
But, 'twas his purpose, should the foe advance,
To make a stand at Leeds, or Ferry-bridge.
Yet, if the Yorkists linger in the south,
His march, I hope, will be direct on London.
Would that our summons were this very hour!
Come, dear revenge ! whene'er thou call'st, I'm ready.

Enter MATILDA.

Mat. Brother, their majesties will soon be here.

250

As with my sister in the watch-tower,
Gazing I sat, expecting their approach,
Just on the summit of the neighbouring hills,
I saw the royal standard wave aloft :
And a large company of horse and foot,
Is now advancing onwards to the castle.

Cliff. My Lord Northumberland, if it is your pleasure,
We will proceed to meet their majesties.

North. Most willingly, my lord, let's strait depart.

[*Exeunt Northumberland and Clifford.*

SCENE V.

Nevill, Matilda.

Nev. This horrid din of war, and clash of arms,
These threatening sounds of wrathful enterprise,
Accord but ill, Matilda, with our joys,
And sadly wound, I fear, thy gentle heart.
Our nuptial day is still deferred, and hope
Still mocks my ardent wish with disappointment.

Mat. It is, indeed it is a fearful period.
And when I think, perhaps some few days hence,
Our army may be summoned to the field ;
And that among the foremost, you my lord,
As it becomes your noble birth and station,
Must in those direful conflicts be engaged ;
My heart sinks in me, I already see
My love, my Nevill, my intended husband,
Stretched on the plain among the vulgar dead.

Nev. Banish, my love, these melancholy thoughts,
Dwell not on evils which may never come.
Think, that perhaps this hateful civil broil,

B 2

This fatal discord, which so many years,
Has like a tempest raged throughout the land,
May soon, exhausted, of itself expire.
Or if another battle be decreed,
Think of our mighty force, our valiant chiefs,
And of our late decisive victories.
Think of thy Nevil's glory; life's a breath,
Destroyed by accident in war or peace.

 Mat. Talk not of accidents, the word alarms me.

 Nev. O with what rapturous transport, to thy sight,
Shall I return, when flushed with victory,
To thy applauding eyes I show this sword
Spotted with hostile blood; regale thine ears
With deeds of valour, by this arm atchieved;
And twining in one wreath, the lover's myrtle,
With the bright laurel, the fair meed of conquest,
Back to thy arms restore thy youthful soldier,
And claim the youthful soldier's just reward.
Let such gay fancies animate thy breast,
And swell Matilda's heart with joy and love,

 Mat. Alas! my lord, our days of joy and love,
Are flown, I fear, and never to return.
Some sad presentiment of future woe
Reigns o'er my heart, and spite of all my efforts,
Saddens my gloomy fancy with despair.
Unbidden tears oft rush into my eyes,
Involuntary sighs convulse my breast.
In fearful dreams, each night it haunts my pillow.
From broken slumbers starting with affright,
For visionary griefs I wake and weep.

 Nev. Thy soft and tender nature, sweetest love,
Is too susceptible of sad impressions.
O strive against them, let not fancied ills,
Or melancholy dreams oppress your spirits.
O hush these wild emotions of thy heart.

Be not alarmed by shadows, wear again
Thy wonted smiles, and trust me all will prosper.
 Mat. I will implore the sacred powers of love,
To make me docile to such sweet injunctions.
But tell me, Nevill, should the enemy
Advance against you, in these northern parts,
Is it a matter of necessity
That you should march to battle?——
 Nev. Surely, love,
It is my place and duty——
 Mat. But is it not
Of more importance, that within the castle
You should remain, and fortify a post
Of so much consequence? while your brave father,
And other generals, who before have led
Our troops to victory, may again display
Their well-tried skill, and conduct in the field.
Your youth, my lord, and inexperience,
Unfit you for these hazardous encounters.
 Nev. And therefore should I go, so much the more,
By all occasions to improve my skill.
 Mat. Consider also, if left here alone,
My sister, with her children, and myself,
What groundless apprehensions, what alarms,
Of danger, and imaginary fears,
Would vex and harrass us, from day to day, .
And rob us of all comfort: then, dear Nevill,
Be this your station, and your post of honour;
And should the foe assail these flinty walls,
Matilda's voice and looks shall fire your courage,
And her hands crown you with the wreaths of conquest.
 Nev. Urge not, dear love, this fruitless suit, in vain
Would you propose it to my friends or me.
To be with thee, is all my happiness,

The only object of my thoughts and wishes.
Thou art the sacred idol of my heart,
To whom, with holy and religious duty,
My ardent vows of love are daily offered.
To gaze with wonder on thy heavenly charms,
To feast with rapture on thy looks and smiles,
To listen to the music of thy voice,
And in sweet converse, through the livelong day,
To pass with thee, the swiftly-flying hours ;
This were to taste the joys of Paradise—
And from this rapturous Elysian scene,
By the stern clamour of blood-thirsty war,
To be thus rudely summoned—Oh! Matilda
Need I seek words to paint the cruel thought?
But honour, a soldier's honour tears me from thee :
My admiration of thy excellence,
Thy peerless beauty, and thy matchless worth,
Command me to deserve thy just esteem.
Thy very name would proudly rise against me—
Shall Clifford's sister be the wife of him
Who shunned the field of glory?——

   Mat. No more, my lord ;
Your gallant spirit, and high-minded valour,
Enhance your noble virtues in my thoughts,
And heighten all your merit to my eyes.
I only wish, it were within my power,
To attend you to the field, and there in person,
To witness your exploits; or by your side,
Along with you, to share your perils——

                [A flourish of Trumpets.

Hark !
The king is entering the castle gates.
Should angry Fate suspend the dreadful blow,
Or give thee back victorious from the foe,

We still may hope, blest by the powers above,
To pass our days in happiness and love.
Freed from this savage and unnatural broil,
Which now depopulates our native soil,
The peaceful blessings of domestic joy,
Would fill our hearts, and all our cares employ.

[Exeunt.

ACT. II.

SCENE I.—A Room of State.—King Henry VI.
is seated with the Abbot of Fountains-Abbey.
—Guards, and Attendants.

King. How grand and awful is this antique pile !
Did you observe, my lord, its wondrous strength ?
Fixed on the edge of the projecting rock,
Which overhangs the flood, its lofty towers,
And threatening battlements, appear to brave
The assaults of foes, and Time's resistless hand.
This is a seat of heroes ; much, my lord,
Am I indebted to this loyal house.
Abb. It is, my liege, a worthy family.
The pious lady too, is much renowned
For virtuous and charitable deeds.
The poor and wretched, through their wide domains,
Pour daily blessings—but my lord approaches—
             [*Enter Northumberland and Clifford.*

SCENE II.

The KING, ABBOT, NORTHUMBERLAND, CLIFFORD.

Cliff. Health, and all happiness to my lord the king.
Most gracious liege, for this distinguished honour,
My grateful heart shall ever render thanks.
             [*They kneel and kiss the King's hand.*

Most reverend lord, I crave your holy blessing.

[*To the Abbot.*

King. Clifford, it is from me that thanks are due.
In my unhappy cause, alas! your father,
And other much-lamented kinsmen fell.
Who, on my side, first gained a victory?
Who, with his heaven-directed falchion slew,
Richard of York, that overbearing chief,
And father of this hydra-headed race?
Who, in the battle of St. Alban's town,
A second time dispersed my enemies,
Released me from my hard captivity,
And gave me back, once more, with joy and triumph,
To the embraces of my wife and child?
Who still supports my rights, and in the north,
Preserves the people loyal to their king?
To you, my lord, and to your friends, through you,
I am indebted for these countless services.

Cliff. These praises, my good liege, I share in common,
With many others of your loyal subjects.
The Dukes of Somerset and Exeter,
The Earls Northumberland, and Westmoreland,
My gallant kinsmen in these northern parts,
And sundry more among your valiant nobles,
Still fan the rising flame of loyalty,
And burn with ardour in their sovereign's cause.
With firm alliance, and true faith of heart,
To your imperial throne, and royal house,
My dearest interests, my life, and honour,
Are all devoted ; while I proudly feel,
My duteous service is its own reward.

King. Language, brave friend, would fail me, to express
My inward sense of your heroic worth,
And grateful feeling of your high desert.   [*To Clifford.*
My Lord Northumberland, I rejoice to see you.

What a stout legion of intrepid vassals,
And lusty tenantry, your lordship owns,
In Alnwick, and Northumbria's vast domains !
A liberal, valiant, active, wealthy race.
The bulwark of our kingdom against Scotland.
The noble Percy, famed in days of yore,
Still bears aloft his undiminished crest,
And deathless lustre of his high-traced lineage.

   North. Most gracious sovereign, long-honoured liege,
Your majesty is pleased, with too much favour
To weigh our deeds, and estimate our worth.
If our adventurous ancestors, of old,
Won with their swords those fair possessions,
Confirmed to them, and their posterity,
By their indulgent sovereign's just decree,
That, in all dangers and emergencies,
They might be ready, both with hand and heart,
To fight the battles of their king and country—
By the same tenure, are we also bound,
To grasp our weapons, at our monarch's call,
And by our valour, loyalty, and prowess,
To vindicate the honours of our blood,
And emulate the glories of our race.
If, by our birth and station, we are raised
Above the level of our fellow-subjects,
So much it doth import us to excell
In every part of manliness and virtue.

   King. Tis sweet to hear such noble sentiments.

   Abb. Whilst others praise the martial enterprise,
The far-famed deeds and valorous exploits,
Of the illustrious sons of Percy's line,
Let me bear witness to their piety.
From the foundation of our monastery,
Those pious lords have ever been distinguished,
By benefactions to that holy place.

The tombs of many of his lordship's fathers,
Adorn our cloisters, and proclaim their virtues.
 Cliff. We hear no tidings of this upstart York.
Pleased with his new-got dignities, perhaps,
The flattery of his fawning parasites,
And servile shouts, and noises of the rabble,
Are sweeter music to his princely ears,
Than the loud roaring of the cannon's mouth,
Or clang of hostile trumpet. Oh ! how I long,
With fifty thousand of our northern men,
To wake him from his dream of royalty.
I see the queen approach—with what an air
Of inborn majesty, and native state,
Conscious of worth, she moves with godlike step !

Enter QUEEN MARGARET, *with the* PRINCE, LADY CLIF-
 FORD, *and* MATILDA, *on one side,* WESTMORELAND, *and*
 NEVILL, *on the other.*

 Cliff. Illustrious queen ! bright wonder of our days !
The boast of England ! glory of thy sex !
Heroic princess ! filled with joy and pride,
I see your majesty beneath my roof.
 Queen. With heartfelt joy, my lord, I meet you here.
'Tis not the pomp and pageants of a court,
Nor smiles of royal favour, that can add
A lustre to the place where Clifford dwells.
Ourselves are honoured by your glorious deeds,
And firm attachment to our wavering cause.
Your gallant conduct in the king's defence,
Commands, my lord, my warm acknowledgements.
 Cliff. Duty, and honour, and a vowed revenge,
Will ever bind me to your sacred rights.
Yes, my whole soul is bent upon the ruin
And extirpation of this cursed line

Of York ; while life this arm upholds, this arm
Shall still uphold the house of Lancaster.

    [The King and Abbot converse together apart,
        also Nevill and Matilda.

    Lady Cl. This is a splendid day for Skipton-castle,
And in our archives shall be duly noted.
Our late descendants will reflect with pride,
That by the presence of our virtuous king,
And his heroic consort, these old walls
Were graced and honoured. O! that from this day,
A happier era of returning peace,
And long-lost concord might dawn upon us.

    Queen. These wishes, my good lady, much I fear,
Are vain and fruitless. Had we now to deal
With an upright and generous adversary ;
Or were the wrongs less poignant, which we all
Have felt, and suffered from these vile usurpers :
Were their accumulated crimes and guilt,
Not of so frightful and so black a die ;
Some ray of hope, to end these grievous ills,
By terms of friendship and accommodation,
Might cheer the gloomy prospect now before us.
But, perjury, rebellion, murder, treason—
And obstinate adherence to such malice—
Tis not by softness, and persuasive arts,
But by the wrathful rigour of the sword,
And the whole thunder of our lawful power,
That such abominations must be crushed,
Cut off, and blasted with extermination.

    North. High-souled princess! worthy of better times,
Formed to command your subjects' grateful hearts,
Accept the homage of your northern friends.

    Queen. Right valiant lords, whose constancy and
        courage
Are the chief props and pillars of the state,

Receive my warmest and sincerest thanks.
It was the fame of such high-minded peers,
Spread far and near throughout the continent,
Which first induced my mind to entertain
The high ambition, one day to become
The queen of this great kingdom.   When I heard
Each tongue repeating with redoubled praise,
The brave atchievements of our English knights;
Their gallantry and chivalrous exploits,
Raised to the skies; and above all, my lords,
Their true devotion to their king and country:
My youthful heart, I own, did not refuse
Freely to welcome the aspiring hope,
I might be one day worthy to command
The willing homage of a freeborn people.
In you, my lords, these pleasing flattering hopes,
And dreams of greatness, have been more than realized.

West. Long may we merit such trancendant praise,
And still prove worthy of our native land!
Dastards, indeed, we justly might be styled,
Unfit to bear our great forefathers' names,
If, at the call of beauty in distress,
And in the cause of injured majesty,
We did not fly with ardour to our post,
And in the blood of the rebellious foe,
Nobly avenge their wrongs.   Dreadful, I trust,
Shall be our vengeance on these odious traitors.

Cliff. Not one, not one shall escape our just revenge.
O that this ancient blade were crimsoned o'er
With the heart-blood of all the loathsome race.

Queen. I have no fears about the final issue.
Would that this boy were now of age, and strength,
To guard the honours of his father's throne!
The soaring spirit of his grandfather,

Who well upheld the crown his father won,)
Would fire his opening soul with emulation.

Cliff. His princely mien, and masculine deportment,
Give happy earnest of his future worth.
I've heard some aged persons say, the prince
Has a great look of that immortal king.

Prince. The queen, my mother, tells me I must strive
To be more like him in his deeds than looks.
I wish, my lord, I could go with you now,
I long to see a battle——

Cliff. Your highness,
Is of too tender years, as yet to bear
The toils and dangerous fatigues of war.
The time will come, when 'mid the shock of spears,
And in the ranks of heroes, you'll aspire
To emulate your grandsire's deathless fame.
Long may you live to equal his renown,
And act again the glories of his reign.

Queen. He has a manly spirit, and shewed it well,
On our way hither, a few days ago.
By a strange accident, we had almost perished.

Lady Cl. Heavens! my most gracious liege, you fill
    my ears
With wonder, terror and astonishment.
What could this dreadful accident have been?

Queen. It did alarm me much. When we arrived
At Richmond, from the north, his majesty
Expressed a wish to sojourn a few days,
In holy privacy, at Fountains-abbey;
And for that purpose, took the road direct
Thither, by Ripon. A few days after,
I set out with the prince a different way.
In Wensley Dale, we passed a spacious forest,
Which, by its coolness and umbrageous shade,
Invited our approach; we entered it,

And following a path, which seemed to lead
Strait through the shady covert of the wood,
Ordered our train to meet us, where the track
Should again issue to the common road.

   Lady Cl. I know the spot, 'tis a delightful valley.

   Queen. Fatigued with riding in the heat, and pleased
To be at liberty among the trees,
Like a young roebuck on the hills, the prince
Bounded along with airy sprightliness,
In search of nests, wild flowers and strawberries,
The game of sportive childhood: when behold!
From a deep thicket, suddenly burst forth,
Three horrid murderous ruffians, with drawn daggers—

   Lady Cl. Merciful heaven! what a dreadful shock!

   Queen. And, with such violence they assailed us,
That, ere I could form a thought or purpose,
They robbed and stripped us both ; and strait made off,
Leaving us almost naked.

   North. Desperate villains!

   West. Abominable wretches.

   Queen. Instantly,
I snatched the prince into my trembling arms,
And fled along the path ; but there again,
We met another of the bloody gang,
Advancing towards us, sword in hand: his arms
Were bare, and his fierce eye-balls glared like fire.

   Lady Cl. Methinks, I should have sunk, and died
       with terror.

   Queen. Resolving to address him, I set down,
The prince, who strait with manly air marched on,
Fearless of the savage murderer, and said,
" I am your prince, King Henry's son, and there,
You see your queen, my mother."

   Cliff.   This evinced
A courage, far beyond his years.

Queen. The wretch
Astonished at so strange an incident,
Struck with his pretty helpless innocence,
Or with the sight of grandeur in distress,
Let fall his sword, threw up his hands and eyes,
And then dropped prostrate on his knees before us,
Assuring him, that what the prince had said,
Was strictly true, he humbly craved my mercy ;
Expressed the greatest sorrow for the crime
His comrades had committed, and declared,
Without delay, he would conduct us safe
Out of the forest, to the king's highway :
Which he performed, and there, well-pleased, we met
Our horses and attendants.

Lady Cl. How wonderful!
It was a most miraculous escape.

Cliff. Now, that your majesties have graciously
Vouched to visit us in this old castle,
May we not hope for some time to be honoured
With the loved presence of our royal guests?

Queen. Our stay must be determined, my good lord,
By the intelligence we may receive
From York, or from his grace of Somerset.
I like this castle much, your ancestors
Spared no expence, nor labour, to erect
This strong and goodly pile.

North. These northern parts
Abound with such vast massy structures, this
'Tis said, was founded in the conqueror's reign.

Lady Cl. We have prepared a pageant to amuse
Our royal guests ; and now if 'tis their pleasure,
Without delay it may be introduced.

Queen. It will delight us greatly, let it enter.

Cliff. My sister, madam, has, for some months past,
Been plighted to her cousin, young lord Nevill ;

But these distracted times, and the large share
Which I have taken in these late events,
Have hitherto deferred their marriage day.
It would be highly grateful to us all,
To the young couple an unlooked-for glory,
And happy omen of their future bliss,
If, in the presence of their king and queen,
They here might pledge their mutual vows; and now,
Should your most gracious majesties approve,
In a few days we here might solemnize,
With feast and revelry the nuptial rites.

King. With heartfelt pleasure shall we see their union.

Queen. Such an event would double the delight
We had expected from our visit here.

SCENE III.

The KING *and* QUEEN *are seated.*

Enter a PAGEANT.

(*In the midst of it, Enter the Warder, and a Messenger,
hastily.*)

Cliff. In God's name, and the king's, say who you are,
And why, thus clad in steel, you burst upon us.
What tidings, or what message of importance
Has brought you hither in such breathless haste?

Mess. I come, my lord, directly from his grace
Of Somerset, who charged me, swift as horse
Could carry me, to speed, without delay,
To Skipton-castle, and inform your lordship,
Last night his grace received intelligence,
The Duke of York, with forty thousand men,
Had reached the neighbourhood of Ferry-bridge.

[*Exit Warder.*

C

Cliff. Now, by my sword, this news is great indeed.

North. Astonishing, and scarcely credible.

Lady Cl. Good God forbid! 'tis most unseasonable.

Mess. 'Twas by forced marches, chiefly in the night,
He had advanced so far, before his grace
Knew of their movements; the Lord Fitzwater,
And Warwick's bastard brother led the van.

West. How much unlooked for is this expedition!

Cliff. And has his grace advanced to check their
        progress?

Mess. The duke of Exeter, two days ago
Had marched to guard the pass at Ferry-bridge;
But when he heard the Yorkists had advanced,
He strait resolved to attack them, and this morn,
Ere break of day surprised them in their beds,
Cut off the vanguard, while in the hurry,
The Lord Fitzwater, and Earl Warwick's brother,
Were both slain.

Queen. Most prosperous beginning!
Health to our warriors, and brave friends in arms.
Rejoice, my lords, I bid you all rejoice,
On this auspicious opening to our cause.

Mess. By a deserter we have since been told,
The Earl of Warwick, furious at this loss,
Rode to the Duke of York, and mad with rage,
Drawing his sword, stabbed on the spot, before him,
His favourite charger; then, with oaths and vows,
Chiefly against Lord Clifford, kissed the cross
Fixed on his ponderous sword-hilt, and protested,
That he would never sheathe his bloody weapon,
Till his dear comrades' slaughter was revenged.

Queen. This fiery Warwick is a valiant boaster:
Has he forgot St. Albans? what did he next?

Mess. Without delay, he took a chosen band
Of horse and foot, and higher up the river,

Forded the stream ; then falling unawares
On my Lord Exeter, forced him to retreat.
His grace of Somerset, who before had pushed
As far as Tadcaster, again advanced ;
And now, in orderly array of battle,
Has drawn up his whole army on a plain
Not far from Tadcaster, betwixt the villages
Saxton and Towton, there to wait the foe.
He charged me earnestly to press your lordship,
The Earls Northumberland, and Westmorland,
And other lords, who haply might be here,
To join him instantly, without delay.

    Mat. O me! come near me—Oh! my heart.—
                       [*Faints in Nevill's arms.*

    Nev. Help, help!
    Cliff. What now? Matilda! how!
    Queen. Poor girl ! she faints !
Her lover now must quit her for the field.
    Lady Cl. Madam, with your permission, I'll retire ;
This sudden news has overwhelmed my spirits.
    Queen. Do so, dear lady, and pray let the prince
Go along with you ; our discourse, I fear,
Must tire his youthful mind.
    Lady Cl. Come, my dear lord.
[*Exeunt Lady Clifford, the Prince, Matilda and Nevill.*

SCENE IV.

KING *and* QUEEN, NORTHUMBERLAND, WESTMORELAND,
    CLIFFORD, ABBOT, *and* MESSENGER.

    Cliff. This urgent business will not brook delay.
The field, the field demands our presence now,
Honour and vengeance summon us to arms.

What answer, may it please your majesties,
Shall we deliver by this messenger ?

King. Oh ! how this civil rage afflicts my soul!
It wounds me to the heart, to think such malice
Should dwell in kindred bosoms ; that this land,
So famed for Christian faith and piety,
Should be polluted by such foul misdeeds.
Is it not possible, even now, my lords,
To offer terms of amity and peace,
And save the shedding of each other's blood?

Queen. Banish the thought, my liege, 'twould but
    prolong
Our melancholy state. You dwell too much
On mercy and forgiveness. These are rebels,
Obstinate traitors to their lawful king:
And had they not, by base insidious arts,
Deluded their unhappy followers,
To rise in arms, and join with them against you,
Long since they would have suffered, by the hands
Of public justice, ignominious death.
To offer mercy to such hardened wretches,
Is to betray your rights, your crown and people.
Successful treason is the grave of kings.
Then let not words, but deeds revenge our wrongs.

King. Spite of their crimes, they are my subjects still.

West. O, that his majesty's paternal wish
Could be fulfilled ! One drop of blood, my lords,
Drawn from our native land, should grieve us more
Than streams from foreign foes.

North. Good Westmoreland,
At such a juncture, to discourse of peace,
Of concord, friendship, or humanity,
Must sure be vain; our own, and country's wounds
Demand another course; they are too deep
For any remed y, but blows anddeath.

'Tis by our swords alone, and in the blood
Of the usurpers, we can end the quarrel.

West. May some propitious power inspire our hearts,
And touch the springs of human feeling in us.

King. O, miserable land! alas! my country!
Where, where is justice, loyalty and truth!

Cliff. Our resolutions will not bear debate.
This is no time for counsel, or discourse.
With sixty thousand valiant sons of war,
Panting with ardour to destroy their foes,
His grace of Somerset awaits our coming.

Queen. Thrice, noble Clifford, 'tis resolutely spoke.
What terms can we expect from perjured rebels,
Or what advantage from a truce with traitors ?

Abb. You are, my liege, our true anointed king,
And 'tis the will of heaven, you should maintain,
With all your lawful power, your royal throne.

King. I thank you for these words, God's will be done.
Would I were dead! if 'twere his holy will.
For what is in this world, but sin and grief?
Oppressed with heaviness and care, my lords,
To you, and to the queen I must resign
These sad affairs ; Lord Abbot, we'll retire,
And strive, by humble prayer, to deprecate
The wrath of heaven from our suffering realm.

[*Exeunt King and Abbot.*

SCENE V.

QUEEN, NORTHUMBERLAND, WESTMORELAND, CLIFFORD,
MESSENGER.

Cliff. Madam, if 'tis your pleasure, we'll dispatch
This messenger forthwith.

Queen. Immediately ;
It cheers my heart to see your forwardness.
Go with your utmost speed, inform the duke,
Within this hour we shall quit the castle,
And join his camp with swiftest diligence.

 Mess. His grace enjoined me, if the king and queen
Were here, to add, it was his wish, the queen
Should strait repair to York : the king, he thought,
Might, by his presence in the camp, contribute
To animate the soldiers to their duty.

 Queen. Go, and inform his grace, all shall be done
According to his wishes. Haste away. [*Exit Messenger.*
When last I saw his grace of Somerset,
It was his plan, that in the next engagement,
Himself should lead the centre, the right wing
Be under Lord Northumberland, the left
Follow our noble host, and the reserve
Be headed by Lord Westmoreland. Most surely,
A happier distribution of our force,
And skilful leaders, could not be devised.

 Cliff. If your most gracious majesty approve,
Methinks it would be most advisable
An escort should accompany the king,
Which my Lord Westmoreland's accomplished son,
Lord Nevill, might command.

 Queen. Let it be so.
And now, most noble lords, I trust the term
Of all your generous toils on our behalf,
Is near at hand ; and the delightful task,
Justly to recompense such high deserts,
Alone remains with us. I must no more
Detain you from the field ; my lords, farewell.

 Cliff. Allow me, madam, freely to express
The deep regret my friends and self must feel
At this abrupt departure ; we had hoped,

In the soft quiet of domestic life,
Within these walls, more nearly to have witnessed
The pleasing virtues of our royal guests.

Queen. Such interruption, in a time like this,
Was to be looked for; once again, farewell.
When next we meet, I trust, with joyful smiles,
With shouts of victory, and hostile spoils,
The feast and song shall chase past cares away,
And hymns of triumph crown the happy day.

[*Exeunt,*

ACT III.

SCENE I.—The Armoury.

Enter CLIFFORD.

Cliff. The blackening clouds which overspread my view,
And darkened all the prospect are dispersed :
Now, with his golden beams, the sun of hope
Illumines the horizon wide around,
And warms my heart with his meridian ray.
These lingering cold delays, and tardy hours
Of tedious expectation are no more.
Our foe advances towards us ; now, with swords
Of tempered steel, well-tried, already stained
In his best blood, we soon shall try his mettle,
And fiercely front him on th' embattled plain.
Aspiring York ! thy fated hour is come.
Now may the spirits of my warlike race
Inflame my soul, and urge me on to vengeance.
What heaps of bleeding victims, on this day,
Shall prostrate fall beneath our raging spears !
What names of slaughtered heroes ! O my father !
If in thy bloody and untimely grave,
The accents of my voice can reach thine ear ;
If, from the seat of bliss, thy sainted spirit
Can e'er descend to witness mortal cares,
And converse hold with those thou lov'dst below ;
Be present with me now—brace my strong arm,
Give edge and vigour to my vengeful weapon ;
Steel all the tender fibres of my heart,

That no compunctious feelings of compassion
May stop the ruthless fury of my course,
Or shake the settled temper of my soul:

Enter LADY CLIFFORD *and* MATILDA.

Thy death shall be revenged, or my own life
Be lost in the attempt : revenge——
   Lady Cl. My lord—
   Cliff. Who's there? my Isabella? what in tears?
This melting softness suits not with the thoughts
That now inspire my breast : the hour is come
Which puts these hot brained rebels in our power,
And gives them up to final vengeance, now
You should rejoice, that ere this sun be set,
Triumphant shouts will hail us conquerors.
   Lady Cl. Alas! my lord, the doubtful chance of war ;
The savage rancour of our enemies,
And the dire horrors—Oh ! my aching heart !
The foe so near us—should he prove victorious ;
Think of thy widowed wife, thy orphan babes,
Left here alone defenceless—horrid thought !
Exposed to all the brutal rage, and malice,
Of merciless exasperated wretches.
No Clifford then to shield us—none—no father,
No husband, brother,—oh ! Matilda oh !
   Cliff. Forbear, my love, these dismal presages,
Fy! on such girlish weakness! come, no more.
Think you, that doubt, or fear can ever shake
The rooted firmness of my settled purpose ?
A life of honour, or a glorious grave,
A bloody triumph o'er my fallen foes,
These are the topics and the themes for me.
   Lady Cl. Oh ! had I lived in happier days of peace !

273

Cliff. Peace ! peace has its evils worse than those of war.
But why this vain unnecessary grief?
Have you not seen me twice return from battle,
Victorious and unhurt ? And, with what joy,
Did you not then receive me ? With much more,
Than if, inglorious, skulking from the field,
I here had hid my cowardice and shame.
Then weep no more, repress those sobs and sighs :
O be not downcast now, when every hope,
And favouring omen shines propitious on us.

    Lady Cl. May Heaven continue its protection,
And all good angels spread their wings around you.
On evil days, ah me! on woeful times,
On days of blood and horror are we fallen.
What scenes of desolation have we witnessed!
Each day is big with some new tale of woe.
None smile, or play, but all the country wears
A face of care or misery——

    Cliff. 'Twill be so ;
Unnatural deeds beget unnatural troubles :
Faction and treason rage throughout the land,
And will, till they be crushed, produce confusion.

    Lady Cl. 'Tis now above six years, I have been yours,
And in that time, I scarce have passed a day
Without alarm or sorrow. Oft have I sighed
To read in history of dreadful wars,
Of havoc, bloodshed, and destruction,
Of ruined families, and wasted realms,
Of widows' wailing and of orphans' cries ;
And now, alas ! the dismal tale is come
Home to myself, my own sad bitter portion.

    Cliff. You move me, Isabella, 'tis not right :
I should have left the castle, on the spot,
Nor have consented to this interview.

Dry up these foolish tears, come Matilda,
You have more courage, and must comfort her.

Lady Cl. O my dear lord! permit me in your bosom
To pour forth all my griefs : it is perhaps
The last—ah! what did I say? oh? no—
You'll sure be back to-night— I know you will.
Think of the many woes, the bitter pangs,
From loss of friends I have already suffered.

Cliff. You shall have vengeance, I'll have vengeance
    too.

Lady Cl. An insulated monument of woe,
Of all my house I am the sole survivor.
An only child, my parents gone, on you,
On you alone my hopes and fears are fixed.
You are my all, my husband, father, brother—
Should I lose you—O my poor little ones !
Think of the darling prattling innocents—
Where shall we hide them, dear Matilda, where
Shall we seek refuge from the murderers ?

                              [*Matilda weeps.*

Cliff. Why this is frenzy, surely, more than sorrow.
I wonder, sister, that on this occasion,
You should be so alarmed : Our force, you know,
Is far superior to the enemy.
Within this year, twice have we conquered them ;
And therefore justly may presume once more,
Victory will prove decisive for us.
All's in our favour——

Mat. Brother, we are told
That strange portents, and wondrous prodigies,
Such, as 'tis thought, foretell the fall of kings
And states ; or mighty changes in the world,
In various places have of late been seen.

Cliff. And what, forsooth, are these, dear sister?

Mat. Some monstrous births, they say, and apparitions:

Spirits have walked, and ghosts broke up their graves ;
Some rivers have run red as if with blood ;
Terrific meteors in a flaming sky
Have suddenly appeared, and strait dispersed :
And hideous howlings in the woods, and mountains,
Have oft been heard at midnight. I myself
Have seen a raven flap against the casement,
And for some nights, have heard the screech-owls
     shriek,
In the old haunted tower——
    Lady Cl. All through the country,
Such things are rumoured, and of late, my lord,
I have observed your sleep is sadly broken.
You start convulsed, call for your sword, scream out,
And seem to labour with some deep oppression.
    Cliff. Some vapourish fumes of indigestion,
A nightmare, or delirium, I suppose.
Nor peace, nor sleep shall I enjoy again,
Till my dear father's murder is revenged.
    Lady Cl. Oft am I terrified with dreams of horror.
Last night, I dreamt, just in the dead of night,
The warder and his son, in blood-stained weeds,
Rushed through my curtains, screaming with dismay,
" The castle is in flames, my lord is dead."
Methought, I started up, and looking round,
Saw my Lord Nevill, and my loved Matilda,
Stretched on a bier, mangled with ghastly wounds,
And, by their side, your armour on the ground,
Purpled with blood : I shrieked aloud, and asked
The warder, if my boys were safe ; he said,
That an old shepherd, who by chance was near,
And first descried the fire, had snatched the children
Out of the flames, and strait conveyed them safe,
Across the river to his neighbouring hut.
I woke in agony, my hair on end ;

A shuddering tremor ran through all my frame;
A sudden damp struck to my beating heart;
The big cold drops ran down my trembling limbs,
And scarce could I believe 'twas but a dream.
It did alarm and shake me terribly.

   Cliff. And, is it then your dreams and prodigies,
Which thus have staggered and appalled your hearts?
A soldier, Isabella, draws his sword,
To fight the battles of his king and country,
And needs no better omen. Heaven, he knows,
Has hid from human eyes the scroll of fate,
And in the womb of dark futurity,
Conceals the issues of all mortal things.
But what's a dream? a shooting star? a noise
Heard in the day, or night? Chimeras all?
The false creations of a fevered brain,
Or sickly superstition's groundless fears.
You keep me here too long, I must away,
My friends await, all ready for the field.

   Lady Cl. O speak some soothing words to cheer my
       spirits.
Look on me, tell me, when will you return?
You must not go before you see the children ;
Give them one parting kiss—perhaps the last—
How my heart bleeds to utter such a thought !
What shall I say to Henry when you're gone?
If you come back no more—Oh !—tell me now,
How shall I bring him up? dear little wretch !
He longs to be a soldier like his father,
And cries for drums and trumpets—hapless mother !
All forms of misery will meet in mine.
Poor dear unhappy babes ! all I shall leave you,
Is but a sad inheritance of woe.
When will my sorrows cease? oh ! never, never—

Cliff. What was that call? who's there? did you not
    hear it?

Mat. No, I heard nothing, all is silent now.

  Cliff. Methought I heard my father's voice, it said
In broken tones of anguish and despair,
" Clifford, revenge—my son revenge my death—"
If I do not, heaven be revenged on me!
O my loved father! ever-honoured shade!
Where is my horse? bring me my lance—my horse,
I say, tis growing late, we must depart.
Farewell, Matilda, come, come, Isabella,
To-morrow's sun will see you clad in smiles,
And chide you for these tears, and childish grief.

                        [Exeunt.

SCENE III.—*A Private Apartment.*

Enter MATILDA.

Mat. O my poor sister! how I pity her!
Her sighs and groans would pierce a marble heart.
But I must stop these tears, and turn my thoughts
To my own enterprise ; Heaven grant it prosper!

Enter MICHAEL.

Mat. Who's there? Michael, come in, I must reveal
A secret scheme to you, in which you may
Afford me great assistance. You know, 'tis settled,
That with an escort of five hundred men,
Commanded by Lord Nevill, the king should join
The army now at Towton.   I suppose,
In half an hour, he will leave the castle.
Therefore, good Michael, we must use dispatch.
It is my wish, if possible, in disguise

To accompany the king; 'tis probable
He will be stationed at some distant post
From the main army; and there, I think, with you,
I might unseen observe the battle, or,   .
Should any danger threaten, could return
Home to the castle : what think you of it?

Mich. Madam, I think this might be safely done.

Mat. I am glad you think so, now for my disguise.
You know, that in the gallery, there is
A little suit of gilded armour, which,
I've often heard my father say, was made
For my great-grandsire, of famous memory,
Lord Henry Percy, who was surnamed Hotspur.

Mich. Madam, I know it well, and oft have heard
My father say, that it was worn by Hotspur.

Mat. It was ; he showed so soon his love of war,
That when but twelve years old, he would not rest,
Till his good father had those polished arms
Made to indulge his warlike humour, and,
When to my grandfather, Hotspur's only daughter
Was wedded, she brought with her to this castle,
That suit of armour : to please my sister,
I oft have tried it on, and know 'twill fit me.
Therefore, good Michael, get it all prepared,
And lay it secretly in my apartment.

Mich. Depend upon me, it shall strait be done.

    ‘   [*Exit Michael.*

Mat. I almost fear this project is too rash.
My heart forebodes I know not what of evil.
I will however soon return; should I
Bring back the tidings of a victory,
How will this bold romantic enterprise
Delight us all ; hush! my Lord Nevill comes—
Ye powers! who guard the innocent, and weak,
O guide, protect, and take me to your care.

SCENE IV.

Nevill, Matilda.

Mat. Welcome, my lord, I had begun to fear
You might perhaps be forced to leave the castle
Without a last farewell: say, is the queen
Departed, with the prince, for York?——
Nev. She is;
They have this moment left the castle gates.
Mat. Is the Lord Abbot gone?——
Nev. No, he will remain
During our absence, with you in the castle.
Leave you, my love, without a last farewell!
My fluttering heart flew on the wings of love
To snatch this tender interview, and now
I am delighted to perceive, Matilda,
Your spirits seem much lighter, that no more,
By sad anticipation of the worst,
You suffer grief to prey upon your heart.
    Mat. It has revived my sad and drooping thoughts,
To know, that in the battle you will not
Be much exposed ; but stationed with the king,
Should the worst happen, it will be your duty,
To guard his sacred person, and retreat
By timely marches to a place of safety.
A dawn of hope has lighted up my heart.
'Tis this, dear Nevill, which has raised my spirits,
And shot a gleam of comfort through my breast.
    Nev. Exquisite pattern of all female goodness !
How thy words fire and transport my soul !
O charming maiden! O exalted virtue !

Why must it be, that all our joys should thus
Be nipped and blasted in the opening bud!
O luckless fate! O mad accursed war!
Offspring of hell! which thus can rend assunder
The ties of peace, of harmony, and love.
When shall we meet again, Matilda, when?
My hopes and fears distract me——
   Mat. Oh! forbear,
Be calm, dear Nevill, and compose your thoughts.
Courage, and comfort, all shall yet be well.
The brightest days have clouds ; and when this storm
Of civil rage and discord is gone by,
It will enhance our pleasure, to recount
The various fortune of this boisterous time.
Our love is pure and spotless, and I trust
Approving Heaven will complete our bliss.
   Nev. Thou art the empress, mistress of my soul!

        Enter the WARDER.

May all the blessings of connubial love!—
   Ward. My lord, your noble father is below
Accoutred for the field, and fain would see you.
   Nev. Tell him, I shall be with him instantly.
                        [Exit Warder.
Farewell, Matilda, we must part—your brother
Would chide me, if he saw this softness in me.
O may no wayward fate divide us more!
My life, my heart is thine, my soul hangs on thee.
Here could I gaze, dwell on thy charms for ever.
But I must tear myself away—farewell.

   [Matilda takes from a drawer an ornamented military
      Scarf, presents it to Nevill.]

            D

Mat. Farewell, dear Nevill, and accept this scarf,
Wrought by these hands—oft have I wept upon it.
For my sake wear it ; and should any chance
Detain you longer absent from my sight,
Than what we now expect, send it me back :
Oh! send it as a pledge of mutual love,
And precious token of your health and safety:
My life is wrapt in thine—be careful of it.

> [*Nevill kisses the Scarf in great agitation, they
> embrace and part.*]

Nev. O God! O God! such struggles—oh ! adieu.
> [*Exeunt.*

SCENE V.—*An Oratory.*

The KING, *and* ABBOT, *in Conversation.*

King. Your obsersation, my good lord, is just.
Empires, like men, and other mortal things,
Must have their seasons of decline and fall.
   all has its destined period—all is change.
Abb. At the first birth of this revolving sphere,
Such was the fiat of Almighty Will.
King. Ceaseless vicissitude, and revolution,
Pervade the universe: poor, short-lived man !
The fluttering insect of a summer's day,
Sees generations rise, and sink around him :
While with more flow, but not less certain aim,
Relentless Time, sweeps with his wasteful scythe
Proud states and empires from their crumbling base.
Abb. Virtue alone survives the general wreck.
King. The various page of history is filled,
With mighty images of past renown ;
With far-famed names of towns and kingdoms, once

The boast and wonder of the world, but now,
Their date and place forgotten, swallowed up,
In the dark gulph of all-devouring Time,
Like unsubstantial pageants of a dream,
They all are vanished! and such, most reverend lord,
Shall one day be the fate of this fair country.

   Abb. The ways of heaven are inscrutable,
Beyond the limits of our narrow sense.

   King. It must be so—the fated hour will come.
Ah! me! what is this world, what changes in it!
The puissant princes of this favoured isle,
My royal ancestors in ages past,
Who held the awful sceptre of this realm,
Sleep in their tombs, unconscious of the storm
Whose factious billows threaten to o'erwhelm
Our native land. Would I were gathered to them!
Locked in the cold embrace of death, no more,
My eyes would view the crimes of this bad age,
Nor my heart bleed in anguish for the woes,
And ruin of my friends, my house, and family.

   Abb. This low, desponding humour, my good liege,
Accords not with the holy resignation,
And well-poised thoughts, which heretofore have swayed
Your royal breast. The path of life, we know,
Is dark and intricate, beset with snares,
Entangled and perplexed ; encompassed round
With storms and perils : but 'tis a transient scene,
A passing state ; and the all-seeing eye
Of him, who rules the various turns of fate,
Is still the polar star, to guide our course,
Safe and unhurt amidst the shoals around us.
Let not despair usurp the throne of reason,
But armed with pious confidence, expect
In silent fortitude, the final issue.

D 2

King. The sins of my forefathers are avenged
On me, their ill-starred son.   Oh! had I waked
To life, to sleep again in death! or while a babe,
Rocked in my royal cradle, had I felt
The gentle sting of infant dissolution—
Unexercised in pain, secure from grief,
And all the miseries of poor mortality;
From this precarious throne, this thorny crown,
Smiling, on angel-wings I then had flown
A happy innocent to realms of bliss.
But, as your lordship piously directs,
This fiery ordeal I must still endure,
Till it shall please our Sovereign Master,
And merciful disposer of events,
To call me from this world of evils, see,
Where young Lord Nevill comes this way in haste:
He comes, alas! to summon me away,
To horrid scenes of bloodshed and destruction.

Enter NEVILL.

Nev. Most gracious liege, the escort, which attends
Your royal person to the field, is ready:
Our noble host, and other lords assembled,
Wait in the hall, impatient of delay.
    King. I shall attend your lordship, instantly.
                                        [*Exit Nevill.*
Most reverend lord, we must depart; your stay,
Within this castle, as yourself proposed,
To wait the issue of this deadly conflict,
Will to our noble hostess be, no doubt,
During the absence of her lord, and friends,
Most pleasing and acceptable: farewell,
I recommend myself, and luckless cause
To your devout and earnest supplications.

Abb. My daily orisons, most gracious liege,
Shall still, in your behalf, be poured forth,
With holy violence to the throne of mercy.

  King. Would pitying Heaven compose this civil feud,
Should dove-eyed Peace extend her olive wand,
And blissful concord once more reign among us;
These forms of royalty, this princely state,
This sceptered dignity, and all its honours,
With heartfelt satisfaction would I leave.
To pass the tranquil evening of my days,
Under your saintly rule, in Fountains-abbey.
Ah! what a life were this! how sweet! how lovely!
Blest vale of peace! where angels walk with men.
Happy retirement! were it only mine.
But we must separate, once more adieu.   [*Exeunt.*

SCENE VI.—*The Hall.*

Enter CLIFFORD *and* WARDER.

  Cliff. Is all completely ready?——
  Ward. Yes my lord.
  Cliff. My visor furbished? the rivets all closed up?
My leaden mace, and iron gauntlets too,
You've tried them thoroughly? I shall wear the spear,
My father used to call Lord Mortimer's.
  Ward. All is prepared, my lord, and set in order:
The barbed steeds stand in the stables, each
Neighing and pawing for the distant field.
Your lordship has not said what favourite charger,
You would have fitted out for this encounter.
  Cliff. As far as Towton, I shall ride black Percy,
But in the field shall mount Pendragon ; now,

Keep up an active watch, good Warder, strive
To calm your lady's fears ; see, no reports,
Or idle rumours spread about the castle.
Look to the gates—we shall dispatch your son
With earliest tidings of the victory.

    Ward. Would I now saw your lordship safe returned!
My boding heart—but now—good lord—farewell.

                                      [Exit.

SCENE VII.—*The same.*

A grand Military Procession, with a Band of Music ; flourish of Trumpets, and discharges of Artillery. The Royal Standard is borne aloft, and other Banners, ornamented with red Roses, and the words " King Henry VI.—The House of Lancaster for ever."

Enter the KING, ABBOT, NORTHUMBERLAND, WESTMORE-
LAND, NEVILL, *and* OFFICERS.

    Cliff. Welcome, dread sovereign, to our warlike
    march,
Welcome, thrice welcome, all my valiant peers.
With what delight I see you here assembled !
What guardian angel, or what favouring saint,
Has thus impelled the foe into our toils,
And given him up, an easy certain prey,
To our avenging weapons ! All-righteous Heaven !
I humbly give thee thanks.   Now, my brave friends,
Let us be mindful of our customed prowess ;
Let all the wrongs we heretofore have suffered ;
Let all the blood, which in our rightful cause

Has hitherto been shed ; let our strong oaths,
And solemn league, oft vowed inviolable;
Let all the sacred ties, which bind our hearts,
And hands together, in one common union ;
Our king, and country, the throne, and altar ;
Our lives and property, and peaceful homes ;
Our wives and children, our fondest, dearest hopes;
Most precious motives ! strongest knots of love !
Let all together rise in one before us,
And fire our souls to vengeance—sweet revenge !
Sanctioned by laws both human and divine.
What ! shall it e'er be said, or even thought,
We tamely suffered such indignities ?
O shall it for a moment be supposed,
A Percy, or a Nevill, shunned the field?
Shall such unheard of miscreants tread the earth,
Polluted with the basest blackest crimes,
And in the face of men and angels, thus
Unpunished, brave the wrath of God and man ?
Forbid it Heaven ! no : let our bows and spears
Be in our hands the ministers of justice,
To scourge these lawless traitors from the land,
And free the nation from such damned rebels.
But let us, first, beseech our reverend guest,
The venerable lord of Fountains-abbey,
To consecrate our arms, and by his prayers,
To draw the blessing of the Lord upon us.
Abb. The God of armies bless your enterprise,
O'erwhelm the power of your adversary,
And guide you back victorious from the field.
May conquest ride triumphant through your ranks,
And guardian spirits spread their watch around you.
Go forth, with confidence, be brave, and conquer.

Cliff. Strike up the drums, sound trumpets, let's
    away,
My fiery soul's impatient of delay.
Ye all are eager for th' approaching fight,
Then in our cause let each exert his might,
God and St. George, England, and Henry's right.

                         [Exeunt.

ACT IV.

*SCENE I.—A Field of Battle, between Saxton
and Towton.—Banners, with the words, " Edward IV.—The House of* York *for ever."
—Shouts, flourish of Trumpets, Drums.*

Enter Edward IV., Earl *of* Warwick, *and* Others, *with
white Roses, in their Helmets.*

Edw. Thus far, my valiant friends, our hasty march
Is crowned by fortune with deserved success.
These fierce Lancastrians, driven from their post,
Dispirited and broken fly before us,
And scatter terror through their trembling ranks.
With her loud trumpet, Fame proclaims our deeds,
In thundering blasts of horror and dismay;
While o'er our brightening crests, and quivering spears,
Auspicious Victory hovering leads us on,
Fans with her crimson wing our royal banners,
And points the way to glory. Noble Warwick,
This brave achievement claims my warmest thanks,
And twines your merits closer round my heart.

War. To die, or conquer in your rightful cause,
Is, my good liege, the summit of my hopes,
The crown of my ambition. And, when I think
Of all the deadly wrongs, myself and friends
Have from this factious band already suffered;
When I behold your throne, and kingly sceptre,
In the weak hands of a deluded prince,

More fitted for a cowl, than for a crown:
When I behold our native English land,
Our laws and liberties, and chartered rights,
Spurned at, and mocked by an imperious queen,
A haughty stranger to our soil, and people—

 Edw. O England! England! miserable country!
How art thou fallen! how betrayed, and ruined!

 War. Oft do I wish, if such the form of things,
Such be the state that we are doomed to live in,
Such the condition of our future days,
Oft do I wish, soon may some hostile spear
Tear from this bosom my indignant heart,
And save my weeping eyes the woeful sight,
The melancholy fall of England's glory.

 Edw. This day is likely to decide our fate,
To crush these base pretenders to our crown,
And firmly fix us in our regal seat.
What tidings have the scouts or spies brought in,
Of the advance or movements of the foe?

 War. They are, my liege, already within reach
Of our stout bowmen; headed by his grace
Of Somerset; Northumberland, proud Clifford,
(Boiling with fury at this forced retreat
Of their best troops) and other northern lords,
Have also joined their camp: their force, 'tis said,
Is much superior to your highness, and
I fear this difference of numbers, joined
With vengeful Clifford's fierce and bloody name
May strike a panic through our southern men.

 Edw. Strait through the camp be proclamation made,
That he who dreads these base Lancastrian rebels,
And fears to front them on this hostile plain,
May, without hindrance, instantly depart,
And tell their numbers to his friends at home.
Edward of York lists only with the brave.

But of the few, who may with us remain,
To share the perils of this glorious day,
If any flinch, or once desert his post,
Our instant vengeance shall o'ertake the traitor.
We want not numbers, Warwick, all we want,
Is Englishmen and soldiers——
 War. Now, by St. George,
This shows you worthy of your princely race.
 Edw. Let this forthwith be done, while we prepare '
Our ranks for battle. Trust me, brave Warwick,
         [Exit an Officer.
Our friends who are not with us on this day,
Shall more regret their absence from the fight,
Than if, when crowned with laurels we return,
They should be banished from our triumph, or
Excluded from our coronation feast.
Know you the name of yonder straggling village?
 An Off. My liege, they call it Towton, and it is
From your good town of York 'bout thirteen miles.
 Edw. Then Towton-field shall henceforth be renowned;
And to our future chroniclers and bards,
Shall be the theme of many a tragic tale.
England's Pharsalia shall it hence be styled;
For on this day, I guess, more English blood
Shall here be shed, and all by English hands,
Than e'er was known before, or shall hereafter.

   [Loud shouts.]—Enter an OFFICER.

What say the soldiers to our proclamation?
 Off. With one acclaim, they shouted to the skies
Edward the Fourth, the house of York for ever.
 War. Now, if my fluttering heart, and towering hopes
Deceive me not, before this sun be set,
Edward of York, on this ensanguined plain
Amid the cries and groans of vanquished rebels,

Shall be proclaimed fair England's lawful king.
The star of York shall rise this night in glory.
This day confirms the sceptre in thy hand.
This day shall be our ruin or our rise,
Edward shall win, or Warwick here shall die.

   Edw. We thank thee, Warwick, for these cheering
       words;
Now to the battle, on my valiant friends,
And give no quarter to the recreant foe.
There will be work anon, this thirsty soil
Shall drink the blood of many a gallant knight.
Bestride your foaming steeds, and once again
Join in the shock of slaughter, blows and death.
Charge, charge the base degenerate traitors;
Victory, and triumph, God, and St. George be with us,
                       [Exeunt.

   [*Flourish of Drums and Trumpets.*]

*SCENE II.—Another part of the Field.—The
Duke of Somerset's Tent.*

      Enter SOMERSET *and* EXETER.

   Som. This sudden check, most noble Exeter,
Has not dispirited our valiant men.
Your grace's hasty, but well-timed retreat,
Has saved the vanguard of our force, and brought
These hot and daring rebels on the plain.
Our force is far superior, with the troops,
Which with Lord Dacre, and from Skipton-castle
Have just arrived, we fairly, now may count
A matchless force of sixty thousand men.
   Ex. They are, my lord, all eager for the fight;
Each bosom fired to actions of renown.

292

From rank to rank, they stand in proud array,
Threatening defiance to their furious foes,
And longing to begin the work of death.
This wrathful rage of civil butchery,
And sad effusion of each other's blood,'
Afflicts my soul; but there's no time for grief:
All is prepared, and now we only wait
Your grace's orders——
   Som. Each moment I expect
Lord Clifford, and his friends, from Skipton, when
They've joined the camp, and have consulted with us,
Without delay we will lead on our men
To charge these rash adventurers—behold!
Where, as I speak, they come——

SCENE III.—*The same.*

SOMERSET, EXETER, NORTHUMBERLAND, CLIFFORD.

   Som. My noble lords,
Your presence is most welcome, scarce can we keep
Our lion-hearted heroes from the fight:
Scarce will they wait their gallant leaders, now
Nothing remains but that we strait repair
To our respective posts, and give the word
To fall or conquer in King Henry's cause.
   North. My lords of Somerset and Exeter,
Most valiant friends, all hail! with utmost speed
We have obeyed your summons, and are now
Prepared to meet your further orders, say,
Have our hot-blooded foes advanced upon us!
   Som. Their foremost ranks are almost joined with ours;
And some slight skirmish has already passed.
Say, my Lord Clifford, did you leave the king
And queen at Skipton-castle?——

Cliff. The king, my lord,
Is in the field, and stationed on a height,
Crowned by yon lofty wood ; a place of safety,
Where a brave troop commanded by Lord Nevill,
Has orders to attend his sacred person.
The queen and prince are on their way to York.

 Ex. Your grace was pleased to order that the right
Should be led on by Lord Northumberland,
The left wing by Lord Clifford ; shall we now
Each to our station, and exhort our men
Without delay to rush upon the foe.

> [*Soldiers run across the Stage, with Bows and Spears,
> and Stands of Colours; shouts, huzzas, Drums,
> Trumpets, and discharges of Artillery.*]

 Cliff. Methinks the battle is in part begun.
A thousand spirits in my single breast,
Seem to rise up, and goad me to the field.
Your grace, I may presume, has issued orders
To give no quarter to the enemy.

 Som. It is his majesty's express command
To spare his vanquished subjects——

 Cliff. Subjects ! my lord,
Infernal villains, vile, perjured rebels,
Unnatural murderers, foul, bloody traitors !
Now, by the tombs of all our ancestors !
By all their warlike deeds, and sacred blood,
Shed through past ages in their country's cause ;
I here protest, in sight of earth and heaven,
And by the hope I have of heavenly bliss,
Here on my knee, I vow to God above,
Ne'er will I cease till I have hewn them down,
And bathed my weapon in their reeking blood.
Worse than the gates of hell, I'll hate the man,
Who bids me show compassion, or relent
From my fixed purpose of revenge and death.

Not one of all the accursed race shall live,
Nor man, nor boy, I swear, shall 'scape my vengeance.
North. We swear, upon our swords we swear the same.
Som. We will give orders to cut off the chiefs,
And factious leaders of the rebel host.
But to their followers be some mercy shown.
Now let us forth, my lords, and join our powers:
Think of our rightful cause, our deadly wrongs,
Fight for our lives, our country, and our king,
And o'er the slaughtered legions of the foe,
March on to glory, conquest, and renown.
Cliff. Blood, and revenge, a victory or death.
[Exeunt.

SCENE IV.—*A Field of Battle.—Soldiers run across the Stage, fighting; some fall.*

Enter WARWICK, *and* OTHERS.

War. I cannot meet fierce Clifford in the field.
Like a fierce tyger, through the ranks of war,
Onward he rushes, and where'er he treads
He leaves the print of blood. Clifford, proud lord,
Come forth; I call, and challenge thee to arms.
Fierce, bloody cannibal! fain would I lose
My life, if dying, I could see thee fall. *[Exeunt.*

SCENE V.

Enter CLIFFORD, *sword in hand, and* OTHERS.

Cliff. St. George, and victory! fight, soldiers fight.
It is a hot and desperate encounter;
But they begin to yield; pale, trembling cowards!

Their guilty terrors paralyse their strength.
Now let our conquering colours wave aloft,
Now die their roses in their own hearts-blood.
Disorder, and dismay have seized their ranks.
On, on, my friends, bring me another horse,
Quick, quick pursue the fugitives, come on,
Strike home, and give no quarter, spare not one.

[Exeunt.

SCENE VI.

Enter WARWICK, *and* OTHERS.

War. Methought I saw him pass by yonder wood,
And there he comes——

Enter CLIFFORD *and* SOLDIERS.

Clifford of Westmoreland
I am rejoiced we've met; all through the plain
Long have I sought thee in this work of death.
Villainous butcher! dark, bloody cannibal!
Too long unpunished hast thou shocked the land
With thy foul acts of murder and revenge,
But now thy hour is come, and Warwick's hand
Shall with unerring blow avenge the wrongs,
The bleeding wrongs of our afflicted country.

Cliff. Warwick, thy tongue is swifter than thy sword;
Men fight with blows, and not with empty words.
Fly to thy upstart, bloody-sceptered tyrant,
The false usurper York ; there strut and boast,
And shake thy harmless weapon; fly from hence,
Unless thou seek'st here by this arm to die.
Go tell thy ruffian master, Clifford has sworn
Not one of all his race, no, not a babe
Shall 'scape the point of this remorseless weapon.

296

War. Cowardly, cruel, ungenerous monster!
Here's to thy heart, perfidious rebel—now—

[*They fight, Warwick, and his party are beat off,
followed by Clifford.*]

*Soldiers rush on the Stage, crying mercy, quarter, mercy;
oh! save my life, oh spare me, save me.*

SCENE VII.—*Opens, and discovers a Wood;
Henry VI. and Matilda, disguised in Armour,
in conversation.*

King. You are, methinks, a very youthful soldier.
I should conjecture 'tis your first essay,
And enterprise of manhood in the field.
Mat. My gracious liege has fairly guessed the truth;
Unused to bear this iron weight, my limbs
Languish beneath its pressure, while the sounds,
And sights of horror, which from every side
Assail my senses, strike me to the heart,
Unman my frame, and overwhelm my spirits.
A field of battle is a ghastly scene.
King. Truly it is, therefore I marvel much,
Your loving parents would consent so soon,
To let you, at your tender age incur
Such mortal hazard; were they not averse
To your adventurous spirit? Sure they must
Be sadly anxious for your safe return.
Mat. Alas! my liege, they feel no pain for me.
Both are at rest in their untimely graves.
My honoured father, in his glorious prime,
Fell at St. Albans, in that bloody fight,
The opening act of this sad civil war.
My mother, pierced by sorrow's deadly dart,

E

Sunk underneath the shock, and left her child,
A helpless orphan in this world of woe.

King. O melancholy times! heart-rending scenes!
Disorder, havoc—a full tide of woes
Is rushing on this worried land at once.
Unnatural discord, rapine, and revenge,
Wide-wasting rage, inexorable hate—
Hell, and its offspring are let loose upon us.
All ties of law and nature torn asunder,
The father kills his son, the son his father.·
Each day is gashed with wounds, with deeds of horror.
The air is rent with howlings of despair ;
The earth is drenched with blood, with kindred blood.
Religion, justice, are forgotten names :
Heaven has abandoned, left us to our fate.

Mat. O pity, pity, gentle Heaven! pity.
Give peace, O give our bleeding country peace.

King. Uproar, and wild confusion at the helm,
The vessel of the state, a shattered wreck,
Is tost, and foundered in the whelming wave.
Like a fierce vulture, screaming for her prey,
Outrageous Anarchy has fixed his claws
Deep in the fallen body of the realm,
And preys upon our vitals——

Mat. Your grace has drawn
Too true a picture of this awful time.
A black and dismal prospect spreads around us,
A deep and settled gloom o'ershades the land.
Domestic peace and happiness are gone.
Brothers, and sisters, and heart-broken friends,
Weep in sad concert o'er their mutual woes.
Just in the moment of expected bliss,
Lovers are severed from each other's arms,
Their hopes and tender wishes crushed at once.
Distress, and bitter anguish——

King. No more, no more,
Each word plants daggers in my bleeding heart.
O if my crown or life could——

                                  [Alarms, shouts.

   Mat. Hark—my liege
I hear a hostile shout; alas! I fear
Some danger is at hand; look there, I see
Lord Nevill rushing in a furious haste.
I will ascend the hill; I may perhaps
Discover from that height, how goes the day.
Ye guardian spirits! O protect me now.   *[Exit.*

Enter Nevill.

   Nev. My liege, my liege, we are surrounded, fly,
Fly through the thicket, where a horse awaits you.
O lose no time, the foe is just upon us.
   King. O ill-starred Lancaster! devoted race!

                                   [Exeunt.

SCENE VIII.—The same.

Enter Edward IV. *and* Others.

   Edw. The rebels run before, pursue, pursue.
Let our swift vengeance overtake their flight.
Both Somerset and Exeter are slain.
Is not King Henry stationed on that hill?
   Off. He was, my liege, but now, I think, he's fled.
   Edw. Follow him up, follow with utmost speed.
Who brings him to our tent, alive or dead,
Shall, crowned with honours, from our hands, receive
The highest recompense we can bestow.
On my brave friends, God and his saints are with us.

                                   [Exeunt.

E 2

SCENE IX.—*Another part of the Field.*

Enter MATILDA, *wounded, leaning on* MICHAEL.

Mat. The wound, I fear, is mortal——
Mich. Say not so,
O do not think it madam——
Mat. I am sick,
And very faint—I'll sit down here,
Under this spreading oak—think you we are safe?
Mich. I see no signs of danger, now I hear
No clang of hostile arms, no noise, nor shout.
Mat. Alas! I have been too rash—O ill-starred fate!
Poor luckless maïd! unfortunate Matilda!
What can I do? ah me! the pangs of death—
My end approaches fast——
Mich. Comfort, good lady,
Your words affright me, freeze me with despair.
Mat. Is there no hut, no sheltered hovel nigh,
Where I might breathe my last, and die in peace?
O think, good Michael, should some savage wretch,
Some rude relentless ruffian pass this way.
My brother—where's Lord Nevill? O my sister!
What can she think or say! I'm very faint.   [*Faints.*

Enter NEVILL.

SCENE X.

NEVILL, MATILDA, MICHAEL.

Nev. Matilda! Michael! do my eyes deceive me?
How can this be? tell me—'tis she—my love,

My angel, my Matilda—speak—awake,
Sure 'tis a dream—O look upon me——
   Mat. Yes,
It was an angel's voice—me thought I heard
My love, my Nevill——
   Nev. It is thy Nevill, speak,
O speak again—look up—let me support thee.
Wounded and bleeding! ha! what dire mischance!
What ruffian hand——
   Mat. How merciful and kind
To let my love go with me! we are safe,
Nothing shall part us more—by day or night,
One grave will hold us both—how cold and dark!
Alas! the frozen hand of death is on me,
And I have only time—farewell—farewell.
It is my Nevill—my dear, my only husband—
Michael will tell you all—its' time to go—
The beckoning angels call us—come dear love—
When we are in heaven, you'll love me still, and oh!
                                  [Dies.

   Nev. Death and confusion! answer on thy life,
Perfidious villain! say, what brought you here?
Who did this murderous deed? Matilda! oh!
Matilda! my love—my life—speak, speak once more—
Bleeding, and dead! impossible!—I rave,
My brain turns round—was ever scene like this?
If this be not revenged—bear witness, earth!
And heaven! O cruel stroke! ah! dead—dead—
O soft-eyed beauty thus untimely slain!
Torn like a rose-bud in her vernal bloom,
Pale as a drooping lily!—bloody villain!
Murder—hoa—murder——

Enter EDWARD IV.

   Edw. What Lancastrian rebel,

Is this, who with his rude and barbarous shouts,
Affrights the echoes of this peaceful wood?

Nev. Thou art the man—vile, bloody-minded tyrant!
Whose mad destructive rage has caused this deed,
This piteous deed, at which all nature weeps.
Matilda! O my love! my murdered love!
Could not thy beauty, innocence, and youth,
Thy helpless innocence disarm the wretch?
Base, spiritless assassin! see thy work—
Thine, murderer, thine—O hellish act!
Which soon shall draw upon thy guilty head
The thundering terrors of avenging heaven,
Rebel, usurper, traitor——

Edw. We have no time
For these wild ravings now; prepare, come on,
And meet thy fate by Edward's hands; we give
And take no quarter on this field of death.

[They fight, Nevill falls.

Nev. The victory is thine ——
Edw. So perish all,
Who dare oppose in arms our rightful claim.
Where is brave Warwick? ho, my Warwick, ho.

[Exit.

Nev. The thought and sight of thee unmanned me
quite.
Here are we joined in death—to part no more.
I die content, thus by thy side—alas!
To have survived thee! oh! far better thus.
Sure I may take one bridal kiss—cold, cold—
A lifeless corpse—O my adored Matilda!
Lovely and beauteous still—hard cruel fate!
A field of battle for a nuptial couch.
Death—envious death has robbed me of my bride.
Oh! I am dying—stay, one moment stay.

[Takes off his Sash.

This was thy last, sweet, precious gift—thou badst me
Restore it to thee—I'll shroud thee with it.
'Twill help to shade thee from the lawless gaze
Of rude spectators—oh! it was thy love,
Thy pure and spotless love, which brought thee here
To watch thy Nevill, in the dangerous fight.
We soon shall meet, and in a better world.
One parting kiss—and then, a lasting sleep—
To wake—ah no! yes—in thy soft embrace,
In heavenly transports—raptures—see—O now—
See where she glides—look how she soars above—
And there she's lost—I come—oh! help me, help—

[*Dies.*

[*Michael, who had remained stupified and
motionless, falls on his knees, by the dead
bodies, and the scene closes.*]

SCENE XI.—*Another part of the Field.*

Enter NORTHUMBERLAND *and* WESTMORELAND.

North. Alas! my lord, our noble general
His grace of Somerset is slain : his men
O'erwhelmed with horror at this dreadful loss,
Begin to yield, and to desert their ranks.
What force remains, we must without delay
Bring on, and charge the foe——
West. The day will still
Be ours, for gallant Clifford, on the left,
Drives like a raging tempest o'er the plain,
Or like some god of war, with thunder armed,
He strikes dismay and terror through their hearts,
And mows whole ranks with his resistless sword.
North. I only fear he may advance too far.

It is a desperate fight, already
The field is heaped with mountains of the slain.
A dreadful scene of carnage, blood, and horror.

   West. I will this instant bring up the reserve.
Courage brave friend, the victory is ours.   [*Exit.*

SCENE XII.—*The same.*

Enter LORD CLIFFORD, *staggering, his Helmet in one
   hand, and holding with the other a bloody Handkerchief to his throat.—*NOTHUMBERLAND, *runs to his assistance.*

   North. Wounded! my lord, alas! how happened this?
   Cliff. Wounded to death, Northumberland——
   North. Not so,
I hope, dear cousin, O say who did it.
   Cliff. Oppressed with heat, and with the close pursuit,
I had unloosed my casque, and gorget, when
A half-spent arrow, shot by friend or foe,
I know not which—my strength is gone, good cousin;
Lay me down gently—there—life's ebbing fast.
It was a bloody fight—the Yorkists fled.
The day is ours, Northumberland, we're revenged.
I'm going now—you'll see my wife—alas!
Here take my helmet—I pray you give it her—
With her own hands she lined it—poor Isabella!
Tell my dear boys—ah me! my life is done—
Prithee, unclasp my sword, I'd have it laid
Close by my father's in the armoury.
His murder is revenged—come nearer, cousin;
I have at least this—ha, ha, ha, (*laughs*) this comfort left,
No Yorkist e'er shall boast he vanquished Clifford.
I'm sick to death—give me your hand—that's well—

Is the king safe ? my Isabella—now—
Give me my sword—cut off his head—there—-there
Matilda! Nevill! remember—oh ! farewell.   [*Dies.*

SCENE XIII.

Enter MICHAEL.

Mich. Alas ! alas ! my noble master slain !
My beauteous lady too, and brave Lord Nevill,
All killed—all lost at once—O father, father !
Too well you prophesied—where shall I go?
What shall I do? O heavens ! would I were dead !
And buried in the deep——
North. This dreadful stroke
Has overwhelmed and stupefied my brain.
Horror and grief have vanquished all my powers.
Who's there? good Michael, haste away, O haste,
Go with all speed to Skipton-castle, fly,
O save your lady, and her infant children.
Tell her—O tale of horror !—haste away—
Here take this sword and helmet—quick, depart.
Lose not a moment, ride with utmost speed.
Mich. O had I died before I saw this hour.   [*Exit.*
North. Bright flower of chivalry ! brave son of war !
Most valiant leader ! anchor of our hopes !
The rock, and tower, of our loyal cause !
The shield and bulwark of our Henry's throne !
Fallen, oh ! fallen, fallen in his prime,
The bloody victim of remorseless Fate !
O woe of woes ! O grief above all grief !
O Clifford ! Clifford ! flow, flow on my tears—
Why did I live to see this fatal day ?
Here point your weapons, York, and Warwick ; here,

With joy would I receive the stroke of death.
O Skipton-castle!—dreadful, killing thought!
A tender husband, father, brother, friend!
My friend in arms, my loved companion slain!
O sight of horror! woeful, dismal sight!
Pale, cold, and breathless! dead! mere senseless clay!
A bleeding corse! ah! who shall shield thee now?
Who shall protect thy honoured loved remains?
Alas! alas! was ever loss like this!
Where shall I turn me now? Ho, help there, ho—
Now would I gladly here upon this heath,
Pierced through with deadly wounds resign my breath:
Our cause is hopeless, all is ruined, gone—
Proud York triumphant, Lancaster undone.

[*Drags Clifford's body, and exit.*]

ACT V.

SCENE I.—An' Apartment in Skipton-castle.

Lady Clifford *is reclining on a couch, a female Attendant
standing by her.—On one side of the room, a table
with a guittar on it.—Flashes of lightning, and loud
thunder.*

Lady Cl. It is a dreadful, most tempestuous night.
Did you ascend the highest watch-tower?
Att. Madam, I did——
Lady Cl. And could you nought discern?
Saw you no messenger on horse, or foot?
Heard you no sound, no clang of arms, nor shout?
Att. Madam, I was all eye, all ear; I stood
Fixed like a marble statue, on the edge
Of the high battlement; and motionless,
With close attention caught each passing breeze,
Watched every moving object in the air,
Or on the earth, but could discover nothing:
And now the shades of night are gathering round.
                                        [*Distant thunder.*
Lady Cl. Hush—hark—what noise is that?——
Att. I think, it must
Have been the distant thunder, or the wind,
Howling for entrance, through some shattered casement.
Lady Cl. My brain is heated—I am beset with terrors.
My boding fears distract my very soul.

Methinks I hear—I see—look, look what's there?

[*Pointing wildly to the bottom of the stage.*]

Give me your hand—this room is very lonely.

Where is my sister? have you seen her lately?

Att. The nurse informed me, 'bout an hour ago,

She left the castle, as she said, to make

A visit to the good old Friar Lawrence ;

To beg his holy prayers on our behalf.

The pathway to his cell is rough and dreary,

And this fierce tempest may prolong her stay.

Lady Cl. I hope the storm will not disturb the children.

Did the nurse say that they were fast asleep?

Att. She said they were——

Lady Cl. O agonizing state

Of torturing expectation and suspense!

Where is the Abbot?——

Att. I met him in the hall,

As I came hither; he said, it was the hour

Of vespers, and for some time he must retire

Into the oratory to his devotions;

And then he bade me say, he'd meet you here.

Lady Cl. A messenger, no doubt, will soon arrive.

O my disordered thoughts! my heart is torn,

And rent in pieces—I am quite o'ercome.

Strange hopes and fears convulse my throbbing breast.

I know not what to hope—yet secret dread,

And apprehension of the worst prevails.

The very thought of what may happen—oh!

I dread to think, and yet—I'm all distraction.

Att. I trust your fears will soon be turned to joy,

And welcome tidings ease your anxious heart.

Lady Cl. Alas! I fear not—and yet why despond?

This heavy melancholy clogs my spirits.

Perhaps some music would relieve my mind:

Play me some solemn softly-soothing air,

Take the guittar, and sing those pretty words,
Which to a good old tune, some weeks ago,
Lord Nevill made in honour of Matilda.
O that they both were here to hear you sing them.

ATTENDANT *Plays and Sings.*

Though tost on Life's tempestuous ocean,
    I fear no care, nor sorrow nigh;
While gentle Love's heartfelt emotion
    Soothes me with its lullaby.

                        Lullaby, etc.

Is cruel Fate new woes disclosing?
    Safe from all alarms I'd lie;
If in Matilda's arms reposing,
    Soothed by Love's soft lullaby.

                        Lullaby, etc.

Lady Cl. Stop, stop—the music gives me no relief.
How frightful is this conflict of the elements.

                        [*Loud thunder.*

The image of my own tumultuous brain,
How 'twill increase the horrors of the fight!
O my dear lord! sure heaven is leagued against us!
Wild with my fears, I speak, I know not what :
Hush—hush—I hear the sound of footsteps nigh.

Enter the ABBOT.

SCENE II.—*The same.*

LADY CLIFFORD, ABBOT, ATTENDANT.

Lady Cl. Welcome, my lord, we have as yet received
No tidings from the fatal field—I fear
All is not well——

Abb. This awful storm perhaps
May have delayed the messenger ; no doubt
The fight ere this is ended, and I trust,
Some joyful tidings soon will reach our ears.
Be confident, good lady, hope the best.

    Lady Cl. Indeed, my lord, I'm greatly moved, and
       need
All the support your virtue can bestow.
Such dire presentiments o'erwhelm my heart !

Enter Lord Clifford's Ghost.

(*Walks across the Stage, waving a bloody Handkerchief.*)

    Ghost. Away, away, away, the hour is come.
                                [*Exit.*

    Abb. Madam——
    Lady Cl. Come near me, O support me, I shall die.
    Abb. What sudden illness !
    Lady Cl. Did you not see him ?
Did you not hear——

Enter Warder.

O my good warder, tell
Tell me directly—ha! so downcast—oh !
See how he droops his head—my heart will burst,
My brain will split asunder —speak, oh! speak—
Is not a messenger arrived? quick, quick—
Tell me the worst, relieve my pangs—oh! tell it—

    Ward. Oh! that some other could the tale relate!
Madam, we must this moment leave the castle,
And fly to some safe place of refuge.
Our army is defeated, and the foe—

    Lady Cl. Who? what ? each look and word distracts
       me—where—

Where is your lord? what message has he sent?
Will he come back to-night? Oh? he is killed!
I see it in your looks, and now your words
Will kill me also with the horrid tale.

War. Ah me! it must be told, Madam, it is
Too true, alas! my noble lord is—fallen.

Lady Cl. Dead! my life! my husband! oh! my
        Clifford!   [*Faints.*

Abb. Look to her—this is frightful news indeed!
The wrath of heaven has burst in vengeance on us.
Is York victorious? is Lord Clifford slain!
Is your son come?——

War. O melancholy day!
Of all my days the blackest and most dismal.

Lady Cl. Stand off, and hold me not—I will go to him.
Where am I? where? O there he is—come now,
Come my dear lord—oh! do not, do not stab him——
He is, he is, indeed he is my husband.
Cover his pale dead limbs—bind up his wounds——

Enter the Ghost.

(*Walks across the Stage, as before.*)

Ghost. Hear me, O hear, away, away, away. [*Exit.*
Lady Cl. See how it glares upon me! my Clifford!
There, there he goes—O my dear boys! rush on!—
Fix daggers in my heart, here drink my blood—
Let fall your rage on this devoted head—
Blast me with lightning—whelm me in the deep—
Throw me to tygers—tear me to atoms—
But spare, oh! spare my little orphan children—
        [*Runs out, followed by her Attendant.*

SCENE III.—*The same.*

The ABBOT *and* WARDER.

Abb. I fear this dreadful stroke will turn her brain.
What's to be done?——
    War. My son is safe returned,
But oh! what dismal tidings! O my lord,
All is ruined, our army quite o'erthrown;
The king has fled almost alone to York;
The Dukes of Somerset, and Exeter,
And my dear lord—oh! have I lived for this!
The young Lord Nevill, and his beauteous bride,
Who to the field disguised in armour went,
Are also slain——
    Abb. O heavy woe on woe!
How shall we tell your lady! gracious powers!
How give her comfort in such bitter anguish!
Heaven, only heaven can support her now.
Yet something must be done without delay.

Enter a MESSENGER.

Mess. The Yorkists have completely gained the day.
The Earls Northumberland, and Westmoreland,
Steeped in their blood, lie dead upon the field.
The brave Lancastrians, all their leaders slain,
And by their foes enclosed, were overpowered.
A general wreck and massacre ensued.
Full thirty thousand, who this morn arose
In health and vigour, ne'er will see again
The cheerful face of day. O had you seen
The mangled bleeding heaps, dying and dead,
Friends, brothers, fathers, by each other slain,

In horrible confusion : had you but heard
The mingled cries and groans, heart-piercing sounds !
God grant I never see the like again.
The Duke of York has ordered that the head,
And hands of brave Lord Clifford, shall forthwith
Be fixed upon the gates of York ; alas !

Enter another MESSENGER.

Second Mess. A troop of horse is ordered by the Duke
Of York, to ride immediately to Skipton,
To seize the Lady Clifford, and her children ;
They are commanded also to destroy
And burn the castle——
　Abb. No time is to be lost.
What plan can you propose, good Warder, now,
To save your lady, and her children ? speak,
Let not despair o'erwhelm your faculties :
Something must be determined on the spot.
　Ward. O wretched house ! most miserable race !
O my poor lady ! sure 'twill break her heart.
Our only hope, most reverend lord, methinks,
Is to persuade my lady, to retire
Alone, and in disguise, to Sawley Abbey.
There, in that sanctuary, concealed, she may
Remain in safety, for some days at least.
Her eldest son, Lord Henry, I will hide
In a good shepherd's hut, among the hills.
The youngest might accompany yourself,
To Fountains-abbey : divided thus, and hid,
They may elude their fierce and savage foes.
But, oh ! 'twill break my lady's heart, to leave
The castle, and from her darling infants
To be thus rudely torn——
　Abb. This must be done.
Do you, good warder, see immediately

F

313

That all be got in readiness ; I'll repair
Strait to my lady's presence, and endeavour
To calm her sorrows, and compose her thoughts,
To bear with patience the afflicting stroke.
Celestial powers! and guardian saints! to whom
Tis given to watch us in the hour of peril,
Assist, and guide us, with your heavenly care.

Ward. O sad reverse of fate ! O dreadful hour !

[*Exeunt.*

SCENE IV.—*The Armoury.*

Enter WARDER, *and* MICHAEL, *with Lord Clifford's
Sword and Helmet.*

Ward. Here lay them down—ah me! and is this all!
These the sole remnants of my noble lord,
Whom warm in youth, and towering in his pride,
This morn we saw, exulting in his strength,
Elate with hopes of victory and triumph!
Are these the spoils and trophies of the field!
And have my days been lengthened but for this!
Here by his father's armour set them down ;
The bloody enemy, proud York himself
Will venerate these relics of the brave.

Mich. O horror ! horror ! woeful, fatal night !
Alas ! the noble race, the ancient house,
The illustrious line of Clifford is extinguished.
In ruin sunk, and all its glories vanished !
All, all is lost, inevitable ruin,
And black despair, our only prospect now.

Ward. Here I had thought at least to end my days.
Here, where I first drew breath, and fondly hoped
When thou hadst closed my aged eyes, and laid me
Deep in my grave at rest, then here, like me,
In this same honourable service, thou,
Thou my dear son, still in these ancient walls,

314

Mightst by thy faithful duty, have repaid
Our obligations to this noble race.
But all is overwhelmed, destroyed, and ruined.

   Mich. Weep not for me, dear father, rather weep
For our good lady, and her infant sons,
Thrown in an instant from their high estate,
Fallen, alas! O dire calamity!
None, none to help, or to befriend them now.
Where shall they fly for refuge? dreadful state!
O what accumulated woes on woes,
In one short fatal day!——

   Ward. However sad,
We must not here indulge our sorrows now.
Without delay, we must prepare the means
For our departure from the castle, come,
We shall have time, oh! time enough for grief. [*Exeunt.*

SCENE V.—*The same.*

Enter LADY CLIFFORD, *leading a Child;* ATTENDANT *with
another:* ABBOT.

   Lady Cl. Here am I sunk and humbled in the dust!
Without a friend, a refuge, or a home.
Poor miserable wretch! oh! tell me where,
Where shall I look for comfort to my woes?
Heaven has exhausted all its rage upon me.
And yet another shock awaits my heart.
Oh! it will break, it can endure no more.
Dear harmless babes! and would they murder you?
Inhuman, savage, blood-polluted fiends!
O wretched mother! mother now no more!
Torn from my darling babes, my only joy!
Who shall protect the helpless orphans? oh!
Oh! when they miss their tender parents, who
Shall soothe, caress, and kiss them into smiles,
Who wipe away their little tears! oh! oh!

Hen. Why do you cry, Mama? Thomas and I
Like to be shepherd boys——
    Lady Cl. Sweet innocent!
May God protect you from these ravenous wolves.
Oh! I'm a wretch, abandoned, desolate,
By earth and heaven abandoned, plunged at once,
To black despair, to agony, and death.
Left to myself, forsaken, none to help me.
O my dear lord! Matilda! Nevill! oh!
Was ever grief or anguish like to mine!
    Abb. Be comforted, good lady, trust my words,
And deem them as prophetic: this your son,
Though by the dark unsearchable decrees
Of Providence, he now appear forlorn,
Spoiled of his fair inheritance, and left
A helpless orphan without friend or home—
    Lady Cl. O hapless babes! far better had it been
Had you been never born! What had I done
To merit such extremity of woe?
    Abb. O let not grief o'erwhelm your reason thus.
For mark my words, the day shall surely come,
When to his father's honours and possessions,
And with increase of dignity, restored,
In arts, and arms, and every virtuous deed,
His great progenitors he shall outshine.
Then of your widowed age, this boy shall be
The prop, and comfort, your delight, and pride.
    Lady Cl. O there's no hope, no ray of hope for me!
What has a wretch like me to do in life!
My dear, my loved Matilda! thou art happy.
O! how I envy thy untimely fate.
Thou hast no husband slain in battle, none
To lament, no helpless orphan babes,
Torn from thy widowed arms, without a home,
Exposed to want, to misery and death.

Happy, thrice happy, my Matilda! thou,
Thou by the Nevill's side, in one kind grave,
Shall feel no more the pangs and ills of life.
Whilst I must drag a miserable load—

Enter WARDER.

Ward. The guides, and steeds are ready, all's prepared,
Without delay, we now must leave the castle.

  [*Lady Clifford sees Lord Clifford's Helmet and
   Sword; takes up the Helmet.*]

  Lady Cl. Ha! there is his sword and helmet both,
   O God!
Stained with his blood! sad precious relic!
My tears shall wash it off—was it, for this,
With my own hands I lined it? ah! no more
Shall I unclasp thee, as I used with transport
On his return from battle—oh! my heart!
He was the husband of my early love—my lord,
My bosom's lord—strange, cruel destiny!
Sweet, tender pledges of our faithful love!
And were you born for this? O Clifford! Clifford!

Enter MICHAEL.

  Mich. We must depart this instant from the castle.
Some shepherds have run in, who say they heard
The noise of horses at a distance, and
Could see the glare of torches through the wood
Moving this way; no time must now be lost.

  [*The Warder takes hold of one boy, Michael of
   the other.*]

  Lady Cl. What tear my children from me? cruel men!
And in a night like this! Where would you take them?
Are you then leagued with those blood-thirsty fiends?

Oh! I shall never, never see them more.
If they must— must be murdered, let it be here,
Here in their mother's arms, before my eyes;
Here let us perish all together—oh!
Where is your lord? he can defend us all,
He, he alone can save us—darling babes,
Come to your mother's arms—one parting kiss,
One last embrace—O heaven! 'tis over—oh!

> [*Falls insensible on the floor; Attendant goes to
> her assistance; the Abbot kneels.*]

Abb. Protector of the suppliant and wretched!
Look with an eye of pity on her tears.
O save this bleeding land, in mercy save it.
In the sad catalogue of human woes,
Of all the miseries our nature knows,
The fiercest and the bitterest, by far,
Are the curst horrors of a Civil War.
When on the bosom of their mother earth
On the dear soil, to which they owe their birth,
Friends, brothers, kinsmen, 'gainst each other turn,
With fiendlike malice, hellish fury burn;
Blast every blessing with infernal joy,
And all the charities of life destroy.
Avenging Heaven! soon cause such crimes to cease,
And soothe our sorrows with the balm of peace!

> [*Exeunt omnes.*

APPENDIX.

APPENDIX

CONTAINING EXTRACTS FROM VARIOUS AU-
THORS, RELATING TO THE

CLIFFORD FAMILY.

No. I.

From Dugdale's *"Baronage of England,"* Tome I. p. 335.

CLIFFORD.

PONCE.

The first of this ancient and noble family, of whom I
find mention, was called Ponce, who had issue three sons,
viz.: Walter, Drogo, (id est, Dru) and Richard. (1)

WALTER I.

Of Walter and Drogo, the Conqueror's Survey takes notice ; and that Walter did then possess the lordships of

---

(1) I am ignorant of the origin of this name Drogo or Dru ;
but I find it was the name of one of the sons of Pepin Heristal,
grandfather of Charlemagne, and that it was common enough
in those times.

Ailford, Westwell, and Alwoldsbery, in the county of Oxford : as also part of Lece, in the county of Gloucester.

And that Drogo held Segry, etc. in Wiltshire ; Frampton, and part of Lece, in Gloucestershire ; Holim, etc. in Worcesterhire; as also Receford, etc. in the county of Hereford.(1)

RICHARD.

But from Richard it is, that the line was preserved. Which Richard, being called Richard de Pons, obtained by the gift of King Henry the First, the cantref of Bychan, (2) and the castle of Landovery in Wales. Moreover with the consent of Maud, his wife, and Simon, his son, he was a notable benefactor to the priory of Malvern, in the county of Worcester. For it appears that he gave thereunto the church of his castle at Cantarabohath, with two carucates of land, and the whole tithes of his revenues in that place. Likewise the church of Lecton, with one hide, and one yard-land in that town ; together with all the tithes of that lordship ; as also the tithes of his Lordship, in Estraddel, called Beechen. (3) He had issue three sons, viz.: Simon, founder of the priory at Clifford, in the county of Hereford; Walter, who first seating himself there, assumed that place for his surname and Richard.

WALTER II.

Which Walter, being called Walter, the son of Richard,

---

(1) In all fifteen lordships or manors.

(2) Cantref, in Welsh, answers to " hundred" in an English county.

(3) Carucates, and hides, are term employed in Domesday-book, to signify certain portions of land, of which the exact extent is not now known.

son of Ponce, gave to the canons at Hagmon, in the county
of Salop, his mills at Tenbury ; and afterwards, (by the
name of *Walter de Clifford*) gave to the nuns of Godstow, in the county of Oxford, for the healt. of the soul of
Margaret, his wife and for the soul of Rosamond, his
daughter, his mill at Frampton, in the county of Gloucester: as also a little meadow, lying near it, called Lecton, in pure and perpetual alms.

In 3 Hen. 2. this Walter was governor of the castle at
Landovery ; and when Roger, Earl of Clare, (having obtained of King Henry all such lands as he could win from
the Welch, came with an army to Cardigan, and fortified divers castles in those parts), this Walter de Clifford
made an incursion upon the lands of Rees ap Griffith,
Prince of South Wales : slew many of his people, and
returned with much booty.

In 12 Hen. 2. this Walter possessed the lordships of
Corfham, Culminton, Hay, Ernestry, and Lechines, in
the county of Salop. And gave to the monks of St. Peter's
Abbey, at Gloucester, his manor of East Leech, in exchange
for the lordship of Glasbury, excepting to those monks the
advowson of the church at Glasbury. Moreover, he
gave to the before-specified canons of Haghmon, certain
lands in Sinetun.

He left issue two sons, viz. Walter, his son and heir,
and Richard ; from whom the Cliffords of Frampton, in
Gloucestershire, did descend. Which Richard, in
2 Rich. 1. gave three hundred marks fine for livery of his
lands.

This Walter (de Clifford) also had issue two daughters,
viz : Lucia, first married to Hugh de Say, of Ricard's-
castle, afterwards to Bartholomew de Mortimer ; and
Rosamond, the concubine of Henry the Second ; on whom
that king begot William, sirnamed Longsword, Earl of

Salisbury; which Rosamond died in the life-time of her father, and was buried by Margaret, her mother, in the choir of the nunnery of Godstow, near Oxford. For the health of whose soul, Osbert Fitz-Hugh, a great baron in Herefordshire, (at her father's request, and by the assent of King Henry) gave to those nuns a salt-work in Wiche, called the Cow, belonging to his manor of Wichebald.

This was that beautiful lady, for whom King Henry built that famous labyrinth at Woodstock, where he kept her so, that she could not easily be found by his jealous queen; and gave her a cabinet of such admirable workmanship, that on it, the fighting of champions, the moving of cattle, the flying of birds, and swimming of fishes, were so exquisitely represented as if they had been alive. But after the death of King Henry, there was little regard had to her memory: for when Hugh, Bishop of Lincoln, in the year 1191, visiting his diocese, came to Godstow, and went up to the altar to do his devotions, observing a herse covered with silk, and divers lamps burning about it, which the nuns at that time had in great veneration, he inquired of the standers by whose it was: and they answering, it was the Fair Rosamund's, whom King Henry so dearly loved, and for whose sake he had been a munificent benefactor to their poor house, by giving large revenues for the maintenance of those lights, he replied; "Take her hence and bury her out of the church with the others." Whereupon they did so.

It is said elsewhere that her body was buried in the chapter-house of that nunnery with this epitaph:

Hic jacet in tumba, Rosa mundi, non rosa munda,
Non redolet, sed olet, quæ redolere solet.

WALTER III.

I now come to Walter de Clifford, the eldest son of the last Walter. This Walter, whilst his father lived, was called Walter de Clifford Junior, and took to wife Agnes, the sole daughter and heir to Roger de Cundi, lord of the manors of Covenby, and Glentham, in the county of Lincoln.

In the reign of King John he was several times sheriff of Herefordshire; but all that I have further seen of him is, that by the consent of Agnes his wife, he confirmed to the monks of. Barklings, in Lincolnshire, certain lands which they had purchased ; and also that he gave to the Gilbertines, at Brodholme, in Nottinghamshire, the church of St. Helen, and the site of a mill. He departed this life in 7 Hen. 3 ; for it appears that Walter his son and heir, then accounting 100*l.* for his *relief*, had livery of the barony descended to him by the death of his father.

WALTER IV.

In consideration of his good and faithful services to King Henry III. he had a discharge of 94*l*. 6s. out of the sum above-mentioned ; and was afterwards constituted governor of the castles of Carmarthen, and Cardigan.

Upon the death of Roger, his younger brother, he gave 100*l*. fine to the king for the wardship and marriage of his heir ; but afterwards adhering to Richard Marischal, Earl of Pembroke, then in arms upon specious pretences, which the king looked upon as rebellious, he was outlawed, and his lands bestowed on those Poitevins, who then bore all the sway. Whereupon command was given to the sheriff of Shropshire to seize his castle and manor of Corfham. Howbeit, this displeasure did not last long ; for the year following, his castle of Clifford, which he had given up as a pledge for his fidelity, was rendered to him again.

In 25 Hen. 3, upon the accord made betwixt Senena, wife of Griffith, son of Lewelin, Prince of North Wales, and King Henry, this Walter was one of the pledges for her in the name of her husband, that full performance should be made thereof.

In 38 Hen. 3, upon the aid then levied for making the king's eldest son knight, he answered for nine knights fees : and being one of the Barons Marchers, was commanded to assist Humphrey de Bohun, Earl of Hereford, in defending the marches of Wales.

In 42 Hen. 3, he had command to attend the king at Chester, with horse and arms to oppose the incursions of the Welsh; and was required to assist Roger de Mortimer, in defence of the Marches, against the like incursions.

At the coronation of Queen Eleanor, wife of King Henry the Third, he claimed with the rest of the Barons Marchers, as *Jus Marchiæ*, to carry the canopy which belonged to the barons of the Cinque Ports.

As to his works of piety, he gave to the canons of Hagmon in Shropshire, his mills at Culmiton, and Sinetun, for the maintenance of their kitchen, with one yard-land, and a messuage belonging to those mills. To the monks of Dore he gave a large territory, set forth in his grant by metes and bonds, as also divers lands in Canterscliff. And to the nuns of Aconbury in Herefordshire, he bestowed certain lands in Corfham.

He married Margaret, daughter to Lewelyn Prince of Wales : who surviving him, bequeathed her heart to be buried in the church of the nuns at Aconbury, with fifteen marks sterling, for performing the solemntiy at the sepulture thereof. He left issue by her, one only daughter, called Maud, first married to William de Longespée, Earl of Salisbury, and afterwards to Sir John Giffard, of Brimsfield. Which Maud, by his consent, gave to the canons of Barlings, in Lincolnshire, the lordships of Covenby and Glentham, in that county.

This Walter died in the 48 Hen. 3.

ROGER I.

Having now finished my discourse of him, I come to Roger his brother, from whom the succeeding barons of of this family did descend.

In 15 John, he had the honour of Kinton in Hereford-shire committed to his custody ; and in 1 Hen. 3, had a grant of the manor of Axeford, part of the possessions of Ralph de la Bruere, then in arms against the king, to hold during pleasure. Upon levying the scutage of Kery, in in Wales, in regard that he was personally in that expedition, he was acquitted for nineteen knights fees, which were of the inheritance of Sibill, his wife, daughter and coheir of Robert de Ewyas, a great baron in Hereford-shire.

He attended King Henry III. into Britanny ; and being there, obtained a grant of the marriage of Hawise, the widow of John Boterell, for the behoof of Roger, his son and heir.

But more I cannot say of him, than that by the advice of Sibill, his wife he bequeathed his body to be buried in the church of the abbey of Dore, near to the grave of one of his sons, who died in his lifetime: also that he thereupon confirmed to the monks of that house, all those lands which William de Ewyas had formerly given them, for which he himself had formerly questioned their title ; and that he departed this life, in 16 Hen. 3. Hereupon Walter de Clifford, his eldest brother then living, had a grant from the king of the custody of his lands, with the ward-ship and marriage of his heir, whose name also was Roger.

ROGER II.

———

This Roger, upon levying the aid for marrying the king's eldest daughter, paid nineteen pounds for those 19 knights' fees, which he had by descent from Robert de Ewyas, his grandfather by the mother; and afterwards attended king Henry III. in his expedition into France.

By the same king he was prohibited to tilt, or to appear in arms, without licence, especially during the king's abode beyond sea.

In 47 Henry 3, he received a command to attend the king at Hereford, on the third day after the Epiphany, well fitted with horse and arms, to restrain the incursions of the Welsh. The same year, being made governor of the castles of Merleburgh, and Luggarshull in Wiltshire, he was seduced by the rebellious barons under the specious pretence of asserting the laws, and peoples' liberties; and being in arms on that account, did much mischief by divers sacrilegious actings, and otherwise : for which, together with Montfort, Earl of Leicester, and many more, he underwent the sentence of excommunication, pronounced against him by the archbishop of Canterbury. But the next year, he fell off from those seeming patriots, and being with the king at the siege of Northampton, was soon after made governor of the castle at Gloucester and sheriff of that county.

Shortly after this, he hastened into Wales, and with Roger de Mortimer, and other Barons'-Marchers, gave battle to Prince Leweline, who had confederated with Montfort, and his fellow-rebels, to make a disturbance in those parts. But when he heard of the fatal over-

G

throw which the king had received in the battle of Lewes, and that he was a captive in the hands of that insolent rebel Montfort, Earl of Leicester ; disdaining that his so_vereign should long abide in that sad condition, he joined with Mortimer, and other loyal barons, and raised such a power against those proud usurpers, as soon after brought them to ruin in the battle of Evesham.

Moreover, having so stoutly adhered to the king in his greatest distresses ; after his deliverance by that happy victory at Evesham, in part of reward for those eminent services, he obtained the custody of the lands of Isabel, one of the daughters and coheirs of Robert de Vipont, a great baron in the north : and was also made Justice of all the king's forests south of Trent, with a grant of the lordship of Kingsbury in Warwickshire, by reason of the forfeiture of Sir Ralph Bracebrigge, knight.

Robert de Vipont, having been of the party of the rebellious barons, died before his composition was made for that transgression ; but so great were the merits of this Roger de Clifford, whose son Roger married Isabel, that nothing of fine was exacted from her for her father's offence.   Nor was this all, but in further contemplation of the notable assistance, and singular valour of this Roger, manifested in divers sharp conflicts, then had with those rebellious barons, the king totally remitted to him a debt of 399*l.* 17s. which otherwise he was to have paid.

Shortly after, he was constituted one of the Justices Itinerant ; and the same year, was one of the sureties for that great rebel, Robert de Ferrers, Earl of Derby, as to the payment of 50,000*l.*, all upon one day, for the redemption of his forfeited lands.

In 54 Henry 3, being signed with the cross, in order to join an expedition with Prince Edward to the Holy Land, he went thither accordingly.   After this, being at St.

George, near the castle of Beaufort, in France, he contracted matrimony with the Countess of Lauretania, whom he enfeoffed, before marriage, in the manor of Weverham, in Cheshire.

In 2 Edward 1, he was sent in commission with others, to Montgomery, to examine, hear, and reform, the wrongs and trespasses done by Prince Lewelyn, contrary to the form of peace concluded betwixt him and Henry the Third.

In 5 Edw. 1, he was made governor of Erdeslegh-castle in Herefordshire; and was constituted one of the justices of the king's forests in Hampshire, being then called Roger de Clifford, senior; and likewise justice of Wales. In this office, having been somewhat oppressive, as may seem by certain complaints made against him, he was surprised upon Palm Sunday, in Hawardine-castle, in Flintshire, by David, son of the Prince of Wales; who, then contrary to his faith, broke out into open hostility. This being made known to the king, he soon marched thither with an army; but in one of the skirmishes with the Welsh, Roger, his son, called Roger de Clifford, jun. was unhappily slain, on St. Leonard's Day, between Snowden and Anglesea, by inadvertently passing Newy Bridge, over the river Conway. Upon his death, Isabel his widow, daughter and coheir to Robert de Vipont, doing her homage, had livery of her lands.

Roger, his father, surviving him, departed this life about four years afterwards (1286); whereupon command was given to seize all his goods and chattels for certain debts which he owed to the king, but with an exception from meddling with the jewels of the Countess of Lauretania, his wife.

G 2

ROBERT I.

To him succeeded Robert de Clifford, his grandson
and heir, son of Roger his son, so slain, as hath been observed, who paid 100*l*. for his relief.

In the year 1300, he was one of the peers in the parliament then held at Lincoln, who subscribed that letter
to the Pope, whereby they declared king Edward's right
to the superiority in dominion of the realm of Scotland ; in which he is written *Robertus de Clifford, Cas-
tellanus de Appelby*. And being afterwards in the Scottish wars with king Edward, he worthily shared in the
glory of that signal victory, which the English then obtained at Dunbar.

On the death of Richard Fitz-John, a great baron in
Essex, this Robert de Clifford, (son of Isabel, daughter of
Robert de Vipont, by Isabel, his wife, sister and coheir
to Richard Fitz-John) was found to be one of the cousins
and next heirs to the same Richard Fitz-John.

The same year, he was sent with 100 men at arms,
and 20,000 foot, from Carlisle, to plunder in Scotland ;
whence, having made great spoil in Anandale, by burning
of whole towns, and much slaughter, he returned on
Christmas Eve, with store of booty. The same year he
was constituted justice of all the king's forests beyond the
Trent.

In 26 Edw. 1, he was made governor of Nottingham-
castle, and went again to the wars in Scotland.

The following year, being constituted the king's lieutenant, and captain-general, in the counties of Cumberland, Westmoreland, and Lancaster ; as also throughout

all Anandale, and the marches of Scotland ; he was joined
in commission with the bishop of Durham, and divers
other great lords, to consider of garrisoning the castles in that realm, as also for guarding of the marches.

Being again in the wars of Scotland, during several
years, in consideration of his many great services, he obtained a grant from the king of the borough of Hartlepool, and of all the lands of Robert de Brus, Earl of
Carrick, (then called an enemy and a rebel) which lay in
his bishopric of Durham, and belonged to the manor of
Hart, which had formerly been given to this Robert de
Clifford for like services.

In the same year the king himself, marching towards
Scotland with a great army, sent this Robert before him,
against Robert de Brus, who then assumed the title of
King of Scotland, in derogation of King Edward ; and in
further remuneration of his services, he gave him the
lands of Christopher de Seyton, then attainted, which
lay in Cumberland, as also all those lands, which were the
inheritance of Erminia, mother of the same Christopher.

Being again in Scotland, he came to King Edward
when he lay on his death-bed, at Burgh on the Sands, in
Cumberland ; being one of the lords then desired to take
care that Piers Gaveston might not any more return into
England to debauch Prince Edward.

In 1 Edw. 2, he was again made governor of Nottingham-castle ; in which year, by a special instrument under
his seal, bearing date at Boulogne, he joined with that
great prelate, Anthony, then Bishop of Durham, and
other lords, who engaged themselves to support the honor
and dignity of the king with their lives and fortunes.

In 2 Edw. 2, he was constituted warden of the marches
in Scotland, afterwards captain-general, and governor
of that whole realm ; with power to give protection to

all those who should submit to King Edward's authority.

In 3 Edw. 2, he had a grant for life of the castle of Skipton in Craven, performing the like services to the crown, as the Earls of Albemarle, formerly lords thereof, used to do. But afterwards, in exchange for certain lands in Monmouth, with the valley of Monmouth, and the town and wood of Hodenake ; he obtained the inheritance of the castle, manor, lands, knights' fees, and advowsons of churches thereunto belonging, as appeareth by the king's special charter, dated at Newcastle upon Tyne, 7 Sept. 4 Edw. 2.

The same year, receiving command, amongst other great men, to be at Roxburgh, in Scotland, well fitted with horse and arms to march against the Scots ; he was there accordingly.

In 6 Edward 2, he was joined in commission with the Earl of Hereford and others, to continue a treaty with Lodowike, Earl of Evreux, and Bishop of Poitou, concerning matters of great importance to the king himself, and some of the chief men in England ; which treaty was to be held at London, but none of the commissioners, nor any of their retinue were to lodge within the city.

This Robert sat in all the parliaments from 28 Edw, 1, till 7 Edw. 2, inclusive.

He was one of those potent men, who joined with Thomas, Earl of Lancaster, in putting Piers de Gaveston, that great favourite of King Edward's to death ; for which transgressioin he had his pardon about this time.

But being again in the wars of Scotland, he was there slain in that fatal battle at Bannockburn, with many other gallant Englishmen ; but his body was sent to King Edward, then at Berwick, to be buried as he should think fit.

ROGER III.

He left Roger his son, fifteen years of age, during whose minority, the king granted the custody of the castles of Skipton, Appleby, Brougham, and Pendragon, and also two parts of the lands, with the profits of the sheriffalty of Westmorland, to Guy de Beauchamp, Earl of Warwick: and unto Maud, the widow of Robert, was assigned the manor of Tenbury, with other lordships and tenements to hold in dower. Which Maud was afterwards married to Robert de Welle, a great baron in Lincolnshire.

This Roger, before he was full 21 years of age, marched into Scotland, in the expedition then made thither; but after this, being drawn into the party of Thomas, Earl of Lancaster, as also into the consultation at Pomfret, when that Earl was advised to go to his own castle at Dunstanburgh, in Northumberland; and observing that the earl refused so to do, lest he should be suspected of holding intelligence with the Scots; this Roger drew his dagger, and threatened to kill him with his own hands, if he would not go with him. Whereupon thus forced, the earl went to his own, and all their sorrows; for in his march to Boroughbridge, receiving an utter overthrow by the king's forces, he was taken prisoner; and with him this our Roger de Clifford, who soon after suffered death for the same, with the Lord Mowbray, at York.

After this the king granted two parts of his house in London, called Clifford's Inn, which by this his forfeiture came to the crown, unto Ralph de Welle, before mentioned, to hold during pleasure; and some of his lordships in Westmoreland, and Northumberland, with the castle and honor of Skipton, to Anthony de Lacy, and Geoffrey le Scrope, for term of life. This Roger, who thus died, had been twice summoned to parliament by Edward II.

ROBERT II.

To him succeeded Robert de Clifford, his brother and next heir in blood, who in 1 Edw. 3, upon the death of Maud his mother, was 22 years of age, and then doing his homage had livery of his lands.

In 3 Edw. 3, he obtained from Idonea, his great aunt, (the coheiress of Robert de Vipont) all her right and title to her purparty in Westmoreland, who afterwards dying without issue, the right thereunto devolved to him.

In 4 Edw. 3, he procured the king's charter for a market upon Thursday every week, at his manor of Burgh, upon Staynemore in Westmorland; and a fair yearly, to begin two days before the feast of St. Matthew the Apostle, and to continue for two days.

In 7 Edm. 3, being in the wars in Scotland, in consideration of his great expenses and losses in the king's service, command was sent to the king's purveyor at Berwick upon Tweed, to give him a tun of wine and six quarters of wheat, out of the stores there, for his better support in that employment.

About this time Edward de Baliol, King of Scotland, hunting in the woods and chases of this Robert, was entertained by him at his castles of Appelby and Brougham.

In 8 Edw. 3, he was joined in commission with Ranulph de Dacre, in the government of Carlisle, and wardenship of the marches adjacent, with power to make choice of able men for the security of both, and the next year was constituted sole warden of the marches of Cumberland and Westmoreland; as also captain-general of all the forces in those countries, for resisting the power of the Scotch.

In 14 Edw. 3, he gave the moiety of the hamlet of Winderton, in the county of Warwick, to the canons of Hagmon in Shropshire.

In 15 Edw. 3, he was again in the Scottish wars; but in 18 Edw. 3, he departed this life, being then possessed of various manors and castles in the counties of Dorset, Hereford, York, Westmoreland, Cumberland, and the bishopric of Durham.

Isabel his widow, daughter of Maurice, Lord Berkeley, then holding a certain mansion, in the parish of St. Dunstan in the West, in the suburbs of London, demised it to the apprentices of the Bench, (the students of law there being then called by that name) for the rent of ten pounds a year.

ROBERT III.

Robert, his son and heir, being only thirteen years of age, his wardship, with the sheriffalty of Westmorland, was committed to Ralph de Nevill, a great baron of that time; whose daughter Eufemia he took to wife, but died before he attained to his full age.

He had two younger brothers, Roger his successor, and Thomas, who was afterwards a knight, and was grandfather to Richard, Bishop of Worcester.

ROGER IV.

In 28 Edw. 3, he made proof of his age ; and the next year was in the expedition made into Gascony, along with Thomas de Beauchamp, Earl of Warwick, whose daughter Maude he had wedded.

In 30 Edw. 3, he was one of those northern barons who received command to repair to the marches of Scotland, for defence of those parts against the Scotch.

In 33 and 34 Edw. 3, he was again in Gascony.

In 40 Edw. 3, he made the park at Skipton, and inclosed there five hundred acres of land in Greenhill, and Lysterfield, together with Calder woods.

In the latter years of King Edward III. and beginning of the reign of King Richard II. he was several times in the wars in France ; and was appointed by those two monarchs, one of the warders of the marches of Scotland, sheriff of Cumberland, and governor of the castle of Carlisle.

In 8 Rich. 2, being then a knight banneret, he was re tained by indenture to serve the king in his Scottish wars for forty days. Moreover, he had summons to all the parliaments from 31 Edw. 3, until 12 Rich. 2, inclusive. He departed this life the following year, leaving Thomas his son and heir, and two daughters ; Mary, married to Sir Philip Wentworth, and Margaret, to Sir John Melton, knight.

Cotemporary with this last mentioned Roger, was John de Clifford, (his brother as I guess) who in 33 Edw. 3, was in an expedition then made into Gascony ; and in 44 Edw. 3, again in the wars of France ; and of the retinue of Sir Robert Knolles, knight, being then called John de Clifford de Ewias.

In 51 Edw. 3, on the testimony of divers of the English peers in parliament of the singular valour of this John, then a knight, and of his special services in the wars of France, the king at the instance of those peers, and of *the whole commons of England, then assembled in parliament,* pardoned him the murder of John de Coupland.

About this time there was likewise another knight of this family called Sir Thomas de Clifford, (a younger brother as I think of this last-mentioned John) who was of the retinue of William de Windsore, in the wars of Ireland.

In 3 Rich 2, he was in an expedition then made into Britanny, being of the retinue with Thomas de Percy. In 7 Rich. 2, this Sir Thomas was retained to serve the king in his wars in the marches of Scotland, having divers of the king's tenants, at Penrith in Cumberland, under his command in that service. At the same time, he made a covenant by indenture with Sir John Lowther, of Lowther in the county of Westmoreland, knight, touching the government of Thomas Clifford, his son and heir, and his men as well in war as in peace.

THOMAS.

This Thomas was before his father's death, much exercised in military affairs; and in 8 Rich. 2, beng a knight of the king's chamber, was constituted governor of Carlisle for life.

This gallant man had summons to the several parlaliaments held in his time ; but died in the flower of his youth, 15 Rich. 2, leaving issue by Elizabeth, daughter of Thomas Lord Roos of Hamlake, John, his son and heir, then scarce three years of age, and a daughter called Maud, who became the second wife of Richard, Earl of Cambridge, and afterwards of John Nevill, Lord Latimer.

This last mentioned Thomas had two younger brothers, Sir William Clifford, Knt. who in 5 Henry 4, was governor of the town of Berwick upon Tweed, and married Anne, one of the daughters and coheirs of Thomas Lord Bardolph. Which Sir William died in 6 Henry 5, without issue, leaving John Lord Clifford, his cousin, his heir.

The other brother was Sir Lewis Clifford, Knt. whose memory is not a little famous, in two respects : first, that he was one of the companions of the most noble order of the Garter ; and 2dly, that having been seduced by those hotheaded zealots of that time, called Lollards, of whom he was one of the chiefs, and being at length sensible of his error, did cordially repent, as may seem by those remarkable expressions which he used in his last will and testament, a transcript whereof I have thought fit here to exhibit.

In Nomine Patris et Filii et Spiritus Sancti. *Amen.*

The seventeenthe day of September, the yere, of our Lord Jesu Christ, a thousand foure hundred and foure, I Lowys Clyfforth, fals and traytor to my Lord God, and to all the blessed company of heavene, and unworthi to be clepyd a Cristen man, make and ordeyne my testament, and my last will in this manere. At the begynning, I most unworthi and Goddis traytor, recommáunde my wrechid and synfule Soule, hooly to the Grace and to the grete mercy of the blessed trynytie : and my wrechid careyne to be beryed in the ferthest corner of the chirchezerd, in which Pariche my wrechid Soule departeth fro my body. And I pray and charge my survivors and myne executors, as they woollen answere tofore God, and as all myne hoole trust in this matter is in hem, that on my stinking careyne be neyther leyd clothe of gold ne of silke ; but a black clothe, and a taper at myne hed, and another at my fete ; ne stone, ne other thinge, whereby any man may witt where my stinking careyne liggeth. And to that Chirche do mine Executors all thingis which owen duly in such caas to be don, without eny more cost, soaf to poore men. And also I pray my survivors and executors, that eny dette that eny man can axe me, by true title, that hit be payed. And yf eny man kan trewly sey, that I have do hym any harme, in body or in good, that ye make largely his gree, whyles the goodys wole streeche.

And I wole also that none of my executors meddle or mynystre any thinge of my goodys withoutyn avyse and consent of my Survivors, or sum of hem.

Now first I bequethe to Sire Phylype la Vache, Knight, my Masse-booke, and my Porhoose ; and my Booke of Tribulacion to my daughter his wyf.

Et quicquid residuum fuerit omnium et singulorum bonorum et catalorum, etc. etc.

Probat, 5 Dec. 1404. (6 H. 4.)

From which Sir Lewis Clifford, the Cliffords of Kent, Wiltshire, and Devonshire, are lineally descended. And among those of Devonshire, Sir Thomas Clifford, Knight, who for his singular merits, having been first comptroller, then treasurer of the household to his majesty King Charles II. was advanced to the dignity of Lord Clifford of Chudleigh, and soon after to the office of lord high treasurer of England.

JOHN I.

But I return to John, son and heir to Thomas Lord Clifford, who making proof of his age, in 12 Henry 4, had livery of his lands; and in 3 Henry 5, was in the expedition then made into France.

In 4 Henry 5, he was by indenture retained to serve the king, in his navy at sea, towards the north, for the safeguard of those parts, with two hundred men at arms and 400 archers; and to have four shillings *per diem* for himself, and two shillings a piece for his knights.

About this time, Ralph Nevill, the first Earl of Westmorland, holding a great tournament at Carlisle, this Lord Clifford, and six other English justed with as many Scots, in which exercise the English had the prize.

In 6 Henry 5, he was again employed in the wars in France, and in 9 Henry 5, attended the king in person thither.

He was summoned to the several parliaments, from 13 Henry 4, till 8 Henry 5, inclusive.

In 9 Henry 5, he was instituted knight of the most noble order of the Garter. But 10 Henry 5, departed this life, being slain at the sige of Meaux, in France : leaving, by Elizabeth, his wife, daughter to Henry Percy, commonly called Hotspur, son and heir to Henry, Earl of Northumberland, Thomas, his son and heir, seven years of age.

THOMAS II.

Which Thomas, in 13 Henry 6, there being then great apprehensions that the Scotch would lay siege to Berwick, and other strong holds in the marches of Scotland, was joined in commission with the Earl of Nortumberland, to arm and array all knights, esquires, and yeomen, in several counties, and march withthem for the safeguard of those parts.

Iu 24 Henry 6, he gave to the Friars Carmelites, at Appleby, at the request of the Conutess of Cambridge, his aunt, timber for repairing and building their house, to be taken out of the forest of Whinfell.

In 29 Henry 6, he was also joined in commission with the Bishop of Durham, and others, to treat with the ambassadors of James, King of Scotland, for a truce between both kingdoms : and had summons to the several parliaments, from 15 to 31 Henry 6.

But in 33 Hen. 6, having the hard fate to be slain on the king's part, in the battle of St. Albans, was there buried in the Abbey church ; leaving issue, by Joan his wife, daughter of Thomas Lord Dacre, four sons ; John, his son and heir ; Sir Roger Clifford, knight, who married one of the sisters and coheirs of —— Courtenay, of ——, in the county of Devon ; Sir Thomas Clifford, knight, a person of great esteem with King Henry VIII. and by him much employed in affairs of state ; and Robert, who was deep in the business of Perkin Warbeck, in the time of King Henry VII.

JOHN II.

In 38 Hen. 6, he was made commissary-general of the Marches towards Scotland, and the same year summoned to parliament.

In 39 Hen. 6, being in the battle of Wakefield, on the king's part, who gained the victory, he is reported to have made so great a slaughter with his own hands, that he was thenceforth called the butcher. And standing ever firm to the Lancastrian interest, in those bloody wars, betwixt that and the House of York, was at length slain, upon Palm Sunday, at Towton Field in Yorkshire, 1 Edw. 4, leaving by Margaret, his wife, daughter and heir to Henry Bromeflete, Lord Vescy, Henry, his son and heir, and Richard, who died in the Netherlands without issue.

Which Margaret brought the title of Lord Vesci to this noble family.

H

HENRY I.

Of this Henry, before I come to his memorable actions, it will not, I presume, be thought impertinent, to give a brief account of the preservation he had from his childhood, till the time that by God's providence, he came quietly to enjoy all his lands and honours.

There is nothing more certain, than that the eager pursuit of wordly wealth and power, hath often transported multitudes of men to the most bold and desperate adventures imaginable ; and that those ambitious aims have not seldom occasioned bloody wars, with merciless slaughter, and dreadful ruin to many : whereof though examples in all nations have been numerous, I shall here only take notice of that in the houses of York and Lancaster ; which continuing for some ages, produced much misery and destruction to divers great and noble families, wherein this of Clifford shared deeply. Thomas, the grandfather of this our Henry, having been slain in the battle of St. Albans, and John, his father, in that of Towton, stout assertors of the Lancasterian interest. So that it cannot be doubted, but that the house of York, at length potently prevailing, had cause enough to be jealous of those whose ancestors' blood had been spilt in the adverse quarrel ; and not to be slack in their extirpation, before they could be ripe for any considerable attempt, which happened to be the case of this Henry, then but seven years of age, as also Richard, his younger brother.

Concerning whom, strict enquiry being made, and

their sorrowful mother examined about them, she said, she had given directions to convey them beyond the sea, and was ignorant whether they were living or not ; part of which answer was true, for she had really sent the younger into the Netherlands, where he died soon after ; but, the elder she placed at Longsborough, in Yorkshire, where she herself then lived, with a shepherd, who had married one of her inferior servants, an attendant on his nurse ; where, though he was brought up in no better condition than the shepherd's own children ; yet as he grew to discretion, he cheerfully submitted thereto as the only expedient for the preservation of his life, supporting himself with hopes of better days in time.

But no sooner did the death of his grandfather Lord Vesci happen, but rumours were brought to court that the young Lord Clifford was alive. Which being made known to his mother, she, by the help of her second husband, Sir Launcelot Threlkeld, conveyed the honest shepherd, with his wife and family, into Cumberland, where she took a farm towards the Scottish bordres ; and sometimes at Threlkeld, and other places on those borders, visited this her beloved child.

In which obscure condition, he continued until the beginning of King Henry the Seventh's reign, being then no less than thirty-one years of age, and so meanly bred, that he was not taught to read, his estate all the while being possessed by his enemies.

But in 1 Hen. 7, being restored to his lands and honours, he then first learned to write his name ; and having repaired all his castles which were in a ruinous condition, he became a great builder, especially at Barden Tower, in Yorkshire, where, for the most part, he made his residence, by reason of its vicinity to the priory of Bolton ; to the end he might have opportunity to converse with

H 2

some of the canons of that house, who were well versed in Astronomy: unto which study, having a singular affection, perhaps in regard of his solitary shepherd's life, which gave him time for contemplation, he fitted himself with divers instruments for use therein.

As to what is farther memorable of him, all that I have seen is, that in 1 Hen. 7, he had summons to the parliament then held, and to all the succeeding parliaments of that king's reign, and of King Henry VIII. till he died.

In 2 Hen. 7, he had a command in the army raised to march against James IV. King of Scotland; and in 5 Hen. 8, was one of the principal commanders who gave battle to the Scots at Flodden, where the English obtained a glorious victory, the King of Scots being there slain.

He took to wife Anne, daughter of Sir John St. John of Bletso, cousin-german to King Henry VII. and by his last will, bequeathed his body to be buried in the Abbey of Shap, or Bolton in Craven. He departed this life, in 1523, being then about 70 years of age.

HENRY,

FIRST EARL OF CUMBERLAND.

Henry his son and heir, is said in his youth to have been profuse and undutiful, yet in time he was reclaimed, and in 1525 was advanced to the title and dignity of Earl of Cumberland, at the king's royal palace in London, called Bridewell.

In 22 Hen. 8, he was one of the lords then sitting in parliament, who subscribed that letter to Pope Clement VII. whereby they importuned him to ratify King Henry's divorce from Queen Catherine, his first wife.

In 1532, he was made a knight of the most noble order of the Garter; and afterwards constituted warden of the West Marches towards Scotland, governnor of the town and castle of Carlisle, and president of the king's counsel in the North.

In 33 Hen. 8, the monasteries being then totally dissolved, he acquired the scite of the priory of Bolton, with all the lands thereto belonging in the parish of Skipton, together with nine manors in the county of York.

In 34 Hen. 8, he was one of the principal commanders in the army which then invaded Scotland.

This Earl Henry had two wives; first, Margaret, daughter of George Talbot, Earl of Shrewsbury; 2dly, Margaret, daughter of Henry Percy, Earl of Northumberland: by whom he had two sons, Henry Lord Clifford, and Sir Ingelram Clifford, who married Anne, daughter and sole heir of Sir Henry Ratcliff, by whom he had a fair inheritance, but dying issueless, left his nephew George Earl of Cumberland, his heir.

Henry Lord Clifford, first Earl of Cumberland, died in the year 1542.

HENRY.

Henry his son and heir, who succeeded him in all his honors, had two wives; first, Eleanor, daughter and coneir to Charles Brandon, Duke of Suffolk, by Mary, Queen of France, second daughter to King Henry VII. by whom he had a daughter Margaret, afterwards Countess of Derby, and two sons who died young. His second wife was Anne, daughter of William Lord Dacre, by whom he had issue George and Francis, and three daughters. He died in the year 1569, at Brougham-castle, and was buried at Skipton.

GEORGE.

To him succeeded George his son and heir, who in 1592, was elected knight of the Garter, and married Margaret, daughter of Francis Earl of Bedford ; and by her had issue two sons, Francis Lord Clifford, who dying young was buried in the vault at Skipton ; and Robert Lord Clifford, who likewise died young, and was buried at Cheneys, in Buckinghamshire, in the vault with his mother's ancestors : and also, one only danghter and heir called Anne.

Departing this life at the Savoy, in the suburbs of London, on the 3oth of October, 1605, he was honourably buried with his ancestors, in the vault to Skipton in Craven, on the 3oth of March following : leaving the same Lady Anne his sole daughter and heir.

FRANCIS.

To this Earl George succeeded Francis his brother, who took to wife Grisold. daughter of Thomas Hughes of Uxbridge, Esq. : by whom he had one son, called Henry, and two daughters.

This Earl Francis died at Skipton-castle, in 1641, and lies buried with his ancestors in the vault of that chancel.

HENRY.

To him succeeded Henry his only son, who married Frances, only daughter of Robert Cecil, Earl of Salisbury, lord high treasurer of England ; and departing this life at York, in 1643, lies also buried in the same vault at Skipton with his ancestors.

He left issue one only daughter his heir, who married in 1635, Richard Boyle, Viscount Dungarvon, son and heir to Richard Earl of Cork ; who by King Charles I. was created Lord Clifford of Lonsborough, and afterwards by Charles II. Earl of Burlington.

Thus ended the male line of this ancient and right noble family, and consequently the dignity of Earl of Cumberland became extinct.

APPENDIX.---No. II.

From " *Collins's Peerage.*"—Vol. I. p. 262.

Francis Russel, Earl of Bedford, in 13 Eliz. obtained the wardship of George Earl of Cumberland, on which occasion he sent the following letter:

" It may please your most excellent Majestie to be advertised that heretofore (as it is well knowne to many) there hath been communication between my Lord of Cumberland and mee, for the marriage of his sonne to one of my daughters ; and being now informed that he is in some danger, I do presume to be a sutor to your Highness, that I may have the wardship of his sonne, if it shall soe stand with youre Majestie's pleasure ; and herein I shall think myself most bounden (as 1 have every way good cause) to your Highness. And thus I beseech God to send unto your Majestie a most prosperous healthfull raigne, to God's glory, and your heart's desire, etc.

" From Russel-place, this 3d of Jany. 1570."

P. 264.

Lady Margaret Russel, his youngest daughter, married (on 24 June 1577) to George Earl of Cumberland, Baron Clifford, Westmorland, and Vescy, knight of the Garter. She died 24 May 1616 at Brougham-castle, and is buried in the parish church of St. Lawrence of Appleby in Cumberland, with the following memorial.

Here lieth the Body of Lady Margaret, Countess
Dowager of Cumb^d. youngest Child to Francis
Russel, second Earl of Bedford marry'd to George
Clifford, third Earl of Cumb^d. She lived his
wife 29 years, and dy'd his widow at Browham Castle the 24th of May 1616, ten years and seven months
after his decease. She had issue by him, two sons
Francis and Robert, who both died young ; and
one daughter, the Lady Anne Clifford marry'd to
Richard Sackville, third Earl of Dorsett, who erected this Monument Anno Dom. 1617.

Who, faith, love, mercy, Noble Constancy,
To God, to Vertue, to Distress, to Right,
Observ'd, Express'd, shew'd, Held Religiously,
Hath here this Monument, thou seest in light,
The Cover of her Earthy Part, but Passenger
Know Heaven and Fame, contain the best of her.

Vol. II. page 478.

The war ending in a truce in 1412, Sir William Doug-
lass, and the Lord Clifford, were the chief challengers at
a solemn tournament, held by the Earl of Westmorland,
at Carlisle.

P. 486.

James, Duke of Queensberry, married December 1,
1685, Mary Boyle, second daughter of Charles Lord Clifford, eldest son of Richard Earl of Burlington and Cork,
by Jane Seymour, daughter of William Duke of Somerset,
etc.

P. 515.

Sir Henry Pierrepont, being a stout adherer to the house
of York, had in 5 Edw. 4, in recompense of his frequent
and faithful services to King Edw. IV. against the Lan-

castrians, a grant in special tail of the third part of the manour of Staveley, with the advowson of the church (in Com. Derb.) then in the crown, by the attainder of John Lord Clifford.

P. 679.

It appears on record, that in 49 Hen. 3, Roger Lord Clifford had a grant of all the lands and tenements which were Simon de Bruges in Bruges, for his adherence to Simon Montfort, Earl of Leicescer, in his rebellion ; but by the Dictum de Kenilworth, were restored to the owners.

P. 749.

Richard Sackville, third Earl of Dorset, son of Robert by Margaret, only daughter of Thomas Howard, Duke of Norfolk, born 28 March 1589 in the Chartreuse, in London, (after purchased by Mr. Sutton, who founded an hospital there, now called the Charter-House) was married to the Lady Anne Clifford, daughter and heir of George Earl of Cumberland, on the 25th of Feb. 1608, 9, in her mother's chamber, in Augustine-Frier's House, in London ; and two days after his father deceased, whereby he became Earl of Dorset. When he married he was twenty years wanting a month and a day, and his lady was nineteen years and a month. In 1611 his lordship travelled into France and the Low Countries, on a pre-engagement to his grandmother and other friends before he married. He staid beyond the seas about a year, and returned to his seat at Knowle in Kent, on the 8th of April 1612. He lived with great magnificence and hospitality in his houses at Knowle, Bolebrook in Sussex, and Dorset-House in London. This lord died in Great Dorset-House London, when he was just 35 years old, on the 28th March 1624, being Easter Sunday at 12 o'clock at noon, and was buried in the vault in Witherham church in Sussex with his ancestors, the 7th of April following. He had three sons who died infants, and two daughters who survived him : Lady Margaret, born at Dorset-house, the 2d of July, 1614, and in 1629, was married to John Tufton, Earl of Thanet ; and Lady Isabella, born at Knole in Kent, in 1622 ; married in 1647 to James Compton, Earl of Northampton.

Anne, his countess, enjoyed great and extensive possessions of her own family the Cliffords, which she left to her grandson the Earl of Thanet. She was married June 3d, 1630, to Philip Herbert, Earl of Pembroke, lord chamberlain to King Charles I., who left her again a widow in 1650. She was a lady of an admirable judgement, and has left the occurrences of her own life in manuscript, wherein she has given the account before-mentioned of the Earl of Dorset, as also a character of his lordship.

Vol. III. p. 22.

The preamble to the patent of Sir William Wentworth sets forth, that he was lineally descended from John of Gaunt, and from the ancient barons of Newark and Oversley, etc. His ancestors either by father or mother, had matched with divers houses of honour ; as with Maud, Countess of Cambridge, daughter to the Lord Clifford of Westmorland, etc. etc. He married first the Lady Margaret Clifford, daughter to Francis Earl of Cumberland, by whom he had no issue.

P. 81.

Henry Stanley, Earl of Derby, on the 7th Feb. 1555, married Margaret, daughter to Henry Clifford, Earl of Cumberland, and Alianore his wife, one of the daughters and coheirs to Charles Brandon, Duke of Suffolk, by Mary, the Queen Dowager of France, one of King Henry the VIIth's daughters.

P. 351.

John Earl of Thanet, married April 21, 1629, Margaret, the eldest of the two daughters, coheirs to Richard Earl of Dorset, by his wife the Lady Anne Clifford, sole daughter and heir to George Earl of Cumberland, and Baroness Clifford of Westmorland, and Vescy; by whom he had issue six sons. He was succeeded by Nicholas, who in 1664, married Elizabeth, second daughter of Richard Boyle, Earl of Burlington. In the time of the rebellion against King Charles the First, he resided in France, but returned to England before the year 1650. Died in 1679, and was succeeded by his brother John, who in 1676, succeeded his mother Margaret Countess of Thanet, as Baron Clifford, Westmorland, and Vescy. She, by her last will and testament, gave the Yorkshire and Westmorland estates to this John, her second son, for life ; and he also succeeded in 1678, his cousin the Lady Aliathea, sole daughter and heir of James Earl of Northampton, by his first wife the Lady Isabella, his mother's sister, whereby he became vested in the whole inheritance possessed by his grandmother the Countess of Dorset. He was succeeded by his brother Thomas, 1683.

This Thomas Earl of Thanet, as heir to his grandmother Anne, Baroness Clifford, Westmorland, and Vescy, being entitled to those baronies, brought his claim into the House of Lords; whereupon their Lordships came to this resolution, Dec. 12, 1691 ; " That Thomas Earl of Thanet, is the sole lineal and right heir to Robert de Clifford, first summoned to parliament as Lord de Clifford, by writ dated 29th December, 28 Edw. 1 ; and that the said title and barony of Lord Clifford, doth of right belong to the said Earl of Thanet, and his heirs."

Vol. IV. p. 86.

Lord Windsor bequeaths (1585) to the Lord Clifford,

Earl of Cumberland, his best hawke, which he thinks to be the haggard.

P. 274.

Malcolm de Harleigh, about 1290, built that house, now called Clifford's Inn, behind St. Dunstan's church, in Fleet-street, which being seized by the king for certain debts due from the said Malcolm, it was granted in 3 Edw. 2, to Robert de Clifford, Lord Clifford, who made it his habitation, and had thence the name of Clifford's Inn ; but Isabel, the widow of the said Robert, demised it to the students of the law.

P. 689.

Thomas Coke, Earl of Leicester, Viscount Coke of Holkeham, and Lord Lovel, married 1718, the Lady Margaret Tufton, third surviving daughter and coheir to Thomas Earl of Thanet. His majesty was pleased to confirm to his lady and her heirs, the ancient barony of Clifford, together with all the rights, privileges, pre-eminencies, precedencies, immunities, and advantages whatsoever, to the same belonging, or in anywise appertaining, by letters patent, bearing date August 13, 1734, which barony descended to her father, the Earl of Thanet, as lineal heir to the Lady Anne, his grandmother, daughter and heir of George Earl of Cumberland, Baron Clifford, which was adjudged to him by the House of Lords, 12th December 1691.

Vol. V. P. 34.

Henry Lord Percy, in 25 Edw. 1, being with Sir Robert Clifford, commanders of the King of England, in the east parts of Scotland, they were appointed to receive Margery, daughter of Robert Brus, Earl of Carrick, as a hostage for his fidelity to the King of England.

P. 40.

In 8 Edw. 2, on the death of Robert Lord Clifford,

this Lord Percy was constituted one of the commissioners for the custody of the castles of Skipton in Craven, Appleby, Brougham, and Pendragon; and likewise of two parts of the profits of the county of Westmorland, by reason of the minority of Roger de Clifford, son and heir to the said Robert.

P. 50.

He married Idonea, daughter of Robert Lord Clifford. P. 84.

John Lord Clifford married Elizabeth, daughter of Henry Percy, surnamed Hotspur.

Supplement. Vol. II. p. 465.

On the decease of Henry Lord Clifford, last Earl of Cumberland, without issue male, the title of Earl of Cumberland became extinct; and in 19 Car. I. Prince Rupert, grandson of King James I., was created Duke of Cumberland, and Earl of Holderness. But he dying unmarried in 1682, the next who had the title of Duke of Cumberland, was Prince George of Denmark, husband of Queen Anne. He died without issue in 1708. King George II. conferred the dignity of Duke of Cumberland, on his second son Prince William, in the year 1726.

Having thus observed how high and noble those were who had the title of Cumberland, after it became extinct in the family of Clifford, I come now to the Lady Anne, sole daughter and heir to George Earl of Cumberland, in whom the noble titles of Clifford, Westmorland, and Vescy, were existing, as dignities which had their first rise by summons of her ancestors to parliament; and by virtue of the entail, the inheritance of the castles and lands lineally descended to her.

No. III.

From *" Camden's Britannia."*

HEREFORDSHIRE.

Hujus agri partem mediam Vaga, sive Wy intersecat, ad quem in ipso limite occiduo Clivus fortis vulgo Clifford Castrum adsidet, quod Gulielmus Fitz-Osberne Herefordiæ comes in *Wasta sua* (ex Gulielmi Normanni Censuali libro loquor) ædificavit, sed Radulphus de Todeney tenuit. Postea ad Walterum filium Richardi Puntii Normanni devenisse existimatur, ille enim de Cliffordia cognominatus erat, et ad eum illustrissima Cliffordorum Cumbriæ Comitum familia ortum suum vere retulit.

The river Wye runs through the middle of this part of the country, and on its bank, in the very western border, stands Clifford-castle, which William Fitz-Osberne, Earl of Hereford, built on his Waste, (I use the expressions of William the Norman's Domesday Book) but Ranulph de Toeny held it. Afterwards, it is thought to have come to Walter, the son of Richard Ponts, a Norman, for he was surnamed De Clifford, and to him, the most illustrious family of the Cliffords, Earls of Cumberland, truly trace their origin.

WESTMORLAND.

Westmorlandiæ dominus primus (quod sciam) præfuit

Robertus de *Veteriponte,* sive Vipont qui in clypeo rubro sex aureos anellos gestavit. Illi enim donavit Rex Joannes Ballivam et reditus de Westmorland, per servitium qua- tuor militum, unde Cliffordi ejus successores ad nostra usque tempora tenuerunt officium Viseomitatus de West- morland. Robertus enim de Veteriponte ultimus duas so- lummodo filias reliquit, Sibillam Rogeri Domini Cliffordi uxorem, Idoneam Rogero de Leyburne enuptiam.

The first Lord of Westmorland, that I know, was Ro- bert de Veteriponte, or Vipont, who bore on his shield, *Gules, six annulets or.* For King John gave to him the sheriffdom and rents of Westmorland, by the service of four knights' fees; and hence the Cliffords, his successors, held the office of sheriff of Westmorland, down to our times. For the last Robert de Vipont, left only two daughters, Sybilla, the wife of Roger, Lord Clifford, and Idonea, who was married to Roger de Leyburne.

CUMBERLAND.

Comites Cumbriæ ante Henrici Octavi tempora non erant, ille enim Henricum Clifford, qui a dominis de Ve- teriponte sive Vipont genus duxit primum Cumbriæ co- mitem creavit; qui ex Margarita filia Henrici Percy Co- mitis Northumbriæ genuit Henricum Comitem secundum, cui ex prima uxore, filia Caroli Brandon Ducis Suffolciæ nata erat Margareta Comitissa Derbiæ : ex uxore secunda filia Baronis Dacre de Gillesland, duo filii G orgius et Franciscus. Georgius tertius comes navali gloria clarus, ad labores impiger ad pericula fortis obiit 1605. Anna unica filia relicta. Illi autem successit Franciscus frater Comes Quartus, in quo ardor mentis ad virtutem tantis majoribus dignus clarissime elucet.

I

There were no Earls of Cumberland, before the time of King Henry VIII. who created Henry Clifford, descended from the Barons de Vipont, first Earl of Cumberland. By Margaret, daughter of Henry Percy, Earl of Northumberland, he was father of Henry, the second Earl, who by his first wife, daughter of Charles Brandon, Duke of Suffolk, had a daughter, who became Countess of Derby ; by his second wife, daughter of Lord Dacre, of Gillesland, he had two sons, George and Francis. George the third earl, renowned for his naval glory, his ardour for enterprise, and his courage in dangers, died in 1605, leaving Anne, his only daughter. To him succeeded his brother Francis, the fourth Earl, who, on all occasions, has displayed that exalted spirit of honour and virtue, which is worthy of such great and noble ancestors.

No. IV.

From " *Shakespeare's Tragedy of King Henry VI.*"

PART THE SECOND,

Act V.—Scene I.

In the fields near St. Alban's.

Enter York, *attended with drums and colours.*

York. From Ireland thus comes York to claim his
　　right,
And pluck the crown from feeble Henry's head.
Ring bells aloud, burn bonfires clear and bright,
To entertain great England's lawful king.
Let them obey who know not how to rule.

Enter King Henry *aud Attendants,* Queen Margaret
and Somerset.

Q. Marg. Call hither Clifford, bid him come amain,
To say if that the bastard boys of York
Shall be the surety for their traitor father.

Enter Edward *and* Richard.

York. See where they come, I'll warrant they'll make
　　it good.

Enter Clifford.

Q. Marg. And here comes Clifford to deny their bail.

I 2

Cliff. Health and all happiness to my lord the king.

(*Kneels.*

York. We thank thee, Clifford, say, what news with
thee ?
Nay, do not fright us with an angry look,
We are thy sovereign, Clifford, kneel again ;
For thy mistaking so, we pardon thee.

Cliff. This is my king, York, I do not mistake,
But thou mistak'st me much to think I do.
To Bedlam with him ! Is the man grown mad?

K. Henry. Ay, Clifford, a Bedlam and ambitious
humour,
Makes him oppose himself against his king,

Cliff. He is a traitor ; let him to the tower.
And crop away that factious pate of his.

Q. Marg. He is arrested, but will not obey;
His sons, he says, shall give their words for him.

Cliff. Why what a brood of traitors have we here !

York. Look in a glass, and call thy image so.
Call hither to the stake my two brave bears,
Bid Salisbury and Warwick come to me.

Drums—Enter Warwick *and* Salisbury.

Cliff. Are these thy bears? we'll bait thy bears to
death,
And manacle the bear-ward in their chains,
If thou dars't bring them to the baiting place.

York. We shall heat you thoroughly anon.

Cliff. Take heed, lest by your heat you burn yourselves.

K. Henry. Call Buckingham, and bid him arm himself.

York. Call Buckingham and all the friends thou hast,
I am resolved for death, or dignity.

Old Cliff. The first, I warrant thee, if dreams prove
true.

Warw. You had best go to bed and dream again,
To keep thee from the tempest of the field.

Old Cliff. I am resolved to bear a greater storm
Than any thou canst conjure up to-day.
And that I'll write upon thy burgonet, (1)
Might I but know thee by thy house's badge.

Warw. Now by my father's badge, old Nevil's crest,
The rampant bear, chained to the ragged staff,
This day, I'll wear aloft my burgonet,
As on a mountain top the cedar shews,
That keeps his leaves in spite of any storm,
Even to affright thee with the view thereof.

Old Cliff. And from thy burgonet I'll rend thy bear,
And tread it under foot with all contempt,
Despight the bear-ward that protects the bear.

Young Cliff. And so to arms, victorious noble father,
To quell the rebels and their accomplices.

SCENE II.

The Field of Battle near St. Albans.

Enter WARWICK.

War. Clifford of Cumberland ! 'tis Warwick calls.
And if thou dost not hide thee from the bear,
Now when the angry trumpet sounds alarm,
And dying mens' cries do fill the empty air,
Clifford, I say, come forth and fight me!
Proud northern lord, Clifford of Cumberland,
Warwick is hoarse with calling thee to arms.

---

(1) A helmet.

365

Enter York.

How now, my lord, what all a-foot?

York. The deadly-handed Clifford slew my steed;
But match to match I have encountered him,
And made a prey for carrion kites and crows,
Ev'n of the bonny beast he loved so well.

Enter Clifford.

Warw. Of one or both of us the time is come.

York. Hold, Warwick, seek thee out some other chace.
For I myself must hunt this deer to death.

War. Then nobly, York, 'tis for a crown thou fights't.
(*Exit.*

Cliff. What seest thou, in me York, why dost thou
pause?

York. With thy brave bearing should I be in love,
But that thou art so fast mine enemy.

Cliff. Nor should thy prowess want praise and esteem,
But that 'tis shewn ignobly, and in treason.

York. So let it help me now against thy sword,
As I in justice and true right express it!

Cliff. My soul and body on the action both!

York. A dreadful lay! address thee instantly. (*Fight.*

Cliff. La fin couronne les œuvres. (*Dies.*

York. Thus war hath given thee peace, for thou art
still:

Peace with his soul, Heav'n, if it be thy will! *Exit.*

Enter Young Clifford.

Y. Cliff. Shame and confusion! all is on the rout;
Fear frames disorder, and disorder wounds
Where it should guard. O war! thou son of hell,
Whom angry heavens do make their minister,
Throw in the frozen bosoms of our part

Hot coals of vengeance. Let no soldier fly.
He that is truly dedicated to war,
Hath no self-love; and he that loves himself,
Hath not essentially, but by circumstance,
The name of valour.—O! let the vile world end,
And the reserved flames of the last day

(Seeing his dead father.

Knit earth and heaven together! Wast thou ordained, dear
 father,
To loose thy youth in peace, and to obtain
The silver livery of advised age,
And in thy reverence, and thy chair-days, thus
To die in ruffian battle! Even at this sight
My heart is turned to stone; and while 'tis mine,
It shall be stony. York not our old men spares,
No more will I their babes; tears virginal
Shall be to me even as the wood to fire,
And beauty, which the tyrant oft reclaims,
Shall to my flaming wrath be oil and flax.
Henceforth I will not have to do with pity.
Meet I an infant of the house of York,
Into as many gobbets will I cut it,
As wild Medea young Absyrtus did.
In cruelty will I seek out my fame.
Come, thou new ruin of old Clifford's house,
As did Eneas old Anchises bear, *(Taking up the body.*
So I bear thee upon my manly shoulders.
But then Eneas bore a living load!
Nothing so heavy as this woe of mine!   *(Exit.*
     (Fight. Excursions.

Enter King HENRY, *Queen* MARGARET, *and Others.*

Q. Marg. Away, my lord, you are slow, for shame,
 away.

Enter CLIFFORD.

Cliff. But that my heart's on future mischief set,
I would speak blasphemy, ere bid you fly.
But fly you must ; incurable discomfit
Reigns in the hearts of all our present party.
Away, for your relief! and we will live,
To see their day, and them our fortune give.
Away, my lord, away !   (*Exeunt.*

THIRD PART OF KING HENRY VI.

ACT I.—SCENE I.—LONDON.

Alarm. Enter Duke of YORK, WARWICK, *and others,*
with white roses in their hats.

War. I wonder how the king escaped our hands !
York. While we pursued the horsemen of the North,
He slily stole away, and left his men.
Whereat, the great Lord of Northumberland,
Whose warlike ears could never brook retreat,
Cheered up the drooping army ; and himself,
Lord Clifford, and Lord Stafford, all a-breast,
Charged our main battle's front, and breaking in,
Were by the swords of common soldiers slain.
Warw. This is the palace of the fearful king,
And this the regal seat : possess it York,
For this is thine, and not King Henry's heirs.
(Warwick leads York to the throne, who seats himself.

Enter King HENRY, CLIFFORD, *and others.*

K. Henry. My lords look where the sturdy rebel sits,
Even in the chair of state! belike, he means
To aspire unto the crown, and reign as king.
Earl of Northumberland, he slew thy father.
And thine, Lord Clifford ; and you both vowed revenge,
On him, his sons, his favourites, and his friends.

Cliff. The hope thereof makes Clifford mourn in steel.

West. What, shall we suffer this? let's pluck him down.

K. Henry. Be patient, gentle Earl of Westmorland.

Cliff. Patience is for poltroons, and such is he :
He durst not sit there, had your father lived.

K. Henry. Thou factions Duke of York, descend my
        throne,
And kneel for grace and mercy at my feet.
I am thy sovereign.

Warw. Be Duke of Lancaster, let him be king.
We, we are those who chased you from the field,
And slew your fathers, and with colours spread,
Marched through the city to the palace gates.

Cliff. Urge it no more, lest that instead of words,
I send thee, Warwick, such a messenger
As shall revenge their death before I stir.

Warw. Deposed he shall be in despight of thee.

Cliff. King Henry, be thy title right or wrong,
Lord Clifford vows to fight in thy defence.
May the ground gape, and swallow me alive,
Where I shall kneel to him that slew my father !

K. Henry. O Clifford! how thy words revive my
        heart.   *(Exeunt.*

Act II. Scene I.

Near Mortimer's Cross in Wales.

March. Enter EDWARD, RICHARD, *and their power.*

Edw. I wonder how our princely father scaped,
Or whether he be scaped away or not,
From Clifford's and Northumberland's pursuit.
How fares my brother ! why is he so sad ?

Rich. I cannot joy, until I be resolved
Where our right valiant father is become :
I saw him in the battle range about,
And watched him how he singled Clifford forth.
Methought, he bore him in the thickest troop,
As doth a lion in a herd of neat.
See, how the morning opes her golden gates,
And takes her farewell of the glorious sun !

Enter a Messenger.

But who art thou, whose heavy looks foretell
Some dreadful story hanging on thy tongue ?
 Mess. Ah ! one that was a woeful looker on,
When that the noble Duke of York was slain,
Your princely father, and my loving lord.
 Edw. Oh ! speak no more, for I have heard too much !
 Rich. Say how he died, for I will hear it all.
 Mess. Environed he was with many foes,
By many hands your father was subdued,
But only slaughtered by the ireful arm
Of unrelenting Clifford and the queen.
They took his head, and on the gates of York
They set the same ; and there it doth remain
The saddest spectacle that e'er I viewed.
 Edw. Sweet Duke of York, our prop to lean upon,
Now thou art gone, we have no staff, no stay !
O Clifford, boisterous Clifford ! thou hast slain
The flower of Europe for his chivalry.
Never, oh never, shall I see more joy.
 Rich. I cannot weep, for all my body's moisture
Scarce serves to quench my furnace-burning heart.
To weep is to make less the depth of grief.
Tears then for babes ; blows and revenge for me !

Richard, I bear thy name ; I'll venge thy death,
Or die renowned by attempting it.

Enter WARWICK, *and others.*

Edw. O Warwick ! Warwick ! that Plantagenet
Which held thee dearly, as his soul's redemption,
Is by the stern Lord Clifford done to death !
 Warw. Ten days ago, I drowned this news in tears.
I come to tell you things since then befallen.
After the bloody fray at Wakefield fought,
Where your brave father breathed his latest gasp,
Short tale to make, we at St. Alban's met,
Our battles joined, and both sides fiercely fought.
But whether 'twas the coldness of the king
That robbed my soldiers of their heated spleen,
Or more than common fear of Clifford's rigour,
Who thunders to his captives blood and death,
I cannot judge ; but to conclude with truth,
Their weapons like to lightning came and went.
Our soldiers, like the night owl's lazy flight,
Or like an idle thresher with a flail,
Fell gently down as if they struck their friends.
I cheered them up with justice of our cause,
With promises of high pay, and great rewards ;
But all in vain, they had no heart to fight,
And we, in them, no hope to win the day.
So that we fled, your brother, and myself,
In haste, poste-haste, we are come to join with you.
 Edw. Lord Warwick, on thy shoulder will I lean.
 Rich. Now Clifford, were thy heart as hard as steel,
As thou hast shown it flinty by thy deeds,
I come to pierce it, or to give thee mine.
  Edw. Then strike up drums ; God and St. George
   for us !

SCENE IV.

A field of battle near Ferry-bridge, in Yorkshire.

Enter Richard.

Rich. Ah! Warwick, why hast thou withdrawn thyself!
Thy brother's blood the thirsty earth has drunk,
Broached with the steely point of Clifford's lance.

Enter Clifford.

Now Clifford, I have singled thee alone.
　Cliff. Now Richard, I am with thee here alone,
And so have at thee.
　　　　　(*They fight, Warwick enters, Clifford flies.*

SCENE VI.

　A loud alarm.　Enter Clifford *wounded.*
　Cliff. Here burns my candle out, ay, here it dies,
Which while it lasted gave King Henry light.
O Lancaster! I fear thine overthrow
More than my body's parting with my soul.
My love and fear glewed many friends to thee,　(*Falling.*
And now I fall, the tough commixtures melt.
O Henry! hadst thou swayed as kings should do,
Or as thy father, and his father, did,
Giving no ground unto the house of York,
I and ten thousand in this luckless realm,
Had left no mourning widows for our deaths,
And thou this day hadst kept thy throne in peace.
Bootless are plaints, and cureless are my wounds,

No way to fly, nor strength to hold out flight.
The foe is merciless, and will not pity ;
The air hath got into my deadly wounds,
And much effuse of blood doth make me faint—
Come York, and Richard, Warwick, and the rest,
I stabbed your father's bosom, split my breast. *(Faints.*

Alarm and retreat. Enter EDWARD, WARWICK, RICHARD,
and others.

Edw. Now breathe my lords, good fortune bids us
pause
And smooth the frowns of war with peaceful looks.
Some troops pursue the bloody-minded queen ;
But, think you, lords, that Clifford flew with them.
Warw. No, 'tis impossible he should escape ;
For though before his face I speak the word,
Your brother, Richard marked him for the grave.
And whereso'er he is, he's surely dead.
(Clifford groans and dies.
Edw. Whose soul is that which takes its heavy leave.
Rcih. A deadly groan like life and death departing.
Edw. See who it is, and now the battle's ended
If friend or foe, let him be justly used.
Rich. Revoke that doom of mercy for 'tis Clifford.
War. From off the gates of York fetch down the head,
Your father's head which Clifford placed there,
Instead whereof let his supply the room.
And now to London with triumphant march,
There to be crowned England's royal king. *(Exeunt.*

VI.

From the French Biographical Dictionary, entitled,
" *Biographie Universelle.*"

———

CLIFFORD, (George) a lawyer of Amsterdam, who took great delight in Botany and Natural History, and whom Linnæus has immortalised by one of his works. Clifford, being possessed of a very great fortune, had formed at his country seat, at Hartecamp, between Harlem aud Amsterdam, the most magnificent garden, and the richest in plants, from all parts of the world, then in Europe ; together with a menagerie which contained a very great number of foreign quadrupeds and birds, and a museum where he had collected several precious herbals, sent to him from foreign countries, and collections of every kind for the study of Natural History, to which he had added a fine library. No individual, nor even any sovereign, ever assembled at once, with so much taste and magnificence, such numerous collections, or opened them to the learned with so much grandeur and generosity. Linnæus, then a young man, having gone to Leyden, to attend the lectures of the illustrious Boerhaave, and having no means of support, made known his situation to him. This great man felt that he was no ordinary character, and foresaw what he might one day become ; he therefore recommended him to Clifford, to superintend his garden, and to arrange and classify the numerous objects in his museum. Linnæus remained with him about three years,

fully justified the esteem and friendship of his generous
protector, and soon found occasion of associating himself
to his fame, by publishing an account of his valuable collections. He first published a simple catalogue under the
title of " Viridarium Cliffortianum," (1737, 8vo.) a work
now become very scarce. Afterwards the Banana having
flowered, Linnæus took the opportunity of making the
fructification of this singular plant better known than it
had been till then, and pointed out its resemblance with
the palm tree. This was the subject of the " Musa Cli-
fortiana," published at Leyden, with plates. But these
works were only the prelude to a more sumptuous monument which appeared under the title of " Hortus Cliffortianus," a large folio with plates. In this work, Linnæus gave his general views on Botany, and details on
Clifford's garden, but principally descriptions with engravings of a great number of plants cultivated in it. This
work was executed with great perfection, at the expense
of Clifford, to whom it is dedicated. The thirty-two plates
it contains were designed by the celebrated Ehret,
and engraved by Van-der-Laer, the first engraver at that
time. They were the finest that had ever been seen, and
have never yet been surpassed. In a dedicatory Epistle,
and a learned Preface, dated from Clifford's Museum, the
30th July, 1737, Linnæus, in the style of a man of genius, whose heart is penetrated with the most lively gratitude, published to the learned, and to posterity, the
magnanimity and generosity of his benefactor. He dedicated to him, moreover, one of the two genera described
in that work, to which he gave the name of " Cliffortia."
The different species of which it is composed, are shrubs
from the Cape of Good Hope. (1)

_____

(1) I have not had an opportunity of ascertaining in what
degree the illustrious patron of Linnæus was related to the

Clifford family, in England, nor from what branch of it he was descended ; but there is every reason to believe he was of the family. About the middle of the last century, the late Hon. Thomas Clifford, of Tixall, in the county of Stafford, being at Amsterdam, made acquaintance with George Clifford, the friend of Linnæus, who invited him to his house at Hartecamp, and assured him that he was of the same family ; and that he had a pedigree, which showed the descent of his ancestors for many centuries. At the same time, he made him a present of a copy of the Hortus Cliffortianus, which is now in the library at Tixall.

The full title of that beautiful work is " Hortus Cliffortianus, Plantas exhibens, quas in Hortis tam vivis quam siccis, Hartecampi, in Holandia, coluit, vir Nobilissimus ac Generossimus, Georgius Clifford, Juris utriusque Doctor."

THE END.

PARIS: Printed by M. Nouzou,
No. 9, Rue Cléry.

ERRATA.

Part I. p. 11, for *cum*, read eum; p. 15, for 1402, read 1404; p. 41, instead of *Robert, Lord Clifford, and Isabel de Berkeley, only daughter to Maurice, Lord Berkeley, of Berkeley-castle*, read, Roger, Lord Clifford, and Matilda de Beauchamp, daughter of Thomas de Beauchamp, Earl of Warwick.

Part II. p. 103, for *eleventh century*, read twelfth century; p. 140, for *ment hae*, read meat hàc; for *Rosamundæ*, read Rosamunda.

Part III. p. 50, Scene V. *And all*, erase And; p. 57, Act IV. for " The House of *Lancaster* for ever," read " House of York."

FULLY ROOFED
Skipton Castle

This is a miniature of the full size self-guiding tour sheet available at Skipton Castle in English, French or German.

SKIPTON CASTLE, YORKSHIRE

By following the route indicated by the 40 sketches, visitors will make an interesting and complete tour, as well as enjoying the convenience of all proceeding in the same direction.

---

1 Here we are at the Gateway to Skipton Castle.

High above the battlements, in Norman French, the proud challenge of the Cliffords, DESORMAIS (HENCEFORTH), is cut in stone.

2 The admission office is in the Shell Room on the right side of the Archway.

Here admission tickets, tour sheets, brochures etc. may be obtained.

3 The Archway attractively frames the old Castle, with the Watch Tower as the dominant feature.

The old Castle probably dates from 1150 but was massively strengthened with drum towers added by Robert Clifford in 1307.

4 Bearing left one now ascends Lady Anne's steps, with her stone tablet above.

The redoubtable Lady Anne Clifford, born in Skipton Castle, 20th January, 1589, made substantial restorations after the Civil War.

---

5 Now we go forward through the Norman Arch.

This ancient arch is probably one of the oldest parts of the Castle; it is certainly the most recorded.

6 Here we are in the picturesque Conduit Court.

The charming Conduit Court was so named because it was the termination of the spring water supply piped to the Castle.

7 To keep to our route, we ascend the outside steps.

The lead in some stones suggests that they may have come from Skipton's Market Cross demolished about 1840.

8 Arriving in the corner of the Banqueting Hall we immediately go through the door on our left.

The blocked stair was merely for ready access to the kitchen.

---

9 We go forward and turn right.

The serving hatch of considerable age is remarkably practical in its design and construction.

10 We are now in the medieval kitchen used for 300 years between 1300 and 1600.

The ancient stone bread baking ovens face the massive roasting hearth of later date.

11 We retrace our steps back to the Banqueting Hall.

The great hall would be used for every gathering of the Castle garrison and other Castle occupants.

12 Proceeding out of the far end of the Banqueting Hall by the door indicated ...

The Hall had a raised portion at this end, to give status to the top table at which the Lord or senior Officer would preside.

---

13 View from the ladies' retiring room window.

If, as tradition avers, Mary Queen of Scots was temporarily incarcerated in Skipton Castle, this is the view towards Scotland that she must many times have contemplated.

14 Turning our back on the window, we ascend the few wooden steps and at once turn left down to the muniment room.

The Lord's personal accommodation consisted of three rooms, his Muniment Room or Library, his Day Room and his Bedchamber.

15 The muniment room showing the walled-up stairs and the level to which Cromwell demolished the outer walls.

This is the doubly secured room where Castle muniments or Deeds were kept. Unfortunately other raiders, mice and damp, destroyed the most precious possessions.

16 Back into the Lord's day room.

This was a room reserved primarily for the Lord's day time occupation. Some fragments of very early wall paper were presented to the Victoria and Albert Museum.

---

17 With the window behind us, we turn right into the adjoining room, the Lord's bedchamber.

The blocked stairs gave access to the medieval flat roof, dismantled after the Civil War.

18 The Lord's bedchamber is a simple room which we leave by the door at the left of the window.

The recess accommodated a sentry or attendant for the Lord's wellbeing.

19 Straight forward now into the Watch Tower mid-floor.

Immediately one is able to see the level to which Cromwell reduced the outer wall.

20 To reach the top storey of this same Watch Tower, we go through the door indicated and immediately turn right up the spiral stairs.

The oak roof timbers are those added in 1659 after the Civil War when cannon bearing flat roofs were forbidden.

OPEN TO VISITORS

As also is the Seat of Lord Clifford of Chudleigh, Ugbrooke Park, Chudleigh, South Devon.